London - Land's End Cycle Route

Beautiful cycling across southern England

Eric van der Horst

London – Land's End Cycle Route

Beautiful cycling across southern England

Published by EOS Cycling Holidays Ltd
www.london-landsendcycleroutebook.com
www.eoscycling.com
Twitter: @LondonLandsEnd or @EOSCyclingUK

ISBN: 978-0-9576617-0-7

Advice for artwork of maps and elevation charts: Owen Roberts, Bideford, Devon.
Concept book design: Tim Roe, Frome, Somerset (www.auburndesign.co.uk).
Line drawings: Tom Pick, Hällefors, Sweden (email: cybertom@hotmail.com).
Logo "London-Land's End Cycle Route": Marianne Keijser, Blaricum, The Netherlands.
Photography: Dorien van den Berg, Dawn Connor-van der Horst, Eric van der Horst, Eric Keetels, Tom Pales, Dirk van Rens and Martijn Tuinman.
Printed by Toptown Printers, Barnstaple, Devon (www.toptown.co.uk).

About the author

Dutchman Eric van der Horst went on his first cycling holiday when he was 16 and has covered many countries around the world by bike. Today, he lives in the UK and works as a cycle route consultant, Bikeability instructor and author. Follow him on Twitter @DutchmanCycling or http://thecyclingdutchman.blogspot.com.

Appeal to readers

This book contains over 1200 kms (940 miles) of routes. We need your help to keep everything up-to-date. Please report any changes you find and share experiences via Twitter @LondonLandsEnd or via our website (see top left). We publish all important changes on the updates page of the website.

Introduction

A life-long **passion for cycle touring** has taken me all around the globe. I've cycled through great countryside, in fantastic National Parks and in and out of world cities. It was always the combination of both **urban** and **rural** cycling and a fascination for finding routes via **famous landmarks** that thrilled me. I feel that **only by bicycle** you can **experience** what the world is really like. Away from obvious mass-transport corridors and not being enclosed by a "metal box" I can feel my **body and spirit** come to life.

Somewhere along the journey, I met my wife Dawn and we settled in England back in 2007. It didn't take long before **Dutch touring cyclists** started to ask me for a good long-distance cycle route guide for England, but I initially dismissed this concept as a **mission impossible**. Several years of cycling in various part of southern England (as part of my work for Cycle City Guides maps) made the idea of a high quality tourist route from London to Land's End bubble in my head though. A Dutch friend who wanted to visit me by bike sparked this concept further.

Keeping in mind classic Dutch cycle route books like Amsterdam-Rome, I found the discovery of a spectacular **traffic-calmed route** across **London** to be the key to getting the first Dutch version published in 2011. Enthusiastic feedback encouraged me to make the route also available in English. The journey has been long though. Without my wife's support and relentless belief in the project, this book would never have been published. We both hope that this "second and improved edition" will especially inspire **families** with teenage **children** to take up cycling together, just as families do in The Netherlands.

This guidebook is intended to cater for **everyone**, whether you just want to cycle short **route sections** or want to embark on a full-on adventure around the **English Channel**. The best traffic-calmed routes available, the high density of famous English landmarks and an attractive mix of landscapes are a guarantee for great journeys. **Enjoy the ride(s)**!

Eric van der Horst

Contents

The table below shows how the route is divided into 24 sections. It includes a brief summary of the characteristics; traffic-free routes in bold.

Rte	Route Section	Distance	🚲	🥾	🚗	🚗🚗	Grading of terrain	Highlights	Page
1	Dover - Canterbury	52.7 km	24%	70%	6%	-	Moderate, some serious climbing	Dover Castle & White Cliffs, coastal path (castles), Richborough Castle (Roman ruins), Kent fruit orchards	24
2	Canterbury - Rochester	70.7 km	40%	54%	5%	1%	Generally easy, some short climbs	Canterbury Cathedral City, Kent fruit orchards, **River Medway Park**, Chatham Dockyard, Rochester Castle	30
3	Rochester - Woolwich	52.0 km	70%	29%	1%	-	Generally easy, some short climbs	Upnor Castle, Gravesend Promenade, North Downs Quarries, **Thames Path**, Erith Pier, Woolwich Arsenal	38
4	Harwich - Maldon	81.9 km	16%	65%	17%	2%	Generally easy, some short climbs	Harwich Promenade, **Wivenhoe Riverside**, Colchester Castle and Roman Gate, Maldon Promenade Park	42
5	Maldon - Woolwich	76.0 km	9%	72%	17%	2%	Moderate, some serious climbing	Woodham Walter village, Essex countryside, RHS Garden Hyde Hall, cycling into London, Woolwich Ferry	48
6	Woolwich - London Bridge	20.1 km	50%	44%	4%	2%	Easy, but one steep climb into park	**Thames Path**, Thames Barrier, Millennium Dome/O2 Arena, Greenwich Park and Meridian, Tower Bridge	54
7	London Bridge - Kingston	30.2 km	41%	47%	9%	3%	Easy	London Southbank, Westminster, Buckingham Palace, **Hyde Park**, South Kensington, Richmond Park	58
8	Kingston - Windsor & Eton	42.6 km	65%	31%	2%	2%	Easy, but one steep climb into park	Kingston, **Thames Path**, Hampton Court, Weybridge-Shepperton Ferry, Runnymede, Windsor Park & Castle	64
9	Windsor & Eton - Reading	37.9 km	49%	47%	4%	-	Generally easy, some short climbs	Eton College Olympic Rowing Centre, Maidenhead River Bridge, rolling hills Warren Row, Sonning Lock	70
10	Reading - Great Bedwyn	55.1 km	65%	34%	1%	-	Generally easy, some short climbs	**Avon & Kennet Canal route**, Newbury horse racing course, Hungerford and Great Bedwyn countryside	74
11A	GB - AP via Avebury	34.1 km	29%	67%	4%	-	Moderate, some serious climbing	Savernake Forest, historic Marlborough, Fyfield Down reserve, Avebury ancient stone circle, Wiltshire hills	78
11B	GB - AP via Stonehenge	68.5 km	8%	86%	6%	-	Moderate, some serious climbing	Crofton Beam Steam Engines, Salisbury Plains, Wiltshire hills, Stonehenge ancient stone circle	82
12	Alton Priors - Bath	52.1 km	73%	13%	14%	-	Generally easy, some short climbs	White Horses, **Avon & Kennet Canal route**, Caen Hill Locks & aqueducts, historic Bradford & City of Bath	86
13	Bath - Bristol	22.1 km	96%	4%	-	-	Easy	**Bristol and Bath Railway Path**, Cotswolds countryside, Avon Valley heritage railway, cycling into Bristol	92
14	Bristol - Cheddar	58.8 km	48%	48%	3%	1%	Generally easy, some short climbs	Bristol, Clifton Suspension Bridge & **Avon Gorge**, Clevedon Pier & Promenade, **Strawberry Line**, Cheddar	94
15	Cheddar - Taunton	60.5 km	40%	59%	1%	-	Generally easy, some short climbs	Somerset Levels, views at Rughill and Poldon Hills, Bridgwater, **Taunton and Bridgwater Canal route**	100
16	Taunton - Dulverton	50.6 km	4%	87%	9%	-	Hard, serious climbing all the way	Taunton, South West Coast Path transfer option, remote West Somerset hills, scenic Bampton/Dulverton	104
17	Dulverton - Barnstaple	55.0 km	12%	86%	2%	-	Strenuous, some extreme cimbs	Exmoor National Park, Tarr Steps, Two Burrows (highest point of route), Devon hills, historic Barnstaple	108
18	Barnstaple - Sheepwash	54.4 km	68%	30%	2%	-	Generally easy, also serious climbs	**Tarka Trail**, historic Bideford, Westward Ho! Beach, Northam Burrows, Torrington, Tarka Country Park	112
19	Sheepwash - Plymouth	86.1 km	43%	56%	-	1%	Generally easy, also serious climbs	**Devon Coast to Coast cycle route**, Brent Tor, historic Tavistock, Dartmoor National Park, Plymouth Hoe	116
20	Sheepwash - Crackington	47.2 km	9%	78%	13%	-	Hard, also one extreme climb	Devon hills, Bude Beach and Coast Path, Widemouth Bay Beach, Cornish coastal route to Crackington	124
21A	Cr - Bl via Tintagel	37.8 km	-	95%	5%	-	Strenuous, many extreme climbs	Crackington Haven Beach, Cornish coastal route to Tintagel, Tintagel Castle, Trebarwith Beach	128
21B	Cr - Bl via Bodmin Moor	34.2 km	3%	97%	-	-	Moderate, some serious climbing	Cornish hills, Bodmin Moor reserve, Crowdy Reservoir, remote St Breward, descent onto Camel Trail	132
22	Blisland - Newquay	68.9 km	39%	49%	9%	3%	Generally easy, also serious climbs	**Camel Trail**, Bodmin & Wenford steam railway, Wadebridge, Padstow, Harlyn Bay Beach, Newquay coast	134
23	Newquay - Penzance	71.5 km	18%	77%	4%	1%	Moderate, some serious climbing	City of Truro, **Mining Trail**, Redruth and Camborne heritage mining area, Towans Beach, St Michaels Mount	140
24	Land's End Round Trip	51.1 km	10%	64%	23%	3%	Moderate, also one extreme climb	Penzance, Newlyn and Mousehole Harbours, Sennen Cove Beach, Land's End, Cape Cornwall	146

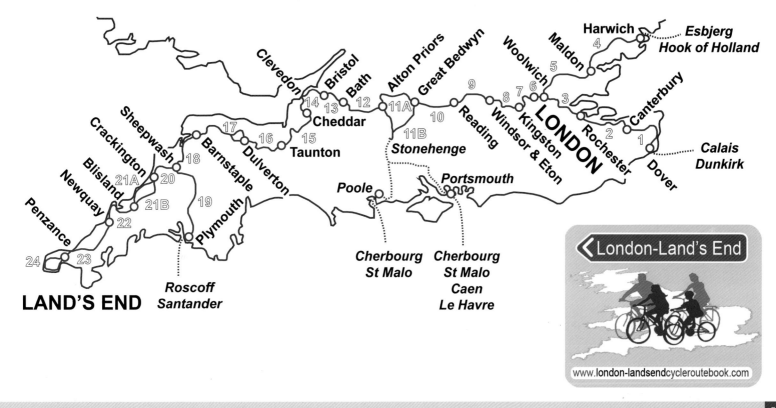

Harwich

Esbjerg
Hook of Holland

Maldon

4

Woolwich

5

Clevedon

Bristol

Bath

Alton Priors

Great Bedwyn

6

7

8

LONDON

Canterbury

14

13

12

11A

9

3

Rochester

Cheddar

10

Reading

Windsor & Eton

Kingston

2

1

Calais
Dunkirk

Sheepwash

17

16

15

Taunton

11B

Stonehenge

Dover

Crackington

18

Barnstaple

Dulverton

Poole

Portsmouth

Blisland

21A

20

Newquay

21B

19

Plymouth

Penzance

22

24

23

LAND'S END

Roscoff
Santander

Cherbourg
St Malo

Cherbourg
St Malo
Caen
Le Havre

< London-Land's End

5

Route Summary

The guidebook contains routes from both **Dover** and **Harwich** ferry ports to London. This makes it possible to cycle around the **English Channel**, when also using the **Plymouth** link. Routes from Stonehenge to **Poole** and **Portsmouth** are not included. Sustrans' "Hampshire & Isle of Wight Cycle Map" will help you to cycle these routes.

The Dover to London route takes you though the fruit orchards of Kent, historic **Canterbury** and the **Medway** estuary with its impressive castles. The Harwich to London route provides pleasant countryside cycling in Essex and takes you through Roman **Colchester**.

Cycling through the heart of **London** is less scary than you'd think if you use this guide book. Even in Great Britain's capital, the route manages to stay away from busy roads, the occasional busy junction crossing excepted. Most of the cycling takes place on towpaths along the **River Thames** with spectacular views to enjoy. If you begin in London it is best to start from **London Bridge Station**, see page 18 for details. You can cycle under the Tower Bridge and you'll pass the London Eye, Big Ben, the Houses of Parliament and Buckingham Palace on the way. Greenwich Park, Hyde Park and Richmond Park all provide superb green traffic-free routes.

Heading west you'll cycle by Windsor Park and **Windsor Castle** before making your way to the **Avon & Kennet Canal**, with the pleasant towns of Newbury, Hungerford and Marlborough to take in. In Sting's "Fields of gold" of Wiltshire you have the choice to cycle either by famous **Stonehenge** or that other beautiful ancient stone circle, **Avebury**. Extraordinary engineering awaits you at the twenty-nine canal locks of **Caen Hill** and the canal aqueducts near Bradford on Avon. You'll cycle through the hilly **Cotswolds** here, with a canal path providing a majestic flat route to magnificent **Bath** with its Roman Baths, Jane Austen Museum and Royal Crescent.

Via the **Bristol & Bath Railway Path** you'll make your way to bustling **Bristol** and its spectacular **Avon Gorge**. If you only wish to cycle "Coast to Coast" from the North Sea or English Channel, you could stop at seaside Clevedon with its striking views over the British Channel. The route continues via the charming **Strawberry Line** to famous **Cheddar** with its cheese museum and gorge.

The **Somerset Levels** provide the last section of truly flat cycling, because from Taunton the big climb starts into **Exmoor National Park**. From here, the route is for determined cyclists only, as there is serious climbing to take in. To get to the ancient Tarr Steps you'll have to take on two major climbs of about a mile long!

Fortunately, from Barnstaple the splendid **Tarka Trail** provides easy cycling on another former railway. You can choose to cycle to **Plymouth** from where you can cross the English Channel to France. This **Devon Coast to Coast route** takes you on high viaducts with fantastic views over **Dartmoor National Park**. The spectacular Plym Valley Way from historic Tavistock down into Plymouth could be a worthy climax to your journey!

Of course, you can also continue into **Cornwall**, but you have to be ready for more serious climbing here. The section between Bude and Tintagel Castle is particularly rugged. **Atlantic Ocean views** are the ultimate reward for all the climbing efforts made, as is cycling on the flat and beautiful **Camel Trail**. This trail leads you to Padstow with its exclusive fish restaurants and the famous surf beaches of Newquay.

The striking mining area of Redruth allows you to cycle briefly through **"lunar landscapes"**, before arriving at beautiful Penzance Bay with its striking **St. Michael's Mount**. The grand finale of the route is a circular route via the spectacular headlands of **Land's End** and **Cape Cornwall**. From Penzance, you can take your bike on the fast train service back to London.

Cycling culture in England

As in many countries in the western world, cycling as a means of transport has been in decline in England since the 1950s. For more than five decades, **road layouts** have been designed with only motorised traffic in mind. Pedestrians were pushed onto fenced pavements and cyclists were largely forgotten. Privatisation of the railways, along with closure of about 15,000 kms (9,000 miles) of the railway network, pushed even more people into cars. These policies have created a **driving-addicted nation**. Many people think that roads are just made for cars and poor role models in the media still make speeding socially acceptable.

Serious change is in the air though. Congested roads, the rising price of fuel, environmental issues and a steady growth of obesity amongst the population have all put cycling back in the spotlight, majorly helped by the recent successes of **British racing cyclists**. The **National Cycle Network** was created and in cities like London and Bristol, cycling is now truly booming.

The problem remains that safe and enjoyable cycle routes for day to day use are still **out of reach** for many people. The English road network is often hostile to cycling and casualties are on the rise, finally causing a **public debate** about the need for proper cycling infrastructure.

Continuity and **quality** are major issues. Even on the National Cycle Network, cycle paths can consist of muddy surfaces or end suddenly, taking cyclists onto busy main roads. Routes are often poorly signposted or can keep you deliberately away from an attraction or view.

This guidebook does everything to **overcome** all problems, principally avoiding main roads and keeping you away from the bad and ugly as much as possible, providing you with a **fully continuous enjoyable route**. Approximately 65% of our route is signposted with **National Cycle Network** signs (see below). This network, created by the Sustrans charity (see page 93) is a great resource for exploring by bike.

The London-Land's End Cycle Route uses large parts of routes 1, 3, 4, 26, 27, 32, 41 and 51, **celebrating the achievements** of the network. Our route is 35% traffic-free. The Thames Path, Avon & Kennet Canal Route, Bristol and Bath Railway Path, Avon Gorge, Strawberry Line, Tarka Trail, Devon Coast to Coast Route and Camel Trail all provide **world-class cycling** with amazing scenery. The connecting friendly lanes take you into rural England, with beautiful towns and villages to be discovered, not to mention all those famous landmarks; the ultimate mix!

Some "new cyclists" or "cyclists to be" might be put off by the fact that 65% of the routes in this book are indeed on-road. Be reassured that the vast majority of the journeys in this book are on **very quiet roads**. UK-based cyclists might like to sign up for a Bikeability adult cycle training session, often offered through local authorities. The key thing is that you learn **to take control** over traffic situations as a cyclist and that you are aware of the main hazards and risks. You'll find some key "Bikeability principles" explained on page 12 and 13; a good read for anyone participating in traffic!

International visitors need to be reminded that the British **keep to the left**, whether they are travelling on a road or a cycle path. If you are used to riding on the right, keeping left is a serious blow to all natural reflexes you normally use when participating in traffic. Be extremely cautious when taking junctions. Work out for yourself where you are supposed to be and look everywhere for traffic before making a move! Also, keep reminding each other to cycle on the left, especially on quiet country lanes or paths and after a break. Most people quickly adapt to ride on the left, but remaining "aware" of being on the left is essential!

How to use this guidebook

This guidebook contains 1,200 kms (just over 940 miles) of routes. All **route directions** are written in telegram style in such a way that you do not need a bike computer. Maps always match the directions on the same page, with visitor information scattered around it.

Due to space restrictions, the route directions of the book only allow you to cycle **from east to west**. If you wish to cycle in the opposite direction you can use the book's maps and/or our GPS-tracks. **GPS-tracks** can be ordered from our website and can easily be loaded onto your outdoor navigation device.

The route is divided into **24 sections**, as displayed on pages 4 and 5. On these pages you'll find characteristics of all route sections, like highlights and grading of the terrain. **Pictorials** show the percentages within a route section of different types of cycling conditions: 🚲 (cycle path), 🏃 (quiet road), 🚗 (road with possibly fast moving traffic or regular traffic flow) and 🚗🚗 (busy main road), see also pages 12 and 13.

Total distances of types of cycling conditions (within a route section) can be found of the first page of every route section. Here, you also find an overview of all **stations** on the way, allowing you to hop on/off trains with the bike and to cycle short route sections. We haven't been able to include **car park** information, but free parking is generally available in the outskirts of towns. Paid parking is widespread in town centres.

You'll also find an **elevation chart** at the start of every route section. Note these charts are generalised for clarity and don't show every incline and decline of the route. Many **steep gradients** are marked on the maps with **arrows**. These arrows always pinpoint down hill!

The scales and style of the **maps** vary per page. Every map has the essential clarity to find your way around. The waypoints on the maps, matching the directions, ensure you are aware of the map scale. For reasons of clarity we decided only to use **kilometres** on the maps and in the directions of this book; divide by 1.6 to get miles!

On the maps you'll also find letters, matching the **facility listings** from page 150. These allow you to quickly find accommodations and/or bike repair shops on or near the route. When a service provider is further away, a dotted line on the map will direct you there, in combination with directions in the listings.

Key to used symbols and abbreviations

→ turn right
← turn left
↑ straight on
↗ smooth turn right
↖ smooth turn left
↘ sharp turn right
↙ sharp turn left
⬏ first turn right, then immediately left
⬐ first turn left, then immediately right

🚲 cyclepath or cycle lane
🚶 quiet road
🚗 road with possibly fast moving traffic or regular traffic flow
🚗🚗 busy main road; an adjacent footpath is always available!

⚑ tourist attraction, view point or location of special interest
⛱ beach or seafront promenade
🛒 shop(s)
☕ cafe/pub with light refreshments
🍴 pub/restaurant serving meals
⛱ picnic area or bench(es) at prominent location

🏠 hotel or bed & breakfast
🏠 hostel or bunkhouse (YHA, YMCA or independent)
⛺ campsite
🔧 bike repair shop

Dover town, village, attraction or rural pub
(note the name of a locality is in ***italic*** if there is a station!)

(1) National Cycle Route number (signposted)

T-jct T-junction
jct junction
cross rds cross roads (four-ways junction)
rndabt roundabout
ep at end of path
1st rd first road
2nd p second path
lhts traffic lights
ped lhts pedestrian lights/pedestrian crossing
car pk car park
imm immediately

street and road names abbreviations:

Br	Bridge	**Mt**	Mount/Market
Cl	Close	**Pd**	Parade
Cr	Crescent	**Pk**	Park
Ct	Court	**Pl**	Place
Dr	Drive	**Rd**	Road
Gdns	Gardens	**Sq**	Square
Gn	Green	**St**	Street
Gr	Grove	**Tc**	Terrace
Is	Island	**Wk**	Walk
Ln	Lane	**Wy**	Way

Route types and your cycling style

Traffic-free cyclepaths 🚲 (35%):

English cycle paths are always **shared** with pedestrians, which may cause conflicts. Cyclists should always **give way** to pedestrians, slowing down when approaching and ringing their bell. You'll notice many pedestrians find it difficult to deal with cyclists. They tend to step out of the way in the direction you don't expect or can be very slow to react. Unfortunately, this means you end up cycling dead-slow quite often, especially if there are dogs and children around. Always try to pass as wide as possible. On narrow canal paths ("tow paths") cyclists are also expected to give way to fishermen and boaters. On cycle paths running parallel to a main road, you are generally expected to give way to traffic moving in and out of side roads. Occasionally, this book takes you onto a **footpath** where cycling is forbidden. Please obey the "dismount" notes in the directions and walk bikes on these sections to avoid conflicts.

Quiet roads 🚶 (58%):

On (very) quiet roads, the biggest risk for a cyclist is being hit by cars moving in and out of **driveways** and **sideroads**. These turning drivers look for other cars, so be where these drivers look! **Be visible** and try to cycle in the **middle of your side of the road** passing sideroads.

Be **always on your guard** for traffic joining the road you are on and be sure to make **eye contact** with any turning drivers to check they've seen you. As a general rule, you should keep **at least one metre** away from the road side.

Another risk for cyclists on quiet roads is **hazardous overtaking** by traffic from behind. You should have an active role to ensure the overtaking takes place safely. If you hear a car approaching from behind, try to move out to the middle of your side of the road before the vehicle gets close. This will **force** traffic to **slow down**!

Looking over your shoulder also helps, as it makes you a person, rather than being an object "in the way". Meanwhile, keep going; it is your right to do so! It is essential to maintain your "middle in the lane position" until you feel it is safe for drivers to overtake you. To show you are happy to be overtaken, pull back to your "normal metre from the road side" position and temporarily stop pedaling, looking again over your shoulder as necessary. If drivers still hesitate you could wave them through! On narrow roads, you might want to pull in and stop to let traffic through.

Avoid cycling through narrow gaps with moving traffic around you. Also stay well away from **parked cars**, **buses** and **lorries**. When overtaking these, wait until it is clear before moving to the opposite side of the road and keep ample space; don't get hit by an opening door, or worse, a vehicle pulling out! Also, **adjust your own speed** to factors such as visibility, surface and weather conditions; know your own brakes!

Roads with fast moving traffic or regular flow 🚗 (6%):

Unfortunately, we haven't been able to create a route just via cycle paths or quiet roads. You will occasionally be exposed to some fast moving traffic or, in towns, to reasonably regular flows of motorised traffic. **Assertive road positioning** is essential to keep safe here. As soon as you start cycling close to the road side, drivers will try to overtake you "in the same lane". You might think this is ok, but the margins of error are large and if something goes wrong, **you** end up in hospital or worse! Also, you expose yourself once again to be **overlooked** and being hit by traffic coming out of driveways and side roads! So, you want to **force** drivers to overtake on the other side of the road. This is only possible by cycling **in the middle of your side of the road**. Adopt this position if you feel it is essential for your safety, especially in blind bends and when turning at junctions. For a turn, look behind before pulling out and signal. Then, make **eye contact** with drivers around you just before making a turn!

Busy main roads 🚗🚗 (1%):

The cycling style explained on these pages is **officially adopted** by the British government (Bikeability). The principles generally work, but on busy roads, where you can't keep up with the speed and the intensive flow of the traffic, it is very hard to enforce these principles. Drivers can get quite hostile, so why bother? Very occasionally, we have no choice but take you via this type of road, but we have ensured you can always **walk** your bikes on pavements; please do!

International cyclists must further know that a general priority for traffic from the right doesn't exist in the UK. At most junctions, clear markings will show the priorities.

Cycling with children:

Always keep to cycle paths until children have achieved **full control** of their bikes. To protect a child on quiet roads, you cycle either **two abreast** (child on the inside, you on the outside) or **behind** him/her. Ensure they listen to your instructions and only move in front of them if you need to show them where to go. If you have multiple children, put the most confident child at the front, but ensure he/she keeps the same speed as the weakest child in your party.

Children should only cycle on roads with a regular flow or fast moving traffic (🚗) if parent and child are both happy and confident to do so. Cycling on main roads (🚗🚗) is only recommended for confident parents and teenagers. You decide on your own limits; there is no shame in walking.

Preparation – gear and equipment

This book is all about sightseeing from your bicycle rather than going as fast as possible. This demands also a specific type of bicycle. **Racing bikes** with their slick tyres are not ideal, as sections of the routes are on gravel. **Mountain bikes** have fat tyres and often have suspension features, lethal to effective energy use on a general smooth surface. If you intend to do touring for multiple days, you are much better off using a **touring/hybrid bike** with semi-slick tyres, rack on the back to carry pannier bags, mud guards and chain cover. Many bikes sold in the UK don't have these features, but these can be added at a reasonably low cost. Whatever the type of bike you choose; have **at least 18 gears** to be able to take in any serious climb. This is also why **BMX-bikes** for children are not ideal (no gears).

A **map holder** for on the bikes' handlebars is advised, as this guide is designed to fit in such holders! A cheap **bike computer** (set on kilometres) is not essential, but makes it even easier to use the guide book's directions; ideal!

Special bikes, such as **tandems**, **recumbent bikes**, **tricycles** etc. will be fine to use most of the way (keeping in mind the hilly sections), but there are some **barriers** which might be impossible to pass. If problems are likely, you'll find pictures of these barriers in this guide, with alternative routes marked on the maps. More barrier pictures can be found on our website. It might be difficult taking special bikes on **trains**; check with the train company before travel!

A set of two **pannier bags** will enable you to carry luggage for a cycling holiday of up to two weeks, providing you stay at indoor accommodation and can do some laundry halfway. Outdoor panniers are the best and German manufacturer Ortlieb sets the standard for this type of bag. It is worth shopping around, but bear in mind that the cheaper you go, the more likely it is the bags will get damaged with regular intense use.

Camping by bike is fun, but physically more demanding than Bed & Breakfast/hostel touring. You'll need **pannier bags** on the **front wheel** (with an additional **rack**) to be able to carry a tent, inflatable matress and sleeping bag on your bike as well. Don't cut down on quality. Good, light-weight materials are essential for happy camping tours by bike! If you have never done any cycle touring before, you should get some experience with a B&B/hostel tour first!

On a cycling holiday with **indoor accommodation** only, you should be able to fit the following in two panniers:

- 2 sets of clothes to be used for cycling during the day, including shirt, jumper and trousers/shorts
- 1 easy set of clothes to wear at night (pyamas)
- 1 nice set of clothes (for non-cycling related travelling and going out; don't use this set for sweaty walking or cycling!)
- More than a sufficient amount of socks and underwear
- Proper waterproofs (coat and trousers), able to withstand cold winds and with a breathable inside layer
- Light outfit for hot weather, including sun cap/shades
- Small bag for toiletries
- Small bicycle repair kit for emergency repairs
- Small rucksack for valuable items (you can bring this with you whilst you leave the pannier bags on the bike during lunch stops or for a short walk away from the bike)

A **repair kit** (see picture) should at least contain:
- Combi tool with spanners and screwdrivers
- Spanner allowing you to take off wheels
- Pump, spare tube, patches and tyre levers (note there are patches on the market which don't need glue!)

If you ensure your bike is in a good state before starting a holiday, you shouldn't get into trouble. Taking bikes to a repair shop for a good check up before departure is best!

Further, bring a good **bike lock**, allowing you to lock frame and wheels to a secure object. Many service providers are still getting used to cycling tourists and might require you to lock up bike(s) outside overnight.

Wear **bright clothes** when cycling on-road. High visibility vests are very popular. It is not legally required to wear **helmets** in the United Kingdom. Many people do, but also many people don't. Whatever you choice is; it is your **cycling style** which will keep you **really** safe, see page 12.

Travelling in England

International visitors should visit from May to September to get the **best of the weather**. The negative image of British weather might do justice to wet weather in Scotland and Northern England, but southern England (where our route is based) is generally milder and with much less rainfall. May and June are generally best, with a high chance of fair weather in September too. Be always ready for some showers though!

English **school holidays** usually start the last week of July and last for six weeks. Also be aware of the **bank holiday weekends** in May and August, dates varying per year. Always make **reservations** in advance for stays on these special weekends. In busy places like London and Bath you should make reservations all year round. Coastal towns can get booked up during the summer holidays. In other areas you should be fine with making bookings on the day itself. Just turning up will be fine on most occasions too, but a call ahead a couple of hours prior to arrival prepares your host and will avoid disappointments.

Bed & Breakfasts are part of England's heritage. The English truly have invented the thing. There are many B&Bs (or guesthouses) around. You may end up in someone's private home with only some rooms open for guests. At the other end of the spectrum, there are large hotels offering "B&B". Note cheap pub accommodation can be noisy. Most B&Bs offer "full English breakfast" with traditional bacon, eggs, baked beans and sausages on toast. "Continental breakfast" (cereal, croissants, etc.) is generally available too. Hosts of smaller and/or rural places often go out of their way to ensure a pleasant stay.

Hostels allow you to sleep in shared dormitory rooms, normally for less than £20 per night per head. Private rooms might be available too. Hostels of the international hostelling organisation YHA are of a high standard and a membership is not compulsory. Independent hostels and bunkhouses are also available, but with varying standards; check out the reviews!

Campsites are generally widely available, except on the routes in and out of London and Bristol. In these areas, it is vital for campers to plan ahead! Most campsites have good amenities, like modern and clean shower/toilet blocks. Most campsites don't have shops, so make arrangements for your evening meals before making your way to the campsite! Note "rough" road-side camping is normally not permitted in England. Landowners don't like trespassing by strangers. If you get stuck, always seek permission of the land owner first before pitching your tent. More information on pricing of all accommodation types can be found on page 150.

For day-time travel (always avoid cycling in the dark!) free public toilets and **pubs** are great facilities for cyclists. Pubs generally open from 11 am or at noon and offer affordable lunches. Just going to the toilet without purchasing any food or drinks is fine. Traditional lunches are a "Ploughmans" (fresh bread with cheese and salad) and a baked potato. Cornish pasties filled with vegetables and meat are popular at take aways. At most pubs, you have to order your food at the bar and immediate payment will be required. **Take aways** like fish and chips, Chinese or Indian make easy evening meals.

Rural pubs and cafés are always listed by their names in the route directions. **Facilities** in towns and villages are indicated by symbols only (see page 11). This allows you to **see at a glance** how far it is to the next en-route facility. Shops are generally open Mon-Sun, banks and post offices Mon-Sat noon. The British Pound is the only accepted currency (no Euros!). Credit card payments are widely accepted, even for small amounts. ATMs (cash machines) are available in most towns.

There are over 60 **stations** where you can join or leave the route. Taking bicycles on trains is free, but capacity is limited. Important is the service from **Penzance** to **London Paddington**, allowing you to cycle from London to the west and to take the bike on the train back to London at various points en-route. The shortest travel time between Penzance and London is 5 hrs and 30 mins, allowing you to travel back from Penzance to Dover/Harwich in one day. See page 18 for train travel across London.

For longer journeys it pays to buy **tickets in advance**, as this will provide you with a fair price and a guaranteed space for your bike. When booking up to three weeks in advance, you'll be able to get fares like Penzance-Dover for £20 per person, but you can travel on the booked train only. If you wait until a couple of days in advance of travel, fares will have gone up to about £50 per person. This is still much better value then turning up on the day in which case you'll have to pay up to £130 per person for such a journey. Buy advance tickets at a station ticket booth, as only railway staff can make **bike reservations**.

International visitors can also buy **unlimited travel** train tickets via www.visitbritain.com, but these tickets don't include bike reservations. The **Night Riviera Sleeper** between Penzance and London has its own reservation system.

London Connections

Starting the main route in London (cycling):

The best point to join the main route in London is **London Bridge Station**. This is the start of route section 7, see page 58. Note sections 1-6 cover the routes from Dover and Harwich to London Bridge Station. **On Your Bike** (next to London Dungeons and London Bridge Station) has a good fleet of **rental bicycles** available, including hybrid bikes with luggage racks and mud guards. You can rent bikes for longer periods (www.onyourbike. com). If you bring your own bike you can also easily join route section 7 at the London Eye (cycle from **Waterloo** Station) or Buckingham Palace (cycle from **Victoria** Station).

With the help of our **London Connection routes** you can also join route section 7 at London Bridge by bike from **Paddington**, **Euston**, **King's Cross-St. Pancras**, **Liverpool Street** and **Monument** stations.

These connection routes, named A, B, C and D, haven't been chosen for their scenic appearance; they just keep you away from busy roads as much as possible. In combination with route section 7, the connection routes also provide a full clockwise circular route in Central London. Only route A has route directions both ways, allowing people arriving at Paddington to make a short-cut to Hyde Park, joining route section 7 there.

Travelling back to Dover/Harwich/Eurostar:

Those who have completed the main route of this guidebook anywhere west of Maidenhead will arrive by train at **Paddington**. From here, use route B to King's Cross-St. Pancras (for Dover Priory station and Eurostar), followed by route C to get to Liverpool Street (for Harwich International station, change at Manningtree). From Paddington, you can also take bicycles on the Underground. The **Circle Line** is just below the street surface, so no long escalators. You'll have to carry your bike on the short stairs though (no lifts!) and you'll probably have to stand most of the journey. No bikes on Circle Line trains 7.30-9.30 am and 4-7 pm (Mon-Fri).

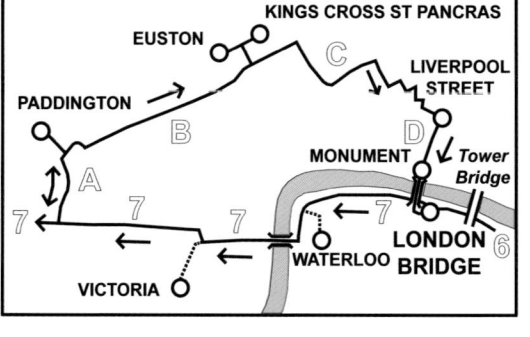

Taking bicycles on trains in and out of London:

You **cannot** take bicycles on trains into London on any trains arriving in London **before 9.30 am** or departing out of London **between 4.30 and 6.30 pm** (Mon-Fri only). At weekends you can take bikes on trains in and out of London at anytime, providing there is space.

Starting the main route at London Bridge (all the way by train):

From the north, west, Dover and Eurostar: join the First Capitol Connect service to Brighton at King's Cross-St. Pancras. This is the only train link from the north to London Bridge station. If arriving at Paddington, Euston or Liverpool Street you'll need to travel on the Circle Line Underground first. If the First Capitol Connect line is closed, use the Circle Line to get to Monument station and cycle to London Bridge from there (route D).

From the south: First Capitol Connect, Southern and Southeastern services make their way to London Bridge. When arriving at Victoria, you could use the Circle Line to Monument (see above). For Victoria and Waterloo stations it is recommended though to join route section 7 directly.

Flying to London (using rental bikes at London Bridge):

If you fly to the UK it is best to start the route at London Bridge Station, so you can use the **On Your Bike** rental.

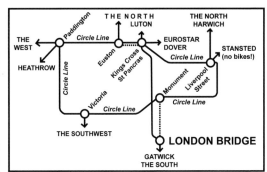

Flying to London (bringing your own bike):

To be able to bring your own bike on a plane, you'll have to find an airline happy to transport your bike at a reasonable rate. Most airlines will require you to **pack your bike** in a carton box or plastic cover. You'll need to turn the handlebars and take off the pedals and the front wheel. You also need to find a way to pack your panniers; only worth doing for **long-haul flights**.

It is best to fly to **Gatwick** or **Luton** airports, as these airports have a direct train link with London Bridge. Note Luton Parkway station is two miles from Luton airport, an easy down-hill ride. When flying to **Heathrow**, you'll have to use the Heathrow Express to Paddington and travel on from there. Note you **cannot** take your own bicycle on trains from/to **Stansted** Airport.

London Connections: Route A and B

Route A: Paddington - Hyde Park (southbound):

0.0 Leave Paddington Station via exit "Praed St/St Mary's Hospital", at lhts ⬅ (London St, see sign "🚲 route to Hyde Park"), keep ⬆
0.5 At rndabt ➡ (Stanhope Tc), 1st rd ⬅ (Brook St)
0.6 At lhts ⬆ into Hyde Park, use 🚲 on left side of rd
1.7 After lake bridge, at 1st 🚲 crossing ⬊, onto 🚲 ⬈ through park, you are now on the Main Cycle Route *(see after 7.6 km on page 60)*

Route A: Hyde Park - Paddington (northbound):

0.0 *(7.6)* Cross rd via 🚲 crossing, then ➡, use 🚲 on left side of rd, follow to end
1.1 **Dismount** at end of Hyde Park and somehow cross ⬆ (Brook St), walk on pavement
1.2 At junction somehow cross ➡ (Stanhope Tc), **resume cycling**
1.3 1st rd ⬅ (Gloucester Square)
1.4 Next jct on Gloucester Square:
    * For **Euston**, **King's Cross-St. Pancras**, **Liverpool Street** and/or **London Bridge** ➡ *(see after 0.4 km on next page)*
    * For **Paddington** ⬆, **dismount** at lhts ahead, ⬆ to Paddington (one way rd with opposite flow; walk on pavement)

If you are in need of **budget accommodation** on the connection routes, there is a YHA youth hostel east of Paddington. See route B on the page below. It is marked with an "A" on the map, see also page 150.

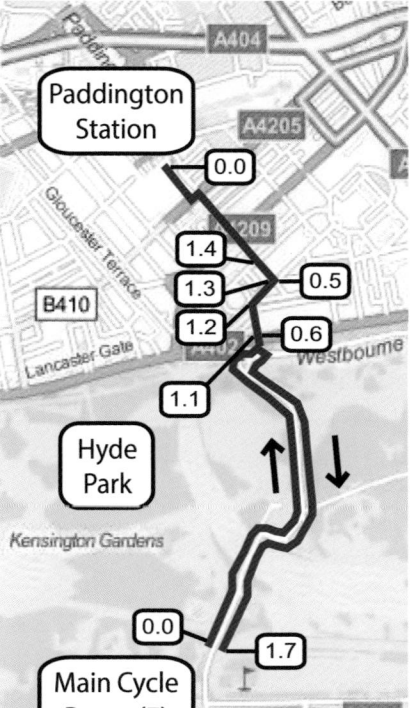

Route B: Paddington - Euston/King's Cross-St. Pancras:

0.0 Leave Paddington Station via exit "Praed St/St Mary's Hospital"; at lhts ⬆ (London St, see sign "🚲 route to Hyde Park"), keep ⬆

0.4 *(1.4: from Hyde Park ➡)* After next jct with lhts, 1st rd ⬅ (Gloucester Sq, later Somers Cr)

0.6 At T-jct ➡ (Hyde Park Cr)

0.8 End of rd ⬅ (Cannaught St), imm ⬅ (Kendal St)

1.3 After 2nd set of lhts, 2nd rd ⬅ (Bryanston Sq)

1.6 At T-jct ⬆ (Wyndham Pl), at T-jct ➡ (Crawford St)

2.2 After 2nd set of lhts, 3rd rd ➡ (Ashland Pl)

2.5 At T-jct ⬆ (Weymouth St), keep going ⬆

3.1 At T-jct ➡ and 1st rd ⬅ (Clipstone St)

3.3 At corner near BT-Tower ⬆ (Maple St), join 🚲

3.7 After lhts, 1st rd ➡ (where 🚲 ends, Hunsley St)

3.9 At give way jct ⬅ via 🚲 (Torrington Pl), keep ⬆

4.5 Jct Tavistock Pl/Marchmont St (4th set of lhts):
   * For **Liverpool Street** and **London Bridge** ⬆
     (see after 0.5 km page 22)
   * For **Euston** ⬅ (Marchmont St), **dismount** at lhts, ⬅
   * For **King's Cross-St. Pancras** ⬅ (Marchmont St), 3rd ➡ (Bidborough St),1st rd ⬅, **dismount** at lhts, ➡

London Connections: Route C and D

Route C: Euston/King's Cross-St. Pancras - Liverpool Street:

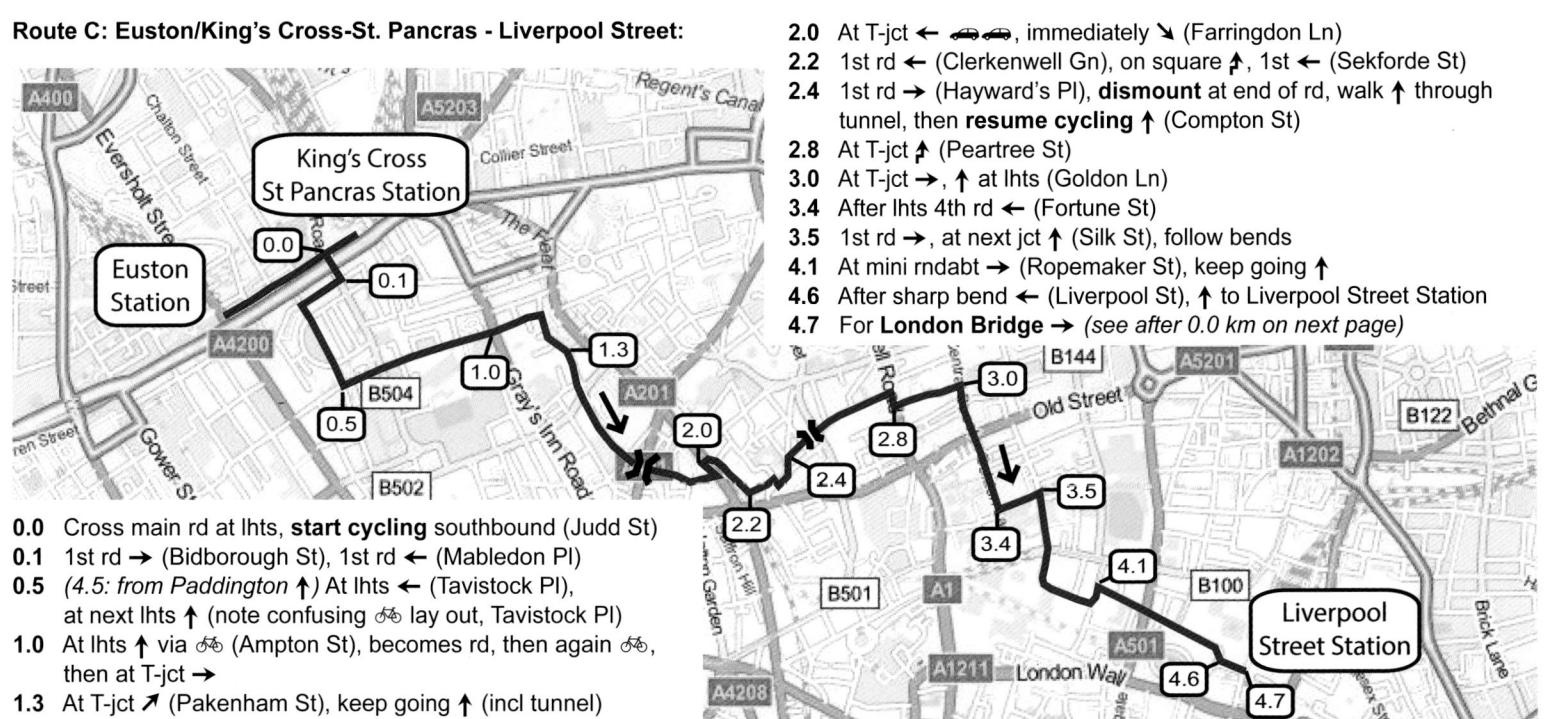

0.0 Cross main rd at lhts, **start cycling** southbound (Judd St)
0.1 1st rd → (Bidborough St), 1st rd ← (Mabledon Pl)
0.5 *(4.5: from Paddington ↑)* At lhts ← (Tavistock Pl),
   at next lhts ↑ (note confusing 🚲 lay out, Tavistock Pl)
1.0 At lhts ↑ via 🚲 (Ampton St), becomes rd, then again 🚲,
   then at T-jct →
1.3 At T-jct ↗ (Pakenham St), keep going ↑ (incl tunnel)

2.0 At T-jct ← 🚗🚗, immediately ↘ (Farringdon Ln)
2.2 1st rd ← (Clerkenwell Gn), on square ↗, 1st ← (Sekforde St)
2.4 1st rd → (Hayward's Pl), **dismount** at end of rd, walk ↑ through
   tunnel, then **resume cycling** ↑ (Compton St)
2.8 At T-jct ↗ (Peartree St)
3.0 At T-jct →, ↑ at lhts (Goldon Ln)
3.4 After lhts 4th rd ← (Fortune St)
3.5 1st rd →, at next jct ↑ (Silk St), follow bends
4.1 At mini rndabt → (Ropemaker St), keep going ↑
4.6 After sharp bend ← (Liverpool St), ↑ to Liverpool Street Station
4.7 For **London Bridge** → *(see after 0.0 km on next page)*

London Paddington Station

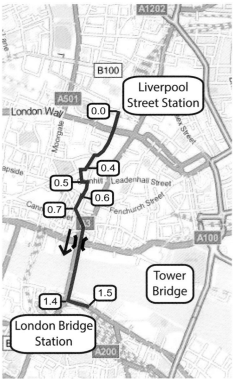

Liverpool Street Station

Tower Bridge

London Bridge Station

Route D: Liverpool Street - London Bridge (via Monument):

0.0 *(4.7: from Euston/King's Cross-St. Pancras →)* Leave Liverpool Street Station via exit "Old Broad St"; ↑ (Old Broad St southbound)

0.4 At end of rd ↗ and **dismount** imm onto pavement, walk ← into pedestrian area, pass George Peabody statue

0.5 At end of pedestrian area cross rd via ped lhts, then ↟ **resume cycling** (Birchin Ln)

0.6 At T-jct ↟ (Nicholas Ln)

0.7 At T-jct ←, at lhts ↗ onto London Bridge (**Monument Tube Station** at busy junction; take extreme care!)

1.4 After London Bridge 1st rd ←

1.5 **London Bridge Station** main entrance; 1st rd ↙, you are now on the Main Cycle Route *(section 7, see page 58)*

Many trains from the west into **Paddington** and some trains from **Liverpool Street** to Manningtree/ Harwich have **bike carriages**, like shown on the middle picture left. Note you must take your pannier bags to the passengers' carriages. On other trains (like the high-speed King's Cross-St. Pancras-Dover route) you'll have to park your bike in the disabled area near the toilets (see picture bottom left).

The International Terminal for Eurostar trains to Paris and Brussels at St. Pancras; bike reservations essential!

Section 1: Dover - Canterbury (52.7 km / 32.5 miles)

🚲 12.7 km, 🚶 36.7 km, 🚗 3.3 km, 🚗🚗 0.0 km
Stations: Dover Priory (please note station "Dovercourt" is in Harwich; very confusing!), Deal (after 16 km), Sandwich (after 25 km), Canterbury East & West

Dover with its striking white cliffs has one of the most spectacular ferry ports in the world. Beyond the majestic promenade though, Dover town is not so scenic. Our route heads for the cliffs straight away, avoiding a winding main road by using a pleasant but steep footpath. It leads to the spectacular **Dover Castle**. Visit its Great Tower with the Royal Court, explore the secret tunnels and learn about the Dunkirk evacuation of 1940 (open daily, £17 pp, English Heritage members and Overseas Visitor Pass holders free). Enjoy spectacular views over the English Channel at the **Langdon Cliffs** and **The White Cliffs of Dover** visitor centre (free).

0.0 **Cycle on left-hand side!** Leave ferry terminal and at rndabt ⬆ onto one-way lay-by rd on right side of main rd (use 🚲 contra flow), reset computer at East Cliff Hotel (house no 28-29), (**1**)

0.2 Just before end of lay-by rd ⬆ cross main rd via lhts, join 🚲 on promenade (to Town Centre, **1**)

0.5 *(For 🏠 🏨 🍴 🛒 🍽 ℹ️ **Dover** ⬆ via promenade 🚲, at "New Bridge" pedestrian area →, ⬆ through tunnel)*

0.5 Imm after Premier Inn → via gap in fence (Douro Pl); **dismount** at end of rd, then walk ↖ via footpath

0.6 Cross main rd → via lhts (Woolcomber St), walk on footpath

0.8 1st rd ↗, **resume cycling** (St James St)

0.9 Keep ↗, then cross main rd ⬆ (Laureston Pl), *(Note; ignore signs 1 at this point!)*

1.1 **Dismount** in sharp bend to right (Victoria Park), ⬆ via footpath, very steep climb!

1.3 At high wall → via footpath (to Dover Castle), ep ↖ **resume cycling** on main rd 🚗 (**1**)

1.3 🚶 🛒 **Dover Castle** *(use pedestrian entrance)*

1.6 1st rd → (Upper Rd, to Deal, **1**)

2.9 🚶 **Langdon Cliffs** *(views Dover Harbour & Castle)*

2.9 In sharp bend to left ↗ via private driveway (**1**)

3.2 🚶 🛒 **The White Cliffs of Dover** *(visitor centre)*

3.2 Follow signs **1** via gravel/tarmac path; pass through 3 gates, short steep climbs!

3.6 Ep ← (**1**), then at T-jct → (to Deal, **1**)

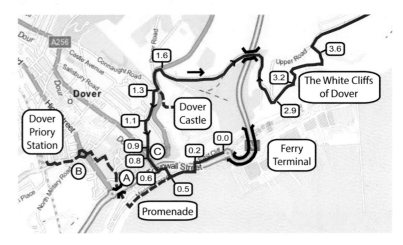

Section 1: Dover - Canterbury (52.7 km / 32.5 miles)

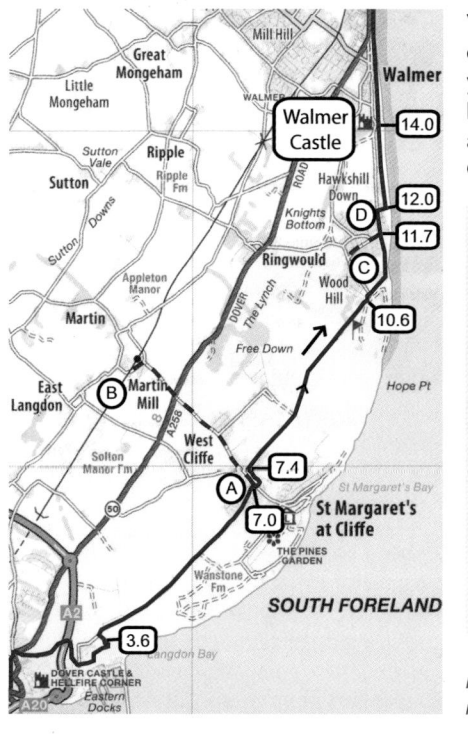

Via the pretty village of **St. Margaret's at Cliffe** you'll make a gradual descent through pleasant rolling hills into **Kingsdown**. From here you'll cycle traffic-free on the seafront to **Deal**, overlooking a shingle beach. On the way, **Walmer Castle** and **Deal Castle** are both worth a visit (open daily, £8 and £5 pp, English Heritage members and Overseas Visitor Pass holders free).

7.0 🏠 ⛺ 🛒 🍴 **St. Margaret's at Cliffe** *(hotel)*
7.0 At T-jct →, then 1st rd ← (Chapel Ln, **1**)
7.4 At T-jct → via dead end rd (to Deal, **1**)
10.6 Ep ↖ via rd with poor surface
11.7 At end of rd ↗ (to Deal, **1**)
11.7 🏠 ⛺ 🏨 🛒 🍴 **Kingsdown** *(pub)*
12.0 1st public rd → (Boundary Rd, **1**), then ← via 🚲
14.0 🍴 🛒 **Walmer Castle and Gardens**
15.5 🍴 **Deal Castle**
15.9 🏠 🚉 🛒 🍴 ⚓ *Deal*
15.9 Ep ↑ join rd 🚌 (to Sandwich, **1**)
17.3 Follow sharp bend ← away from seafront (**1**)
17.7 At T-jct → (Golf Rd), 1st rd ↖ (to Sandwich, **1**), keep going ↑ via golf course, also ↑ at private rd

Pictures on page 27 below: Walmer Castle, the coast at Deal, rolling hills near St Margaret's at Cliffe and the Barbican Toll Gate in Sandwich.

Beyond Deal the route heads inland via flat and open marshland to **Sandwich**, an historic "Cinque Port". In the 12th century, various ports on England's east coast received special royal privileges in return for the availability of ships to be used by the King. By the 16th century, the importance of the royal Cinque Ports had declined, but the system gradually made way for the formation of the Royal Navy. Sandwich's harbour silted up over time and is now well inland. You'll pass Sandwich's historic landmark, the **Barbican Toll Gate**, on arrival. To avoid one way restrictions and long detours we use a handy short footpath link in the town. This route takes you to the High Street, but is not signposted.

19.5	🚲 🍴 **The Chequers** (pub)
24.0	In Sandwich 1st 🚲 ↗ (**1**), at end park ep ↑ join rd
24.5	**Dismount** at lhts and ← on narrow pavement, pass Upper Strand Street on left hand side, then imm → cross rd onto footpath, footpath narrows
24.6	Cross rd, ↑ via footpath, ep → **resume cycling** into High Street 🚲 🏠 🏨 ⛺ 🏧 🚲 🍴 ⚕ *Sandwich*, keep to ↖ at next jct
24.8	At T-jct ↗ and imm ← at T-jct (Breezy Corner) 🚗
25.3	Once rd widens 1st rd → (Richborough Rd, to Canterbury, **1**)

Section 1: Dover - Canterbury (52.7 km / 32.5 miles)

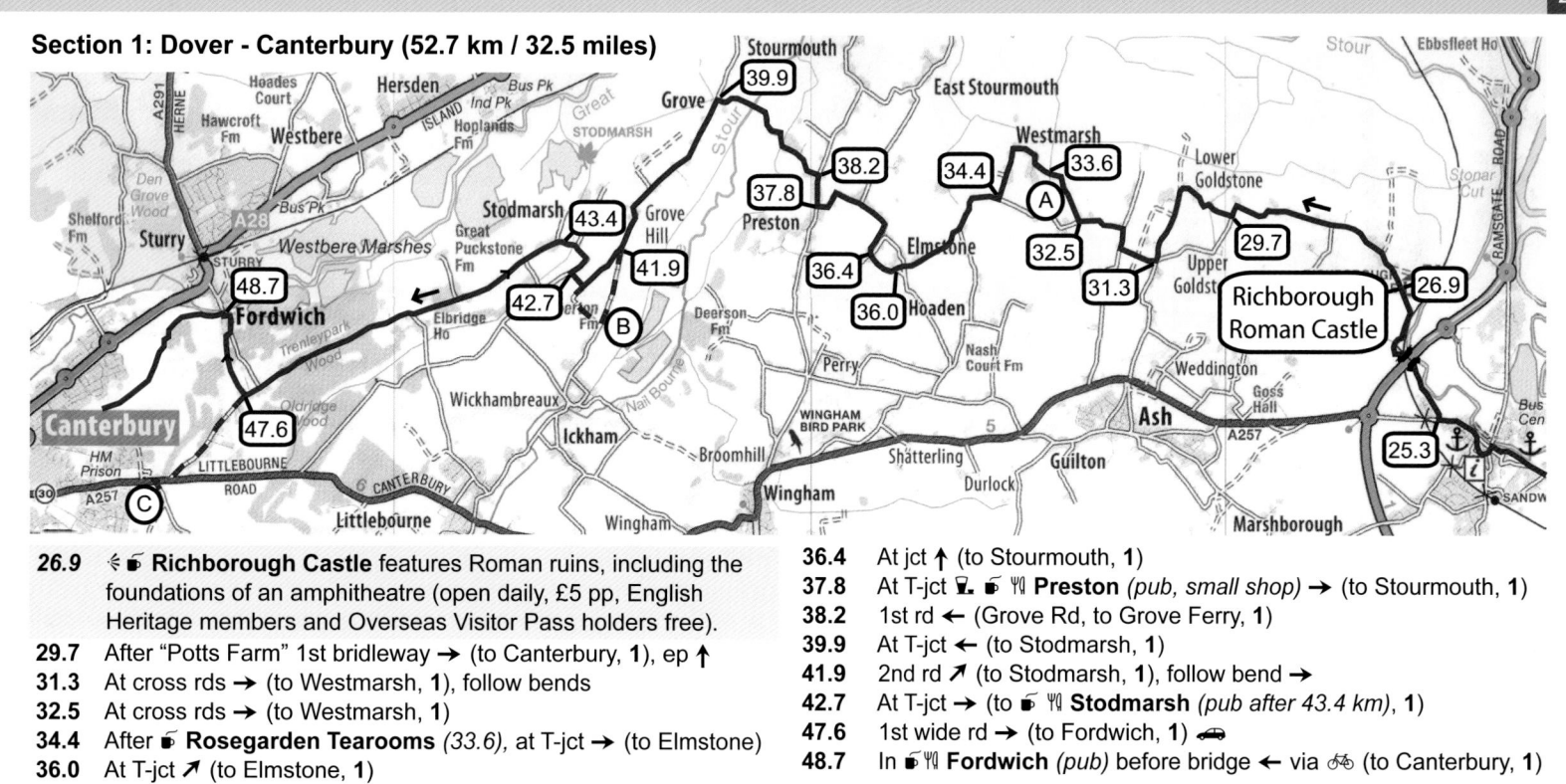

26.9	🥾🚲 **Richborough Castle** features Roman ruins, including the foundations of an amphitheatre (open daily, £5 pp, English Heritage members and Overseas Visitor Pass holders free).
29.7	After "Potts Farm" 1st bridleway → (to Canterbury, **1**), ep ↑
31.3	At cross rds → (to Westmarsh, **1**), follow bends
32.5	At cross rds → (to Westmarsh, **1**)
34.4	After 🚲 **Rosegarden Tearooms** *(33.6),* at T-jct → (to Elmstone)
36.0	At T-jct ↗ (to Elmstone, **1**)
36.4	At jct ↑ (to Stourmouth, **1**)
37.8	At T-jct 🚲 🚲 🍴 **Preston** *(pub, small shop)* → (to Stourmouth, **1**)
38.2	1st rd ← (Grove Rd, to Grove Ferry, **1**)
39.9	At T-jct ← (to Stodmarsh, **1**)
41.9	2nd rd ↗ (to Stodmarsh, **1**), follow bend →
42.7	At T-jct → (to 🚲 🍴 **Stodmarsh** *(pub after 43.4 km),* **1**)
47.6	1st wide rd → (to Fordwich, **1**) 🚗
48.7	In 🚲 🍴 **Fordwich** *(pub)* before bridge ← via 🚲 (to Canterbury, **1**)

Kent is famous for its fruit orchards. Between Sandwich and Preston you'll see plenty. At **Westmarsh Farm Park** you can camp overnight in an orchard, although this might not be for everyone. This farm site has limited amenities, shared with seasonal fruit pickers. Just down the road, **Rosegarden Tearooms** is a great place to have a break. From nondescript **Preston** you cycle into flat marshland, interspersed by some short hill climbs. **Stodmarsh** and **Fordwich** are pretty villages. **Neals Place Farm** is the closest campsite to Canterbury's City Centre (see section 2). To get to the **Cathedral** you must take our route; ignore route 1 signs!

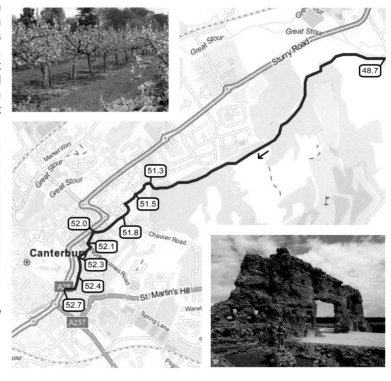

51.3	Ep ← via 🚲 (to City Centre, **1**), ep ↑ via rd
51.5	At T-jct ↖ (Military Rd), then 1st 🚲 ← (to City Centre, **1**), follow bend → at council offices
51.8	Cross Chaucer Rd ↑ via 🚲 (Falala Way, to City Centre, **1**)
52.0	Ep ← via rd (to Dover, **1**)
	*(Note; ignore signs **1** to City Centre/Northgate at this point!)*
52.1	1st rd ← (North Holmes Rd) and imm → (Havelock St)
52.3	1st rd ← (Monastery St, to City Centre)
52.4	At rndabt ↑, then 1st rd → (Church St)
52.7	**Dismount** at end of rd, cross main rd ↑ via lhts

*Don't miss the Roman ruins of **Richborough Castle** (see picture bottom right).*

Canterbury Cathedral on left (see also left picture on page 6).

Section 2: Canterbury - Rochester (71 km / 43.6 miles)

🚲 28.5 km, 🚶 38.3 km, 🚗 3.3 km, 🚗🚗 0.6 km
Stations: *Canterbury East & West, Whitstable (after 10 km), Faversham (after 26 km), Kemsley (after 44 km), Newington (after 50 km), Rainham (after 56 km), Gillingham (after 63 km), Rochester*

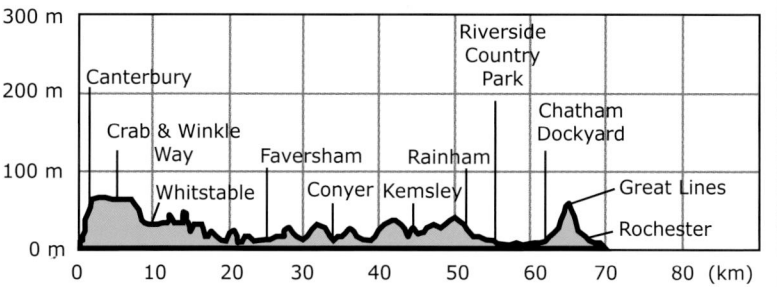

Historic **Canterbury** is a bustling major tourist attraction. Surrounded by fine medieval city walls, the whole city centre is an architectural journey into England's past. At its heart is the majestic **cathedral**, seat of the head of the Anglican Church, the Archbishop of Canterbury (open daily, £10 pp, attendance of church services free). Other attractions are the **Canterbury Heritage Museum** with its **Rupert Bear** exhibition, the **Roman Museum** and the **Westgate Towers Museum** (all open daily, £8, £6 and £4 pp). From the historic West Gate you can also take scenic **canal boat tours**.

0.0 *(52.7)* After crossing A28 via lhts, ↑ (Burgate),
(Note to watch flexible sign regarding current cycle policy)

0.3 ⫷ 🏠 🏛 ⛺ ♨ 🛍 🍴 ⚡ 🅸 *Canterbury*

0.3 At "Butter Market" and ⫷ **Cathedral** ↖ (Mercery Lane),
at next jct → (Parade, to West station)

0.8 End Parade ↑ through ⫷ **West Gate**,
then imm ← (Westgate Grove, becomes 🚲)

0.9 Ep ↖ via rd, then 1st rd → (Whitehall Bridge Rd, to Wincheap, **1**)

1.1 At next jct ↑ (to Whitstable, **1**), traffic free bridge

1.3 At next jct ↖ (Queens Avenue, to Whitstable, **1**)

1.6 At bend to right ↑ via 🚲, cross rd ↗ via lhts, then ↑ (to Blean, **1**),
then 1st 🚲 → (to Whitstable, **1**, becomes Fisher Rd)

2.0 At T-jct ← (to Whitstable, **1**)

2.3 At end of rd ↖ via 🚲 (**1**), then 1st 🚲 → (**1**), follow through route

3.5 At T-jct ← via 🚲 on left side of rd, cross to 🚲 on right side at lhts

3.8 1st 🚲 ↗ (Crab & Winkle Way, to Whitstable, **1**),
at rd crossings ↑ via 🚲 (to Lowes Wood, **1**)

The **Crab & Winkle Way** takes you through pleasant **Lowes Wood** on the course of Britain's first passenger railway (1834). There is no good seafront cycle route in **Whitstable** and beyond, so ignore signposted route 1 and use our inland route. To avoid difficult barriers on the way to Faversham (see picture) use the alternative route, see the maps.
Scenic **Faversham** was once at the forefront of the explosives industry. Historic marvel, but out of town, is 13th century Maison Dieu (weekends only, 14-17hrs, £2 pp)

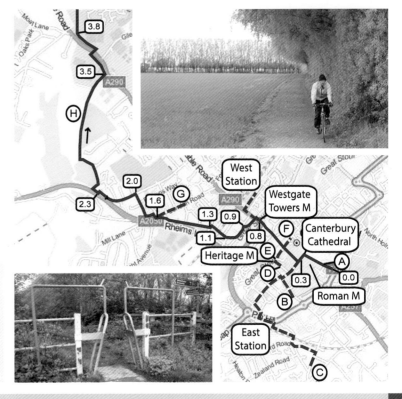

Section 2: Canterbury - Rochester (71 km / 43.6 miles)

7.0 In Lowes Wood, follow sharp bend to →

7.5 At T-jct of paths ← via gravel path

8.5 In bend to right ↖ via gravel path (**1**),
keep following main gravel path, becomes tarmac

10.0 Ep ↖ via rd 🚗 (to Whitstable, **1**)

10.4 ▲ 🛏🚿 🍴 ***Whitstable*** *(super store only)*

10.4 1st 🚲 ↖ (Invicta Way, to Whitstable, **1**)

10.8 Just before viaduct tunnel → via narrow 🚲 (to Faversham, **1**)
(Note; only ↑ via 🚲 for station and bike shop!)

11.1 Ep ↖, cross rd and ← via narrow 🚲 on right hand side of rd (**1**),
leading over viaduct

11.8 At rndabt ↑ via 🚲 on right hand side of rd (**1**)

12.0 Use lhts to cross main rd ↖ onto 🚲 on left hand side of rd,
then 1st rd ← (Golden Hill) *(Note; ignore signs **1** at this point!)*

14.5 Cross main rd ↖ (Pye Alley Lane)

15.5 At T-jct →, at next jct ↖ (Fox Cross Hill)

16.2 At T-jct ↖ (Dargate Rd)

17.3 After sharp bend to right, 1st rd ← (Plumpudding Ln, to Bargate),
then 1st rd → (to Waterham)

18.1 At T-jct ← (to Graveney)

20.6 At T-jct ← 🚗 (to Faversham)

21.4 1st rd → (Sandbanks Ln, **1**)
(↑ to avoid barriers, see picture page 31, use map for diversion)

23.2 1st 🚲 ← (to Faversham, **1**); barrier ahead

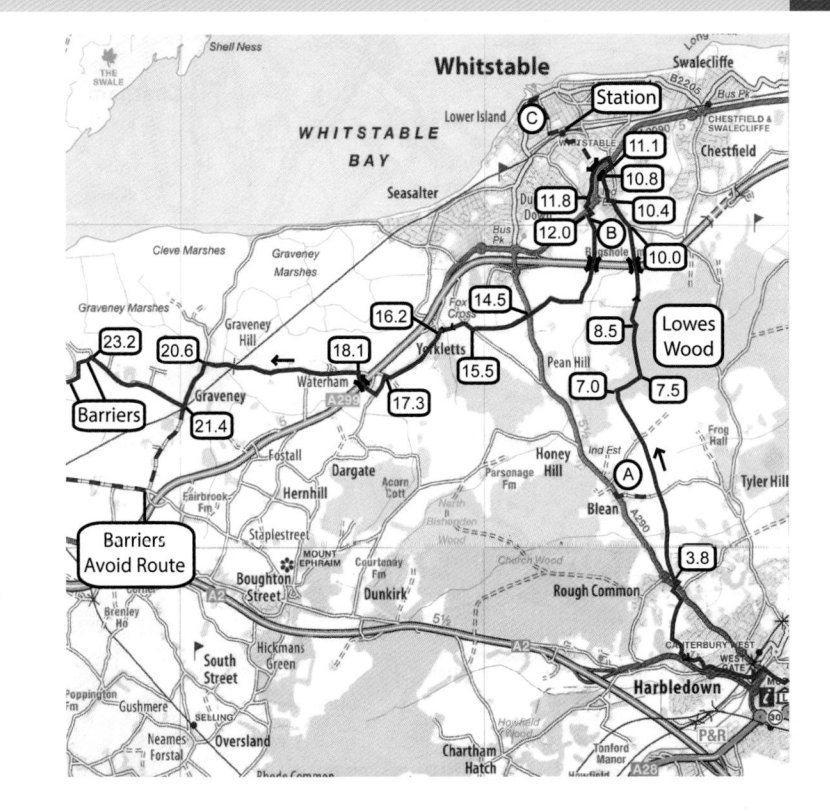

24.2 At jct of paths ← (**1**), barrier ahead at bridge

24.8 Ep ← via rd (**1**), follow bends to right and left

25.8 In built up area 1st 🚲 → (to Sittingbourne, **1**), at rd ↑ via 🚲 (cross Gordon Square, **1**)

26.3 Ep ↑ via rd, at T-jct ← (**1**)

26.5 At give way jct ⚡🏠⛺🍴☕🍴ℹ️ *Faversham* → 🚗 (Quay Ln, **1**)

26.6 1st rd → 🚗 (Bridge Rd, **1**),1st rd ← (Brent Rd, **1**)

27.1 At T-jct → 🚗 (Davington Hill, **1**), at ☕ *(small shop)* 1st rd ← Priory Rd (to Sittingbourne, **1**)

27.5 At T-jct → via 🚲 (Bysing Wood Rd, **1**)

28.2 After ☕🍴 *(super store)* cross rd and ← via 🚲 on right hand side of rd, then imm ↗ (Bysing Wood Rd, to Sittingbourne, **1**)

28.7 1st rd → (Tin Shop Hill, to Sittingbourne, **1**)

29.3 At cross rds ↑ (to Sittingbourne, **1**)

29.5 1st rd ← (**1**)

Painters Farm Camping near Faversham and **Campers Palace Farm Hostel** in Doddington (see page 34) are the last campsites on the way to London. These campsites are both well away from the main route, but worth the detour if you prefer such accommodation.

The flat marshlands around tiny **Conyer** with its pretty harbour are great for bird watching. This should compensate for the uncomfortable cycling on the gravel and grass paths in this area, which might be muddy after heavy rain.

You'll bypass most of industrial **Sittingbourne** by its new River Bourne Bridge. Kent's fruit orchards will resume after suburban **Kemsley**.

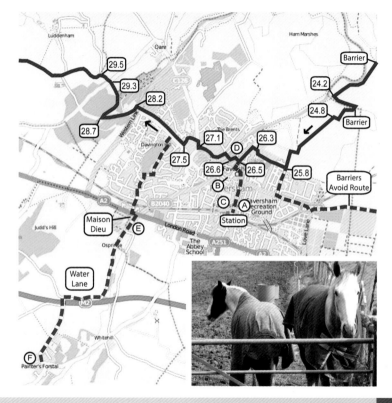

Section 2: Canterbury - Rochester (71 km / 43.6 miles)

32.1 At T-jct → over railway level crossing (**1**)
33.1 2nd rd → (to Deerton Natural Burial Ground, **1**)
35.3 At T-jct ↗ (to Conyer) *(For ⛺ 🏠 ←, see map)*
36.2 ⇇ 🛒 🍴 **Conyer** *(For pub, follow rd → to end)*
36.2 Via entrance "Swale Marina" ↑ and 1st 🚲 ↖ (**1**)
37.6 After bridge over sluice ↖, path away from estuary
38.2 1st path ← (to Sittingbourne, **1**), follow bend to →
38.8 Ep ← via rd (to Sittingbourne, **1**)
39.8 1st rd ↘ (to Sittingbourne, **1**)
    (Note; ignore signs to town centre at this point!)
40.4 At next jct keep ↖ (**1**), keep going ↑
41.0 At end of tarmac ↑ via gravel path *(Note; no signs)*
41.6 At jct of paths →, **dismount** and ↑ across area of fly tipping,
    resume cycling on tarmac rd to ↖, away from travelers' site
41.9 At T-jct → via 🚲 on left hand side of rd
    (Note; new route; ignore old signs 1 at this point!)
42.3 At rndabt ↑ via 🚲 on left hand side of rd
43.8 After river bridge at rndabt with electricity grid mast 1st 🚲 ↖
    away from main rd, 🚲 becomes rd
44.4 After 🍴 🛒 🍴 *(pub/shop)* at rndabt ↗ (Menin Rd)
44.6 At T-jct ← (Ypres Dr) and 1st 🚲 → (to Rainham, **1**),
    becomes rd after bridge over railway
44.9 Cross main rd 🍴 ***Kemsley*** *(small shops)* ⬆
    (Bramblefield Ln, to Rainham, **1**), rd becomes 🚲

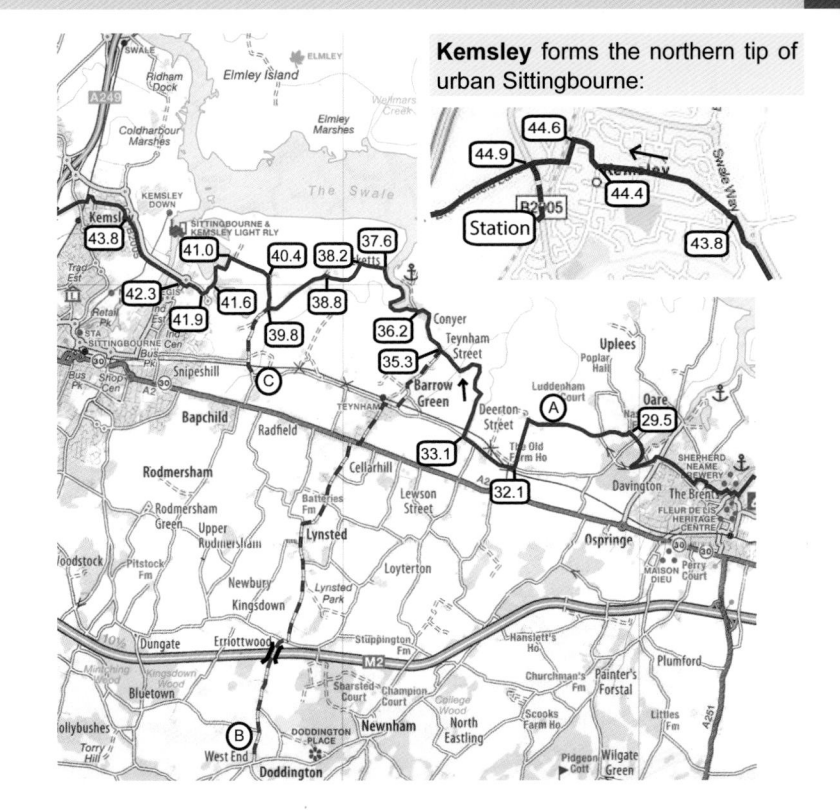

Kemsley forms the northern tip of urban Sittingbourne:

The district of **Swale** provides the last truly rural stretch of Kent's fruit orchards. **Newington** is a quiet village with some fine traditional buildings (see picture on left). In **Rainham** you'll arrive in **Medway**, a large urban area named after the estuary on its northern flanks. The **Riverside Country Park** provides the ultimate escape. Via a causeway you can walk to **Horrid Hill** in the Medway estuary. More great estuary views are available in **The Strand Leisure Park**.

Then, you fully arrive in urban Medway. **Chatham** has been a stronghold for the Royal Navy since the days of Henry VIII. The **Historic Dockyard** is now an open air museum with a tremendous collection of historic ships, dry docks and steam power demonstrations (open daily, £17 pp). Ironically, Chatham is also the site of the worst defeat of the Royal Navy. In 1667, the Dutch navy raided the Medway; reason to build the **Great Lines**, a high line of defences overlooking both river and town.

The guidebook leaves official route 1 to take in these Great Lines, taking you to historic **Rochester** where you enter the world of **Charles Dickens**. Numerous plaques on buildings in the lively high street refer to the locations in the books of the famous author. The **cathedral** dates from 604 AD. (open daily, free entry). The ruins of **Rochester Castle** next to Medway Bridge are a superb sight (open daily, £6 pp, English Heritage members and Overseas Visitor Pass holders free).

Section 2: Canterbury - Rochester (71 km / 43.6 miles)

45.6 Ep ← (to Rainham, **1**)
46.5 1st rd → (Stickfast Lane, to Rainham, **1**)
48.3 At T-jct ← (to Newington, **1**)
50.6 🚲 🛒 🍴 *Newington* (800m to village centre, ←)
50.6 At T-jct → (School Ln, Boxted Ln, to Rainham, **1**)
52.1 At cross rds ↑ (to Rainham, **1**)
52.3 In descent ← (Restricted Byway, to Rainham, **1**)
52.6 1st narrow 🚲 ← via cattle grid (to Rainham, **1**)
53.0 At end of narrow path → via wide gravel path
53.7 🛒 🍴 **River Valley Golf Course** *(open to all public)*
53.7 Ep ← (to Rainham, **1**), 1st rd → (Canterbury Ln, **1**)
54.8 At T-jct ← 🚗 (**1**)
55.0 2nd rd → (Wakeley Rd, to Chatham, **1**)
55.7 After 🚲 🛒 🍴 *(pub/small shops)* before bend to left → (Taswell Rd), then 1st rd ← (Harry St, **1**)
56.1 At T-jct ↑ 🚲 🛒 🍴 *Rainham* ← 🚗 and 1st rd → (Childscroft Rd, to Chatham, **1**)
56.2 1st rd → (Chalky Bank Rd) *(Note; ignore signs 1 at this point!)*
56.8 At T-jct → (Berengrave Lane, **1**) 🚗
57.1 ↑ to join narrow 🚲 on right side of rd
57.4 At rd crossing ↑ (⇐**Riverside Country Park**, **1**)
57.7 Ep ↑ onto car park, then ← via estuary 🚲 (**1**)
59.5 At viewpoint ⇐**Horrid Hill** ← via wide gravel path
59.7 Before gate → via wide gravel path (**1**)

The inset on the right provides a more detailed map of **Rainham**:

61.1 Ep ← via rd with poor surface (**1**) *(Do not go ↑ via riverside path!)*
61.3 At T-jct → via 🚲 on right side of rd (**1**), ↑ at rndabt
61.9 1st rd → (Owens Way, **1**), then follow 🚲 riverside route (**1**)
62.7 At small beach, follow main path ↖, keep going ↑
62.8 ⇐🛒 **The Strand Leisure Park** *(Pavilion)*
62.9 At rndabt → via 🚲 (to Chatham Maritime, **1**)
63.5 After 🚲 *(Pier Rd, shops)* at jct via lhts ↑ to 🚲 on left side of rd (to "Universities of Medway"), keep to path near main rd *(Note; ignore signs 1!)*

63.9 At major jct with lhts 2nd rd ↖ via 🚲 on left side of rd
(to "Universities of Medway"), at T-jct → via rd

64.3 1st rd → (New Kent Rd)

64.5 ↑ (to Liberty Quays, **1**), **dismount** at footbridge, imm ←
(Don't cross bridge!), at end of slope again ←,
resume cycling on paved 🚲 (to Chatham)

65.2 Ep ↗ through gate and ← via 🚲 on left side of rd

65.3 🚲 🏠 ✂ **Chatham Historic Dockyard**
(400m; → via crossing, then →, keep to path on left of roads)

65.3 ↑ at crossing (to Chatham, **1**), join 🚲 lane 🚗

65.9 At rndabt 2nd exit ↖ (Middle Street, to Brompton shops)
*(Note; ignore signs **1** at this point!)*

66.1 At top of hill → (🚇 Brompton High St),
at T-jct ← (Garden St), keep going ↑ (Sally Port)

66.9 Via 🚲 ↑ into 🚲 **Great Lines Heritage Park**, there 1st 🚲 →,
follow main path, ↗ downhill at end

68.0 Ep ↑ via rd, at T-jct ← downhill

68.2 **Dismount** at lhts, cross ↑ via lhts,
resume cycling on traffic free rd ↑ to shops 🏠 🚇 ✂ 🍴 **Chatham**

68.4 → into High St, ↑ at rd crossing, keep going ↑ 🚗

69.6 At major jct with lhts ↑, **dismount** at start High St, ↑ into
🚲 🏠 🚇 ✂ 🍴 ⚕ 🛈 ***Rochester*** *(Note; ignore signs **1**!)*

70.1 Just before big clock hanging over High St ←,
resume cycling (Boley Hill), ↑, keep castle on right

70.3 Imm after castle → and → again (Bakers Walk)

70.4 At T-jct ↘ via riverside rd 🚗, to Medway Bridge

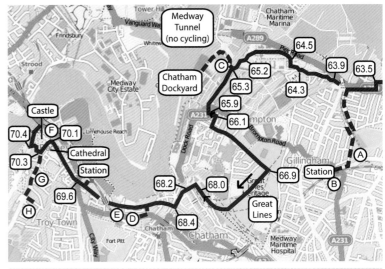

Section 3: Rochester - Woolwich (52 km / 32.1 miles)

🚲 36.3 km, 🚶 15.2 km, 🚗 0.4 km, 🚗🚢 0.1 km

Stations: *Rochester, Lower Higham (after 9 km), Gravesend (after 17 km), Dartford (after 30 km), Erith (after 40 km), Woolwich Arsenal*

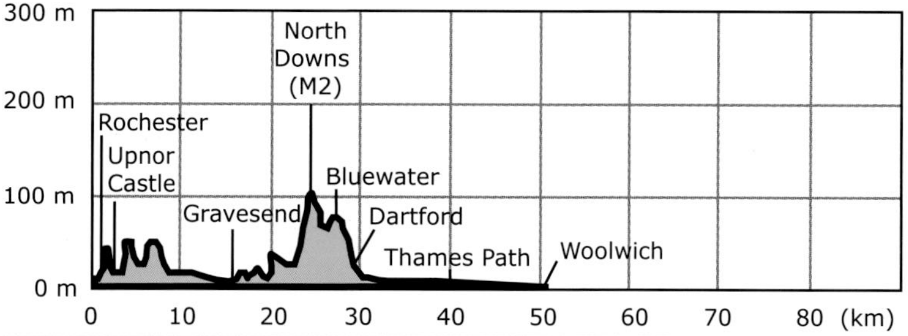

[Elevation profile graph: vertical axis 0 m to 300 m, horizontal axis 0 to 80 km. Labels on the graph: Rochester, Upnor Castle, North Downs (M2), Bluewater, Gravesend, Dartford, Thames Path, Woolwich]

0.0 *(70.4)* Cross Medway Bridge via 🚲 on right side of main rd
0.3 After bridge imm → (Canal Rd, to Upnor, **1**)
1.0 At jct with lhts ↑ via steep path (**1**), becomes rd, then 🚲
1.9 Ep → via 🚲, at lhts ↟ to other side of main rd, follow path ↖ (**1**)
2.9 Ep ↖ join rd *(For ♿🚻 **Upnor Castle** 1st →; open daily, £6 pp)*
3.3 In sharp bend to left ↗ (M.O.D. Rd, **1**)
3.7 At cross rds ↑ (Upchart Rd, to Chattenden, **1**)
4.8 Just before rndabt ↖ via 🚲 (Woodfield Wy, **1**), at ep join rd
5.7 At T-jct before "Construction Engineer Sch" ← (**1**)
6.1 At T-jct → (Higham Rd, **1**), keep going ↑ (to Gravesend, **1**)

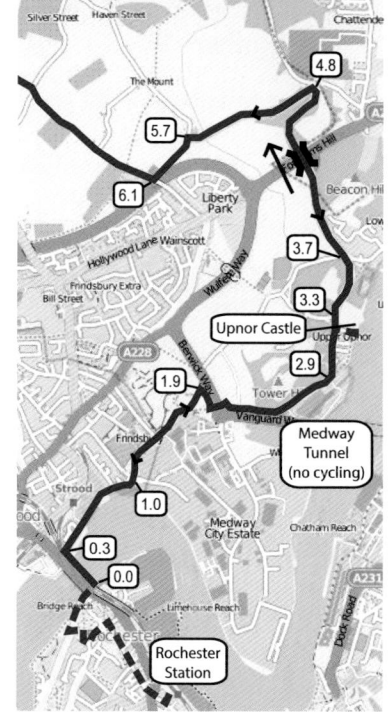

Charles Dickens

Welcome to
Upnor Castle

This Tudor artillery fortress, built in 1559 to protect the new Chatham Dockyard, saw action during the famous Dutch raid of 1667, before undergoing conversion into a huge gunpowder magazine.

Heading west from **Rochester** you'll encounter some short climbs before a cycle path through flat marshland will take you to **Gravesend**. Beyond its derelict industrial buildings you'll find a nice promenade, ideal for a break. You can also be part of the Thames on a **Tilbury Ferry** return trip!

8.2 At T-jct ↗ (Lower Rochester Rd, **1**)

9.5 In sharp bend to left ⬆ (Canal Rd, to Gravesend, **1**)
(For 🏠 🍴 🍽 Lower Higham ←)

11.2 At end of rd ↑ via 🚲 (**1**), becomes rd

15.2 In Gravesend ⬆, at end of rd ↑ through industrial wilderness

16.0 After bridge over lock Gravesham Canal Basin imm ↗ via ramp to ⬳ 🍽 **Gravesend Promenade**

16.4 End park ↖, 1st rd → (The Terrace, to Dartford, **1**)

16.7 At jct → (Royal Pier Rd, **1**)

16.9 At end ↖ via ramp, ↑ via 🚲 on right side of rd

17.1 At Town Pier 🏠 🍴 🍽 🍽 / 🅸 *Gravesend* ⬆ to left side of rd (narrow 🚲, **1**)

17.3 At rndabt follow 🚲 ↖, beyond rndabt → at rd crossing, then back "⬆" (Clifton Rd, to Dartford, **1**)

17.5 At T-jct ⬆ via 🚲 on left side of rd (to Dartford, **1**)

17.6 In front of rndabt → via riverside 🚲 (**1**)

18.0 Ep ↑ via rd, at T-jct → (Clifton Marine Pd, **1**)

18.4 1st 🚲 ← (to Dartford, **1**), ep ↗ via rd with steep climb

18.6 1st rd ←, at T-jct →

18.8 Cross rd ↑ via 🚲 on left side of rd, at next jct ↗ via lhts, continue 🚲 on left side of rd (**1**)

Section 3: Rochester - Woolwich (52 km / 32.1 miles)

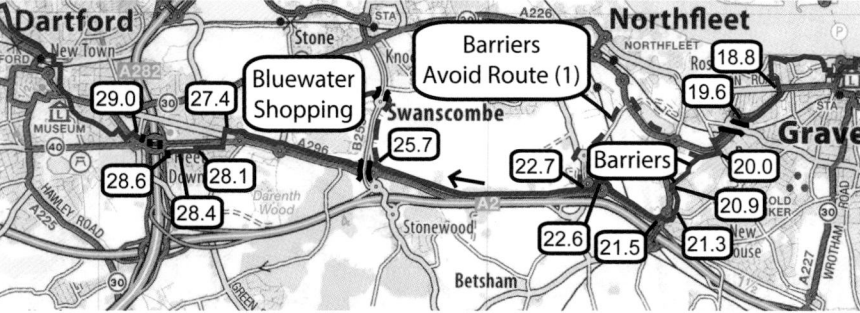

*Disused **chalk quarry** next to Bluewater Shopping Centre on left, **Erith Pier** and the River Thames above. The **Thames Path** west of Dartford is the highlight of this route section, see also picture on page 3.*

Leaving Gravesend you'll encounter two barriers similar to those shown below; use route 1 and the map to avoid. The **North Downs** have been heavily quarried for chalk. You'll cycle on paths along main roads in a surreal landscape, looking down on **Bluewater Shopping Centre**. It is bleak cycling through urban **Dartford** before returning to the Thames.

19.6 At jct with lhts follow ⬡, using rd crossings, ← (to Dartford, **1**)

20.0 At jct with lhts ⬆ to ⬡ on left side (to Ebbsfleet, **1**), then 1st ⬡ ↖ *(Note; ignore signs **1**, unless avoiding barriers)*, keep going ⬆, path narrows onto course of dismantled railway

20.9 Ep ← 🚗🚗, 1st rd ← and 1st rd → (Gwynn Rd)

21.3 At T-jct → via lay-by and imm ⬆ cross rd to ⬡ on left side of rd (to Ebbsfleet), cross ⬆ at rndabt, then ← via ⬡ on right side of rd

21.5 ↗ via lay-by; keep ↗ via narrow path without sign posts, then → via narrow path on right side of M2

22.6 Ep cross rd ⬆ via lhts to ⬡ on left side of rd

22.7 Just beyond rndabt, cross rd → via lhts and ← zigzag uphill (**1**), keep going ⬆ via ⬡ (**1**)

25.7 At rndabt, 2nd ⬡ ← (to Dartford, **1**), 1st ⬡ ↗

27.4 After 2nd rndabt, ⬆ via lhts, then cross bus lane and ↗, join residential rd (to Dartford, **1**)

28.1 At sign "dead end rd" ←, at T-jct → (to Town Centre, 1)

28.3 *(For 🍴 local shops 1st rd ←)*

28.4 At cross rds ⬆ (Hesketh Av), in bend ⬆ via ⬡ (**1**)

28.6 Ep →, imm ↘, through tunnel, then ← via ⬡ bridge over M25 (**1**), then → through next tunnel

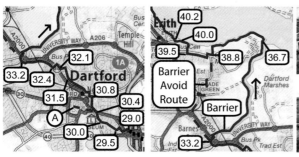

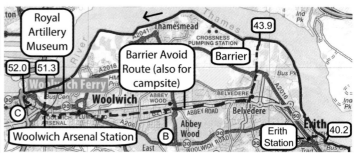

Cycling on the **Thames Path** to **Woolwich** with its **Royal Artillery Museum** (open Tue-Sat, £6 pp) is superb, but watch the barriers! Top picture is barrier on middle map, bottom picture is barrier on right map.

29.0 At jct "Pilgrims Way" ↑ via poor ⚲ on right side (**1**), a bit further, cross ↑ to poor ⚲ on left side, then 1st rd ← (Downs Av, **1**)

29.5 At T-jct →, at next T-jct again → (**1**)

30.0 At T-jct → (Dareth Rd, to Town Centre, **1**), after 100m in bend to right ↖ via ⚲ ramp (**1**)

30.4 At lhts ↑ *(For ▯ ☕ 🍴 ₰ Dartford ←)*, then 1st rd ↗ (Overy St, to Erith) 🚗

30.8 At T-jct ← via ⚲ on left side (**1**), later ↟ to ⚲ on right side, keep going ↑ via ⚲ on right side (Victoria Rd, **1**)

31.5 After rndabt, 2nd rd ↗ (Priory Rd North, **1**), then 2nd rd ← (**1**)

32.1 At T-jct → via ⚲ on right side of main rd (**1**)

32.4 Cross main rd ↟ to other side (to Erith, **1**), go ↑

33.2 After railway viaduct over rd, "round" left side of next rndabt, then cross main rd ↟, 1st rd → (**1**), join ⚲ to gravel river path *(to avoid barrier ↑ via left side of main rd; use map)*

36.7 ⚓ **Dartford Creek Barrier & Dartford Crossing**

38.8 Ep → via ⚲ on right side, later ⚲ on left (Manor Rd, Thames Cycle Route, to Greenwich, **1**)

39.5 After gentle climb → (Appold St, to Greenwich, **1**), end of rd ↟ (James Watt Wy), ↑ onto riverside ⚲ (**1**)

40.0 ⚓ ▯ ☕ 🍴 **Erith** (River Pier and super store)

40.0 At Pier, join rd ↖ and ↟ via ⚲ on right side (**1**)

40.2 At jct →, after slope down →, follow riverside ⚲ ↑ (**1**)

43.9 ↑ via riverside ⚲ *(to avoid barrier and for △ ←; use map)*

51.3 ↑ at Arsenal Piazza *(For ⚓ ▯ ☕ 🍴 ₰ Woolwich Arsenal ←)*

52.0 Cross Woolwich ferry rd ↟ to ⚲ (**1**), continue on page 54

Section 4: Harwich - Maldon (82 km / 50.5 miles)

🚴 *13.3 km,* 🚶 *52.9 km,* 🚗 *14.2 km,* 🚗🚗 *1.5 km*

Stations: *Harwich International, Harwich Dovercourt (after 2 km),*
Wivenhoe (after 33 km), Colchester (after 42 km)

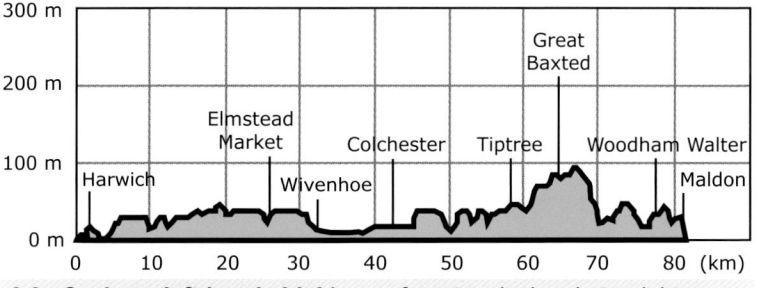

0.0 **Cycle on left-hand side!** Leave ferry terminal and at rndabt →
    (see disused petrol station on left side of rd)

0.1 1st rd ← (Foster Rd) and imm ← (Station Rd)

0.8 At rndabt via 🚴 crossings ↑ (to Old Harwich, **51**)

1.0 1st path ← (to National Cycle Network), around houses onto 🚴

2.3 Ep ↖ (Station Rd, to Old Harwich, **51**)

2.6 At station ↘ (**51**) 🚗, ↑ at lhts 🏠 🛅 📷 🍴 /ℹ️ *Harwich* (Kingsway)

3.0 At T-jct ← (Marine Pd, **51**)

3.1 At end of rd → and imm ↘ down onto beach path

4.0 Leave path and join rd ↗ (to Great Oakley, **51**) 🚗

6.6 At rndabt ← (to Great Oakley, **51**) 🚗

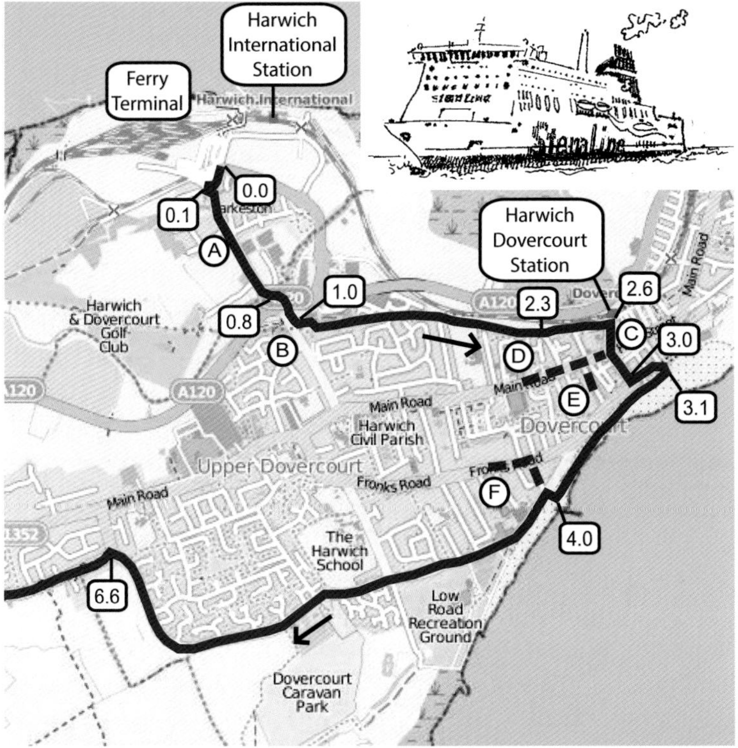

Dutch and Danish cycling enthusiasts can join us in Harwich, but you also use the Hook of Holland ferry to cycle to Amsterdam with our The Netherlands Guidebook (see www.cyclinginholland.com). Harwich's headland between the North Sea and the Stour and Orwell Rivers made the town a Royal Navy stronghold for centuries. Today, the pleasant promenade is Harwich's most significant feature. You'll be exposed to some fast-moving traffic when leaving town.

8.9 At 🍴 🍺 **Cherry Tree** *(pub)* → (Rectory Rd) *(Ignore route 51!)*

10.5 At T-jct ← (to Gt Oakley)

11.8 At T-jct → into 🚲 🍴 🍺 **Great Oakley** 🚗

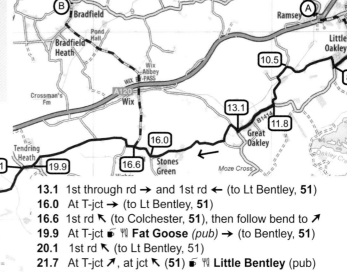

13.1 1st through rd → and 1st rd ← (to Lt Bentley, **51**)

16.0 At T-jct → (to Lt Bentley, **51**)

16.6 1st rd ↖ (to Colchester, **51**), then follow bend to ↗

19.9 At T-jct 🍴 🍺 **Fat Goose** *(pub)* → (to Bentley, **51**)

20.1 1st rd ↖ (to Lt Bentley, **51**)

21.7 At T-jct ↗, at jct ↖ (**51**) 🍴 🍺 **Little Bentley** (pub)

22.5 At T-jct ↖ (**51**)

23.1 At T-jct ← (to Great Bromley, **51**) 🚗

25.0 At jct 🚲 🍴 🍺 **Old Courthouse Inn** *(pub)* ↑ 🚗

27.6 At lhts 🚲 🍴 🍺 **Elmstead Market** → (**51**) 🚗🚗

27.8 1st rd ← (School Rd, **51**)

29.0 1st rd ↗ (**51**), at T-jct ↗ (**51**) 🚗

29.8 1st rd ↖ (to Wivenhoe, **51**)

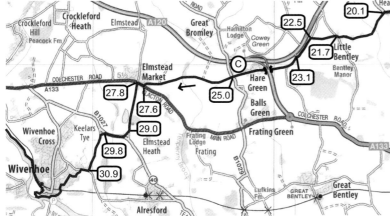

Section 4: Harwich - Maldon (82 km / 50.5 miles)

Wivenhoe has a pleasant quay on the River Colne. A riverside path takes you to **Colchester**. In its **Castle Park** you'll find the impressive **Norman Castle** (open daily, £7 pp). The **Hollytrees Museum** brings 300 years of social history to life (open daily, free). You'll leave town via the Roman **Balkerne Gate**. Beyond Colchester's large housing estates, rural Essex will resume. **Tiptree** is the next village along the way.

30.9 At T-jct → (**51**), 1st rd ← (Bowes Rd, **51**)
31.4 1st rd ← (Claremont Rd, **51**), follow bends to end
31.9 At T-jct ← (**51**), follow bend ←, then → on gravel rd
          (to Cook's Shipyard, **51**), tarmac resumes later
32.7 After fish and chips shop 1st rd ← (Rose Lane, **51**)
32.8 🛏 🍴 **Wivenhoe** *(riverside pub and chips take away)*
32.8 At T-jct → follow paved quay path to end
33.4 Ep ← and 1st rd → (Old Ferry Rd)
33.6 1st rd ← (Admiral Wk), at T-jct ←
33.8 At rndabt ← via car pk onto 🚲
          (Wivenhoe Trail, **51**, to Colchester), keep going ↑
37.3 Cross rd via lhts and → via 🚲 on left side of rd,
          at rndabt ← (Hawkins Rd, to Town Centre, **51**)
38.0 At T-jct ←, cross rd ↟ onto 🚲 bridge,
          then → (to Town Centre, **51**), at end 🚲 join rd (Haddon Pk)
38.2 1st 🚲 → (to Town Centre, **51**), follow to end
39.3 Ep cross rd via 🚲 lhts → into park 🚲 (**51**)

Colchester's Roman **Balkerne Gate**

40.5 At jct in front of park gate → 🚲 (to Town Centre, **51**)

40.7 After footbridge 1st rd ← *(Note; ignore signs* **51***!)*

40.9 1st 🚲 ← (to Town Centre, **51**),
follow tarmac 🚲 ↗ (Stan Ruby Wy), after bridge ↑ via rd

41.4 At bend to right ↑ (to Town Centre, **1**),
dismount at next jct and walk ↑ *(Note; ignore signs* **1***!)*

41.6 ⬱ 🏠 ⛺ 🍴 🛏 ⛽ 🍽 ⚡ **ℹ Colchester** *(for Castle 2x ←)*

41.6 At T-jct →, walk on pavement on right side of rd

42.0 At lhts ↑ **resume cycling** (Balkerne Passage/Gdns)

42.2 **Dismount** at end, walk ↑ via ⬱ **Balkerne Gate**, ↑ via footbridge,
then ↑ **resume cycling** (Popes Ln)

42.4 At jct ↖ (Popes Ln, becomes Rawstorn Rd)

42.6 3rd rd →, cross main rd ← via lhts
(opposite Essex County Hospital) and join rd → (**1**) 🚗🚗

43.7 After "St Mary's School for girls" on right side of rd, 1st rd ←
(Norman Way, to Prettygate, **1**)

43.9 At start private rd → via 🚲 (to Prettygate, **1**)

44.8 Ep ← via rd (Prettygate Rd, to Prettygate, **1**)

45.3 At T-jct 🍴 **Prettygate** ↑ (Prettygate Rd)

45.6 At T-jct ↑ (Baden Powel Dr), follow bends to end

46.3 At T-jct ← (Straight Rd) 🚗

46.5 At T-jct ↑ (Gosbecks Rd, to Mearsea) 🚗

46.8 Via zebra ↑ onto 🚲 on right side of rd

46.9 1st 🚲 →, becomes rd "Gladiator Wy", at jct ← (Temple Rd)

47.1 At rndabt via 🚲 crossings ↑ (Olivers Lane, to Tiptree, **1**), keep ↑

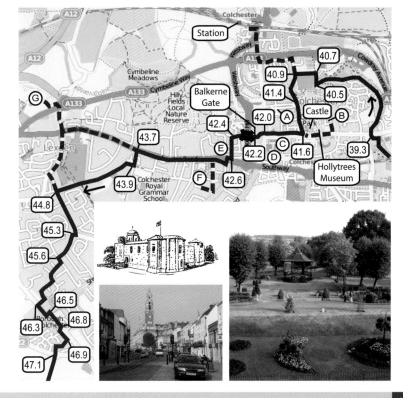

Section 4: Harwich - Maldon (82 km / 50.5 miles)

49.6 After bridge and steep climb, keep to 🚲 ↖ **(1)**

50.3 Ep at rd jct ↑ **(1)**

52.4 Opposite "Breton House" ↖, at T-jct ← (to Gt Wigborough, **1**)
*(Note pub 🏠 🍴 **Hare & Hounds** on your right across field)*

52.8 1st rd → (Shatters Rd, to Layer Marney, **1**)

54.9 At cross rds ← (to Layer Marney, **1**)

55.1 1st rd → (Woodview Rd, **1**), follow through rd

56.4 At cross rds ← (Newbridge Rd, to Tiptree, **1**)

58.1 1st rd → (Crove Rd, **1**), don't follow bcnd to left,
but keep going ↑ and at T-jct ↗ (Grove Rd, **1**)

59.5 🍴 🛒 **Tiptree** *(shops and cafe)*

59.5 At T-jct → **(1)** 🚗🚗, 2nd rd ↖ (Ransom Rd, **1**)

59.9 At cross rds ↑ (Vine Rd, to Witham, **1**)

60.4 At end of rd at house "Little Oaks" → via 🚲 **(1)**

60.8 At T-jct ← (to Witham, **1**)

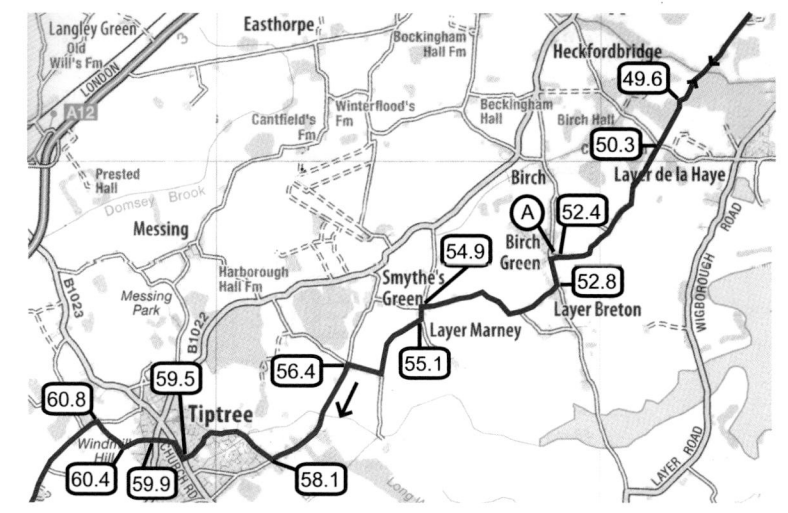

Essex is dominated by crop farming, interspersed by marshland and woodlands on higher ridges. Campers shouldn't miss the special **Opera in the Orchard** site. **Maldon** is well-known for traditional sailing barges. Its **Promenade Park** has great sea views. Note choice of accommodation beyond Maldon is very limited. If you need a B&B before arriving in London, you should make arrangements before leaving Maldon!

64.4 At cross rds ↑ (Tiptree Rd, to Gt Baxted, **1**)

66.3 After Great Baxted, 1st rd ↗ (Braxted Rd, **1**)

67.1 At cross rds → (to Hatfield Paverel, **1**)

67.7 At cross rds ↑ (Church Rd, to Langford, **1**)

67.7 🛒 🍽 **The Chequers** *(pub after 50 m, ← at jct)*

68.2 At T-jct ↗ (Church Rd, **1**)

70.2 At T-jct ↗ (to Hatfield Paverel, **1**) 🚗

70.9 1st rd ← (to Hatfield Paverel), ↑ (Spring Ln, to Maldon)

72.7 At T-jct → (to Hatfield Paverel, **1**) 🚗, 1st rd ← (to Woodham Walter, **1**), follow through rd

74.5 At T-jct ←

77.3 Start 30 mph zone Woodham Walter:
* To bypass Maldon: ↑ *(Note; ignore signs* **1***!)*, continue reading after 4.6 km on page 48
* For Maldon only: ← (Blue Mill Ln, to Beeleigh, **1**)

78.8 2nd rd ← (Manor Rd, **1**)

79.1 1st rd → (Cut-A-Thwart Ln, to Beeleigh, **1**)

80.7 At T-jct → (**1**), at T-jct ← (**1**) 🚗

81.9 ⛵🏠🚉🛒🍽🍴🅷 **Maldon**

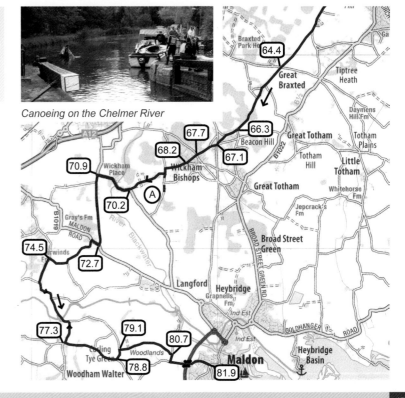

Canoeing on the Chelmer River

Section 5: Maldon - Woolwich (76 km / 46.9 miles)

🚲 7.2 km, 🚶 54.5 km, 🚗 12.8 km, 🚗🚗 1.5 km

Stations: Ingatestone (after 29 km), Seven Kings (after 63 km), Barking (after 67 km), East Ham (after 69 km), Woolwich Arsenal

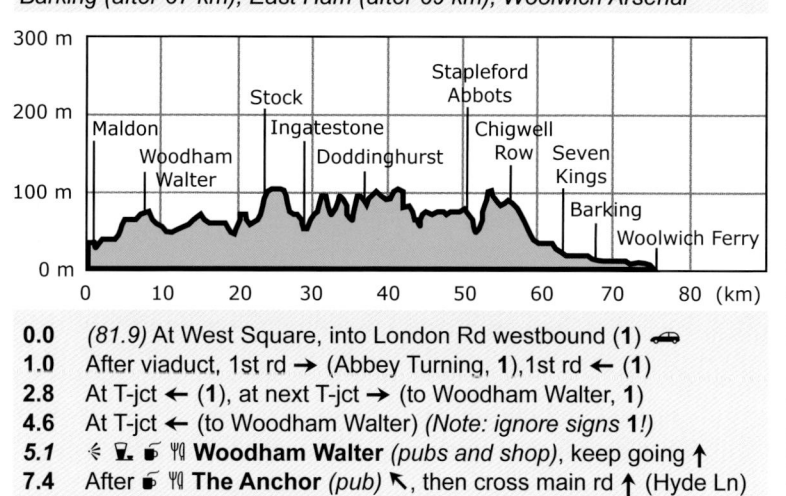

0.0	(81.9) At West Square, into London Rd westbound (1) 🚗	
1.0	After viaduct, 1st rd → (Abbey Turning, 1), 1st rd ← (1)	
2.8	At T-jct ← (1), at next T-jct → (to Woodham Walter, 1)	
4.6	At T-jct ← (to Woodham Walter) *(Note: ignore signs 1!)*	
5.1	⛲ 🍴 🛒 🍽 **Woodham Walter** *(pubs and shop)*, keep going ↑	
7.4	After 🛒 🍽 **The Anchor** *(pub)* ↖, then cross main rd ↑ (Hyde Ln)	
8.3	*(For 🏠 🍴 🛒 🍽 **Danbury** ↘ via Mill Ln, ↗, ← via main rd)*	
8.5	After jct "Mill Lane" 1st rd → (to Gay Bowers)	
8.7	At T-jct ↗, 1st rd ↖ (to Bicknacre)	
10.0	At T-jct ← (to Bicknacre) 🚗, 1st rd → (Moor Hall Ln)	

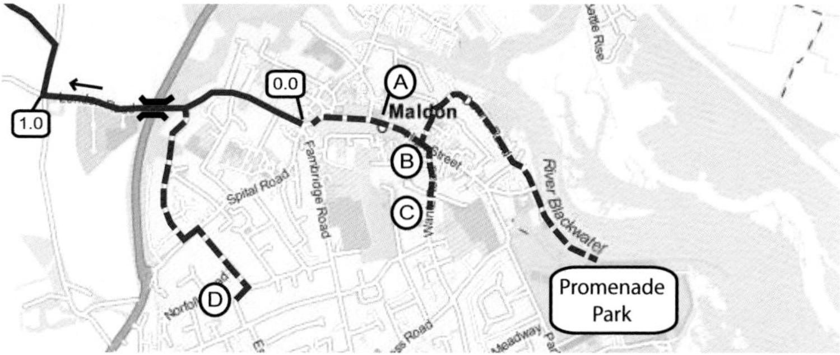

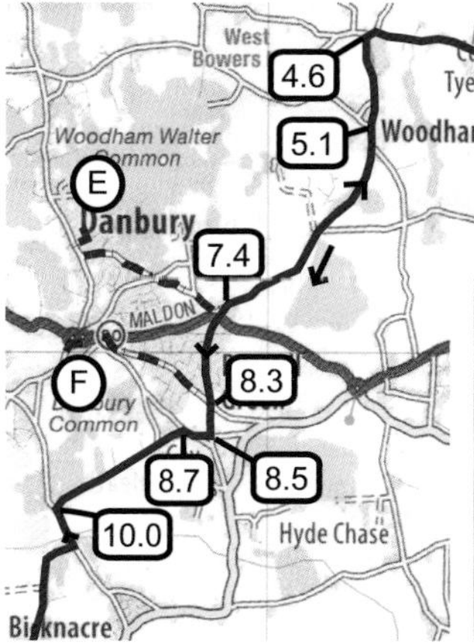

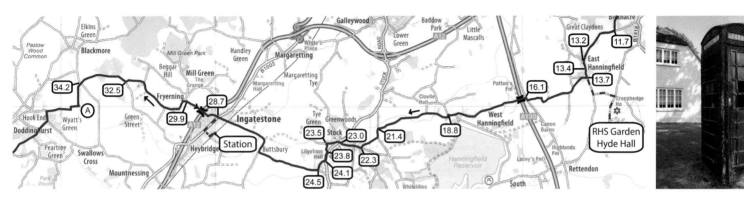

The Essex greenbelt can feel pretty empty. **Woodham Walter** is the liveliest village en-route. Its church (see picture on page above) dates from 1563, the first to be built for the "Church of England" after England's break from Rome. Garden lovers can visit **RHS Garden Hyde Hall** (open daily, £8 pp, RHS-members free). In **Ingatestone** you can briefly feel the proximity of Greater London, but it is still a long way to go!

11.7 At T-jct just beyond house "St Giles Lodge" → 🚗
13.2 At rndabt ↖ (to Rettendon) 🚗
13.4 🚾 🛒 ⑪ **East Hanningfield** *(pubs, for shop 1st rd →)*
13.7 Follow bend → (Old Church Rd, later Pan Ln)
    (For ⛲ RHS Garden Hyde Hall ↖ to Rettendon, 1st rd ←)
16.1 At T-jct ↑ (to West Hanningfield)
18.8 In 🛒 **West Hanningfield** at pub ↖ (to Stock)
21.4 At T-jct ←, 1st rd → (Mill Ln, to Stock)
22.3 After ⛲ **Stock Windmill** at T-jct → (to Stock)
23.0 At cross rds 🛒 ⑪ **Stock** *(pubs)* ↖ (Back Ln)
23.5 At sign "dead end" ← and before "Fosters Cl" ↗
23.8 At T-jct → 🚗🚗 *(note: difficult right turn ahead!)*
24.1 1st rd → (Honeypot Ln, to Ingatestone)
24.5 At T-jct → (to Ingatestone)
28.7 At cross rds 🚾 🛒 ⑪ **Ingatestone** ↑ (Fryerning Ln)
29.9 After viaduct A12, before 🛒 ⑪ **Woolpack Bistro** ↖
    (Blackmore Rd, to Blackmore), near pub again ↖
32.5 At T-jct → (Blackmore Rd, to Blackmore)
34.2 In sharp bend to right, 2nd rd ↖ (Hay Green Ln)

Section 5: Maldon - Woolwich (76 km / 46.9 miles)

36.1 At T-jct ← (to Wyatts Green), follow rd ↗

37.2 🏠 ⛺ 🍺 **Doddinghurst** *(various shops)*

38.4 In bend to right ↖ (Warren Ln, to Bentley)

39.4 At ⛺ **Kelvedon Hatch** ↗ (Frog Ln)

40.4 At T-jct → via path on left side of main rd

40.7 1st rd ↙ (Crown Rd, to Navestock Side),
keep following through rd ↑

44.0 At T-jct ↑ (Church Rd, to Navestock Heath),
keep following through rd ↑ (Havering Lane, to Havering)

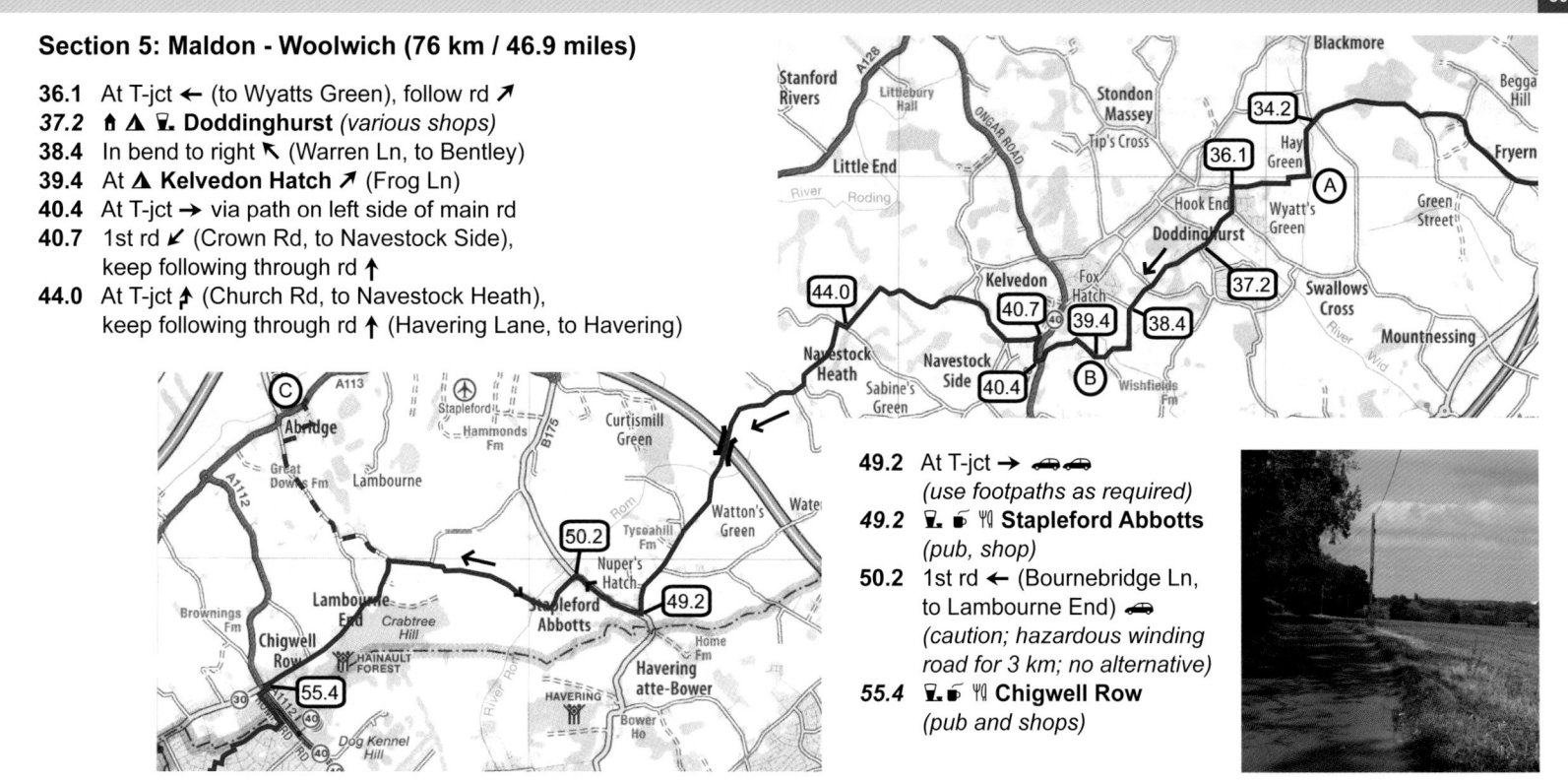

49.2 At T-jct → 🚗🚗
(use footpaths as required)

49.2 🍺 👆 🍴 **Stapleford Abbotts**
(pub, shop)

50.2 1st rd ← (Bournebridge Ln,
to Lambourne End) 🚗
*(caution; hazardous winding
road for 3 km; no alternative)*

55.4 🍺 👆 🍴 **Chigwell Row**
(pub and shops)

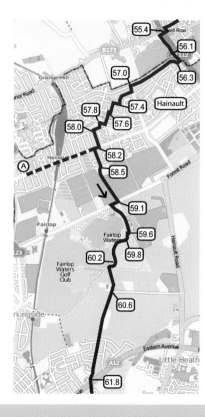

Beyond Ingatestone you'll find Essex at its hilliest. The last campsites before London are near **Doddinghurst**, although you can also camp off-route near Woolwich, see page 41. At **Chigwell Row** you hit the Greater London urban wilderness. An unconventional route via some grass paths is included, see pictures. To keep this vital link open, please give way to pedestrians and horses and walk bikes where instructed to do so.

55.4 **Dismount** at lhts, cross main rd ↑ via pedestrian lhts, then imm ← via path on right side of main rd

56.1 End path ↗ **resume cycling**, 1st rd → (Manford Wy)

56.3 At T-jct → (Brocket Wy)

57.0 3rd rd ← (opposite sports area), 1st rd → (Crossbow Rd)

57.4 At T-jct ↑ (Fawn Rd)

57.6 At T-jct ↑ (Tufter Rd)

57.8 At cross rds ↑ (Covert Rd), ↗ **dismount** for bollards

58.0 **Resume cycling** after bollards, 1st rd ← (Lime Gr)

58.2 At T-jct ↑ (Penrith Rd, dead end rd)

58.5 At end of rd ↑ into park, keep ↗ by sports fields

59.1 At T-jct ↑ (to Fairlop Sailing Centre)

59.6 At end of car park ↑ via tarmac path which stops after 30m, ↗ via grass path

59.8 Where 5 grass paths meet ↑ via grass path, gradually bending ↖

60.2 Where grass path widens (note also some gravel surface) at split of paths ↗ (to "Clubhouse"), then ← and **dismount** at gate ("Horse Ride and footpath to Painters Road"), keep walking bikes!

60.6 End path **resume cycling** ↑ (Aldborough Rd North)

Section 5: Maldon - Woolwich (76 km / 46.9 miles)

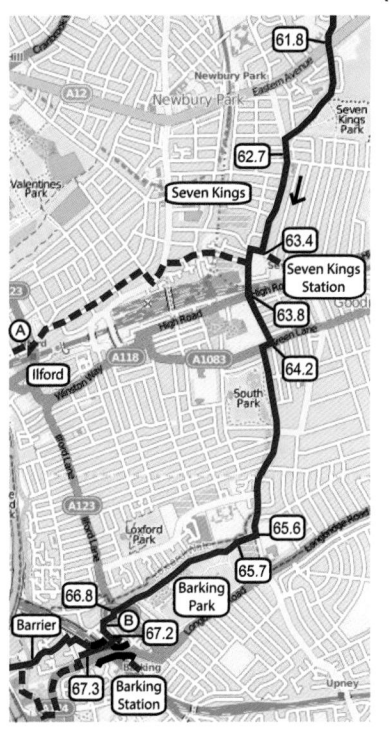

To cycle from the countryside into a world city is a true experience. The lack of an official signposted cycle route in **East Londen** adds to the sense of adventure. You shouldn't encounter any social safety issues on the way, but if you cycle with younger children you might want to skip this section. **Barking Park** is ideal for eating packed lunches. Just down the road, a **barrier** on a cyclepath (see picture) is barely passable by bike. To cross the **Northern Circular Road** we use a footbridge with some steps. Alternative routes are provided for both obstacles. The route navigates to the **Thames ferry** at **Woolwich** with spectacular views over the City.

61.8 At jct with lhts ↑ (Aldborough Rd South) 🚗
62.7 🏪 *Seven Kings (shopping area)*
63.4 At T-jct ⬆ (Aldborough Rd South), join 🚲 ↑ at end
63.8 At lhts 🏪 **Ilford** *(shopping area)* ↑ (Highbury Gdns)
64.2 At cross rds → 🚗🚗, 1st rd ← (South Pk Dr) 🚗
65.6 After house no 279 on left side, 1st path →
65.7 Ignore sign "no entry except council service vehicles", so ↑, then ↖ via waterside path ⛴ 🏕 **Barking Park**
66.8 End park route ↑ (dead end rd), after Barking Park Hotel 1st rd ↖ (Church Rd), ↖ (Pickering Rd)
67.2 At start "Wakering Rd" ↗, **dismount** on corner, then ← at house no 20 via footpath on right side of one way rd
67.3 On railway viaduct ↘ via ramp, ↖ **resume cycling** via 🚲 *(to avoid barrier ahead, keep walking ↑ on viaduct, see page 53)*

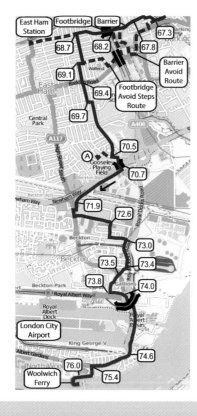

67.3 *(to avoid barrier; walk ↑, join main rd ↟ at lhts, use 🚲 lane, before rndabt ↟ via 🚲, after bridge → 🚲, Roding River Route)*

67.6 Ep ← via rd, at jct ↟ (Harts Ln)

67.8 At sharp bend to right ↑, at end ↖ via path, pass through difficult barrier and cross river bridge ↑ via 🚲

68.2 Ep ↟, **dismount** and join footbridge *(to avoid steps; ←, at end of rd → via footpath under viaduct, 1st residential rd →, at rndabt ←)*

68.7 **Resume cycling** after footbridge, at 2nd rndabt ← (Wall End Rd)

69.1 6th rd → (Kempton Rd), 1st rd ← (Bedford Rd)

69.4 At 🚉 *East Ham* (shopping area) ↑ (Ranelagh Rd)

69.7 2nd rd ← (Market Rd), 1st rd →

70.5 At T-jct ← (Gooseley Lane), at end of rd → via 🚲

70.7 Cross main rd via bridge with ramps, → via 🚲 "superhighway"

71.9 Leave "superhighway", following 🚲 ↖, at ep join rd 🚗🚗, 1st rd ← (Alpine Wy) 🚗

72.6 At rndabt → (County Rd), 2nd rd ← (dead end)

73.0 At end of rd ↑ through gate, 1st 🚲 →

73.4 After rd "Oxleas" (on right), before viaduct → 🚲

73.5 At rndabt ↑ (Ferndale St)

73.8 In sharp bend to right ↖ via path *(note: no signs)*

74.0 Ep follow signs "Gallions Reach DLR Station" to other side of large rndabt, under viaduct → via 🚲 on left side of rd (Sir Steve Redgrave Bridge)

74.6 Ep join rd ↑ 🚗

75.4 After park on left side, 1st rd ← (Pier Rd, to Ferry)

76.0 Cross Thames by free ferry or pedestrian tunnel (see pictures)

Section 6: Woolwich - London Bridge (20 km / 12.4 miles)

6A: 🚲 10.1 km, 🚶 8.8 km, 🚗 0.0 km, 🚗🚗 0.4 km
6B: 🚲 10.1 km, 🚶 9.0 km, 🚗 1.5 km, 🚗🚗 0.4 km
Stations: *Woolwich Arsenal (for access route see map page 41), Greenwich (after 10 km), London Bridge*

Elevation profile:
- 6A: Greenwich River Route — Woolwich, Greenwich, London Bridge
- 6B: Greenwich Park Route — Woolwich, Greenwich Park, Greenwich, London Bridge

0.0 *(52.0/76.0)* Join 🚲 westbound (Thames Cycle Route (TCR), **1**)
1.1 Just before end of path (◁ **Thames Barrier viewpoint**) ←, then → via rd, follow bends (TCR, **1**)
1.3 1st rd → (Ruston Rd), at T-jct → (TCR, **1**)
1.6 At rndabt ↗ (to Greenwich, A206), 🚲 lane, 🚗🚗
2.0 Use 2nd set of lhts to cross rd →, 🚲 (TCR, **1**)
2.4 At ◁ 🚶 **Thames Barrier** ↑ briefly on-road onto 🚲 (TCR, **1**)
3.2 Ep ↑ via 🚶 **Anchor and Hope** *(pub)*, ↑ 🚲 (TCR, **1**)
4.1 After sailing club →, 🚲 (TCR, **1**), keep ↑ on riverside 🚲

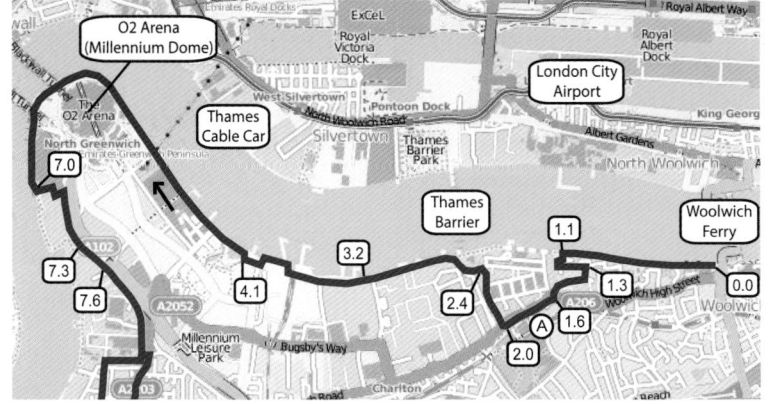

7.0 After "rounding" ⛵**O2 Arena/Millennium Dome** via riverside 🚲 follow 🚲 signs ← away from river *(do not continue on footpath!)*, ep → via lay-by rd (to Greenwich, TCR, **1**)

7.3 Keep ↗ via poor 🚲 on right side of main rd (**1**)

7.6 Ignore 🚲 bridge over main rd, ↑ via lay by-rd on right side (**1**)

8.0 At lhts → via 🚲 on right side of rd (TCR, **1**)

8.1 At bus stop, choose **your Greenwich Route**, see also page 57:

A: Greenwich River Route *(1.7 km: flat, easy):*

8.1 After bus stop ↑ via 🚲, 1st rd → (Mauritius Rd, **1**)

8.7 At T-jct ←, 2nd rd → (at pub, TCR, **1**), follow rd ↑

9.0 At 🍺 **Georgian Free House** *(pub)* ↗ follow 🚲 (TCR, **1**)

9.4 At 🍺 **Trafalgar Tavern** *(pub)* ↟ through gate, → via 🚲

9.8 ⛵🏠 🚉 🍺 🍴 ℹ️ *Greenwich Pier* (end River Route)

B: Greenwich Park Route *(3.4 km: climb into park, great views):*

8.1 After bus stop, cross rd ↟ onto bus lane on main rd 🚗 ↑

8.6 At lhts cross rd 🚗🚗 ↑ (Van Burgh Hill) 🚗

9.6 At T-jct ↖, after 30m cross rd → through wall gap, in ⛵ **Greenwich Park** ↑ via 🚲 (to Rose Garden)

10.1 Follow wide rd with 🚲 ↖, at rndabt →

10.4 At ⛵**Greenwich Royal Observatory** make U-turn, at rndabt ↘

11.0 ↑ at park gates and **dismount** at major jct

11.2 Walk ↑ via pavement on right side of rd (cross main rd via lhts), **resume cycling** ↑ at end of one way rd (to ⛵**Cutty Sark**)

11.5 ⛵🏠 🚉 🍺 🍴 ℹ️ *Greenwich Pier* (end Park Route)

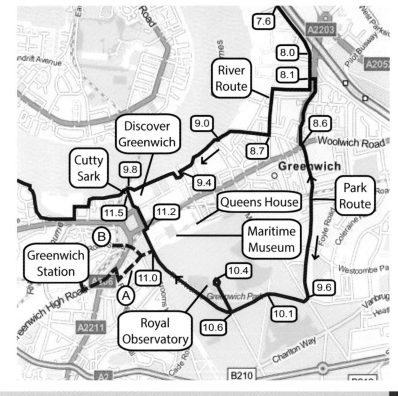

Section 6: Woolwich - London Bridge (20 km / 12.4 miles)

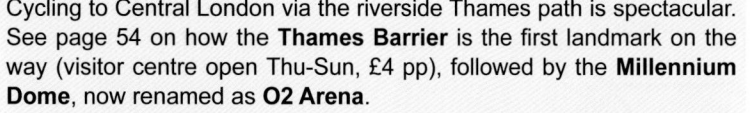

Cycling to Central London via the riverside Thames path is spectacular. See page 54 on how the **Thames Barrier** is the first landmark on the way (visitor centre open Thu-Sun, £4 pp), followed by the **Millennium Dome**, now renamed as **O2 Arena**.
The **Thames Cable Car** (also on page 54) provides a sky ride over the Thames (open daily, £9 pp), but the clear views over the high office blocks of **Canary Wharf** can also be enjoyed from the path around "The Dome". This path ends abruptly at the entrance of the Blackwall Tunnel.

0.0 *(9.8/11.5)* At ⛴ **Cutty Sark/Pier** go westbound (**4**)
0.3 River path leads onto rd, there 1st rd → (TCR, **4**)
0.5 At T-jct → via pavement on right, **dismount** (**4**)
0.7 After bridge, **resume cycling** on 1st 🚲 ↗ to riverside
1.3 Ep ↑ via rd, after 400m 1st rd → (Prince St, **4**)
2.0 Just before T-jct → via cobbled rd, 1st rd ← (**4**)
2.2 At T-jct → (Grove St, **4**), keep going ↑ *(Note: ignore signs route **4**!)*
3.2 At T-jct → (Plough Wy), at rndabt ← (Calypso Wy)
3.4 Cross lock area ↑ and → via 🚲 (**4**)
3.7 At T-jct → via bridge, keep ↑ via rd (**4**)
3.9 At T-jct ←, 1st 🚲 → (Bonding Yard Wk, **4**)
4.1 1st 🚲 ↗ through bushes, before tunnel → by pub *(Note: ignore **4**!)*, after pub ↑ via rd, follow bend ← (to Nelson Dock)
4.4 2nd rd → (Rotherhithe St, to Nelson Dock)
6.2 🏨 🍴 🛒 🍽 **Rotherhithe** *(YHA, eateries, small shop)*

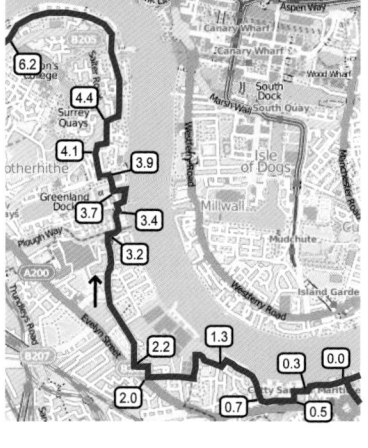

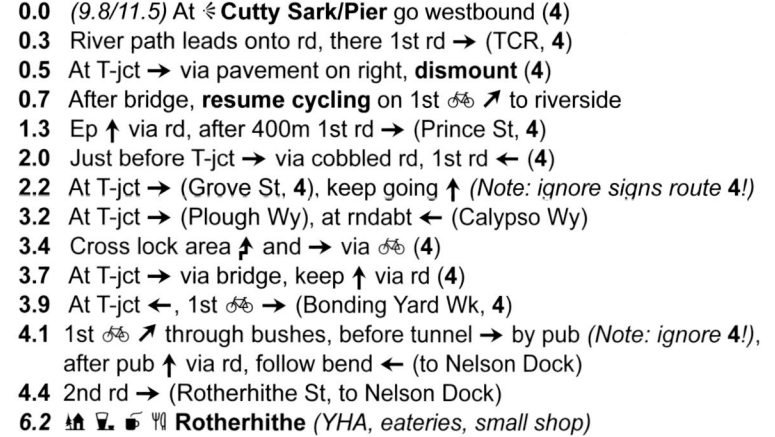

On page 55 you can choose between the official riverside route to **Greenwich** or our route via Greenwich Park. Our park route brings you to a spectacular view point next to the **Royal Observatory** (open daily, free), on the famous **Greenwich Meridian**. Back in the valley, you can visit the **National Maritime Museum**, **Queen's House** and **Discover Greenwich** (all open daily, free). The historic ship **Cutty Sark** can be found on the pier of Greenwich (open daily, £12 pp). This is where our two routes merge.

In **Rotherhithe** (see page 56) you'll find many converted warehouses and an excellent YHA before scenic **St. Saviour's Dock** and **Shad Thames** take you under the **Tower Bridge** (exhibition open daily, £8 pp). Walk the last 600m to London Bridge station. The **Tower of London**, warship **HMS Belfast** and the **London Dungeons** are all within walking distance. The best place to park bikes is at the far end of Tower Bridge Park (on left).

6.9 At end of rd ↑ via 🚲, ↑ via rd, then imm 🚲 ↗ (4)
7.2 Ep ↰ via gravel, ↑ via rd (Bermondsey Wall E, 4)
7.6 ← (Bevington St, 4), 1st rd → (Chambers St, 4)
8.0 At T-jct → (George Row) *(Note ignore signs route 4!)*, **dismount** at end of rd, ← (Bermondsey Wall West)
8.2 At "Mill St" ↰ via walkway "St. Saviour's Dock Bridge"
8.4 1st rd ← **resume cycling** and imm → (Shad Thames)
8.7 **Dismount** at ⟨ **Tower Bridge**, walk ↖ via middle path
8.9 At end of park, walk ↑ (see "3 Norton Rose" on left)
9.0 At square, walk ↖ (see water feature in middle of street)
9.3 Ep walk ↗ via footpath next to main rd (to London Bridge)

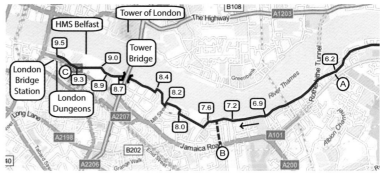

Section 7: London Bridge - Kingston (30 km / 18.6 miles)

🚲 *12.2 km,* 🚶 *14.2 km,* 🚗 *2.7 km,* 🚗🚗 *1.1 km*
Stations: *London Bridge, London Waterloo (after 2.8 km), London Victoria (after 5.0 km), West Brompton (after 11.2 km), Barnes (after 18.6 km), Kingston upon Thames*

Whether you start the route in **London** or cycled from further east, this route section is likely to be one of your favourites. The **spectacular diversity** of (urban) landscapes and density of **London's iconic landmarks** make this a ride you'll remember the rest of your life. Note the cycle route in itself is not perfect. To stay away from heavy traffic, dismount at busy junctions like Blackfriars Road and Parliament Square. Sustrans Route 4 is used for most of the way, but to be able to cycle by **Buckingham Palace** and through **Hyde Park** we have devised our own route through Westminster and Kensington. Stick to our route for the best experience!

From London Bridge, the ride starts on London's popular **Southbank**. Its narrow streets can be packed with tourists. Allow time to take in the Thames views at **Shakespeare's Globe Theatre** (open daily, tours £14 pp) and the **Tate Modern** (open daily, free). Speed up towards the **London Eye** (open daily, £19 pp) and Westminster Bridge, overlooking the **Big Ben** clock tower.

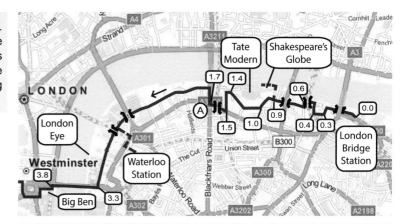

0.0 *(9.5/1.5)* Standing with your back to main entrance London Bridge station ↖ into quiet rd northwestbound (to Southwark Cathedral, **4**)

0.3 After tunnel 2nd rd → (Winchester Wk, **4**)

0.4 At T-jct ↑ (Clink St, **4**)

0.6 After tunnel at T-jct ↖ (Park St, **4**)

0.9 *(For* ⛴ **Shakespeare's Globe Theatre**, **Tate Modern** *and* ⛴ 🍽 **Thames Path** *(pubs)* → *via Emerson St)*

1.0 At T-jct ↗ (Sumner St, **4**), 1st rd → (Holland St, **4**)

1.4 Before barrier ←, follow bend ↖ (Hopton St, **4**)

1.5 At jct → 🚗🚗 (**4**) *(use footpath on right side of road as needed)*

1.7 At lhts → (Blackfriars Rd, **4**) 🚗🚗, before Thames bridge 1st rd ← (**4**) 🚗, keep going ↑

3.3 At end of rd → (Westminster Bridge) 🚗🚗 *(use bus and 🚲 lane; ignore signs route **4** at this point!)*

3.8 After Thames bridge, **dismount** at 2nd lhts next to ⛴ **Big Ben**, walk ↑ around Parliament Sq via pavements, at ⛴ **Westminster Abbey** walk ↑ via pavements around Parliament Square, **resume cycling** on 3rd exit of rndabt (George St) 🚗

Section 7: London Bridge - Kingston (30 km / 18.6 miles)

Remember many tourist attractions in Central London have **luggage restrictions**. Guarded bike parking is non-existent, so if you cycle with a full load, it is easier to visit sites on a separate journey. From the **Houses of Parliament**, **Westminster Abbey** and the **Churchill War Rooms** it is a stone's throw to **Buckingham Palace**. Its classic guard change is at 11.30 (daily April-July, otherwise every two days). It is a traffic-free ride from **Green Park** via monumental **Wellington Arch** into **Hyde Park**. A cycle path allows you to cycle the famous park for its full length from east to west to **Kensington Palace**, home of Prince William.

5.0 In approach of lhts, move ↗ into most right lane (🚗!), ↘ at lhts, after this jct, imm ↖ to ⛪ **Buckingham Palace**

5.1 ↖ via traffic-free zone in front of palace, ↑ at main gate, then use lhts to cross main rd, ← via 🚲 (Constitution Hill)

5.8 Cross rd ↑ at lhts via 🚲 under ⛪ **Wellington Arch**

6.0 Cross rd ↟ at lhts, pass through gate, cross next rd via zebra, then ↖ via 🚲 in ⛪ **Hyde Park**

7.6 *(1.7: From Paddington →)* Ep ↟ cross rd and ↗ via 🚲 park route
  * For **Paddington Station** →, see page 20
  * For ⛪ **Royal Albert Hall** ←, after 100m at jct →

8.4 At crossing of wide traffic-free avenue ← (to Flower Walk)
  *(For ⛪ **Kensington Palace** ↑, after 50m)*

8.7 **Dismount** at end of wide traffic-free avenue,
  walk → via footpath on right side of rd (Kensington Rd)

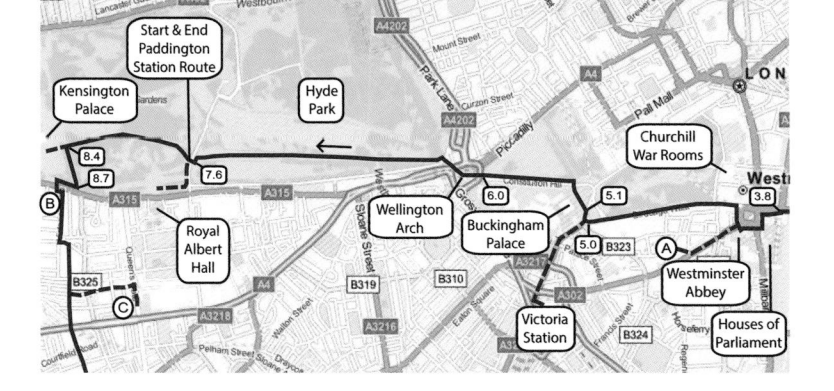

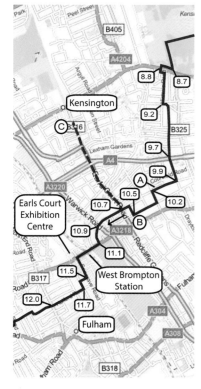

Houses in **South Kensington** are amongst the most expensive in the world, so in this respect it is surprising to find various budget accommodation options in this district. In **West Brompton** you are next to the **Earls Court Exhibition Centre**, check www.eco.co.uk/events/ to see what is on. **Putney Bridge** is where the city promptly ends and where the route turns very green once again. We make our way to **Richmond Park** were you'll completely forget you are still in London!

8.8 ← cross rd via pedestrian lhts,
     then ↑ **resume cycling** (Victoria Rd, to Battersea Bridge)

9.2 At cross rds and "STOP"-sign ← (St Albans Gr),
     1st rd → (Launceston Pl, becomes Grenville Pl)

9.7 At lhts ↑ via 🚲 gap in middle of rd (Ashburn Pl)

9.9 2nd rndabt → (Harrington Gdns)

10.2 1st rndabt ← (Collingham Gdns),
     1st rd → (Bolton Gdns) (🏨 *YHA after 300m on left*)

10.5 2nd rd → (Bramham Gdns No 18-27), at T-jct ←

10.7 At lhts 🍴 ☕ 🍴 ⌁ **Earls Court** *(shopping area)* ↑

10.9 At cross rds ↑ (Kemsford Gdns)

11.1 At T-jct 🍴 ☕ 🍴 ***West Brompton*** *(shopping area)* →
     (Old Brompton Rd) 🚗🚗 (use footpaths as needed),
     1st rd ← (Seagrave Rd) *(For ⌁ **Earls Court Exhibition Centre** →)*

11.5 2nd rndabt → (Hildyard Rd), at T-jct ← (Ongar Rd)

11.7 1st rd → (Halford Rd), keep going ↑

12.0 At 🍴 ☕ 🍴 **Fulham** *(shopping area)* ↟
     (Haldane Rd, becomes St Thomas Wy)

Quiet back streets in South Kensington

Section 7: London Bridge - Kingston (30 km / 18.6 miles)

12.4 At T-jct ← (Rylston Rd),1st rd → (Sherbrooke Rd)
12.5 At cross rds ↖ (Filmer Rd)
12.9 At 2nd rndabt ↗ (Filmer Rd)
(Note; no sign; do not enter Bishops Rd or Rostrevor Rd!)
13.1 At cross rds (Munster Rd) ↟ (Colehill Ln, no sign)
13.5 At T-jct ↟ (Bishop's Park Rd) *(For step-free route ← 🚗🚗)*
13.9 In bend ↑ via 3 steps *(!)* onto 🚲 (Bishop's Park),
near Thames River ← via 🚲, keep ↗ via 🚲
14.6 Ep ↑ through gate, follow ramp up, **dismount** at top,
→ onto Putney Bridge via pavement on right side of main rd
14.9 After bridge imm →, ep **resume cycling** ↑
(Riverside Wk, Thames Cycle Route (TCR), to Barnes, **4**)
15.8 After 🚻 ☕ **The Kings Head** *(pub)* ↑ via gravel 🚲
(Thames Path, to London Wetland Centre)
16.4 1st 🚲 ← (Elizabeth Wk, to Barnes, TCR, **4**)
17.0 ⛲ 🚻 **The London Wetland Centre**
17.2 Before lhts ↖ via 🚲 (to Richmond Park, TCR, **4**)
17.6 Ep cross rd → via lhts,
then ↟ (Ranelagh Av, to Richmond Park, TCR, **4**),
1st rd ← (Laurel Rd, **4**)

The **London Wetland Centre** is a wildfowl and wetland reserve. It features walks and hides for bird watchers (open daily, £10 pp). It is likely you'll encounter some deer in **Richmond Park** on the way to **Ham**.

18.3 **Dismount** at end of rd, ↖ onto narrow footbridge,
imm → via narrow path, 1st rd ← **resume cycling** (Cedars Rd, **4**)

18.5 At T-jct ↑ (Station Rd, to Richmond Park, TCR, **4**)

18.6 1st rd → (Vine Rd, to *Barnes* railway crossings) *(For station ↑)*

19.2 At lhts ↑, join ♽ on right side of rd (Priory Ln, **4**)

20.1 At end of ♽ → (Bank Ln, to Richmond Park, TCR, **4**),
1st rd ← (Roehampton Gate, **4**)

20.7 **Dismount** at T-jct, walk → via path on right side of rd,
after park gate, **resume cycling** ↑ via ♽ on right side of rd (**4**)

21.5 At jct ← (to White Lodge, Ham & Kingston, **4**)

23.0 After car park ⤺ ⊼ **Richmond Park** 1st rd →
(to Isabella Plantation, Ham & Kingston, **4**)

24.5 Before jct, join ♽ on right side, ↑ cross rd (**4**)

24.9 ↑ through "Ham Gate" via ♽ on right side (**4**)

25.9 At lhts ↑ (Ham Common Rd, to Kingston, TCR, **4**)

26.7 At T-jct → (to Kingston, TCR, **4**),
after bus stop imm ← via ♽ (to Teddington Lock, **4**), ↑ via ♽

27.2 Before locks/footbridge ← via ♽ (to Kingston, **4**)

28.5 Ep ↗ via rd (to Kingston, TCR, **4**)

29.0 1st ♽ ↗ (to Kingston, TCR, **4**)

29.8 After 🚲 🍴 ⊼ **The Boaters Inn** *(pub)* 1st rd ←
(to Kingston Town Centre, TCR, **4**), follow bend →

30.0 At lhts, follow signs ♽ (**4**) ↗ to left side of main rd,
then ↖ via bus lane (see "All Routes", **4**)

30.2 🚉 🚲 🍴 *Kingston Upon Thames* (shopping area)

Section 8: Kingston - Windsor & Eton (42 km / 26.3 miles)

8A: 🚲 27.1 km, 🥾 13.0 km, 🚌 0.7 km, 🚗🚗 0.8 km
8B: 🚲 28.4 km, 🥾 13.9 km, 🚌 0.6 km, 🚗🚗 0.8 km
Stations: *Kingston upon Thames, Hampton Court (after 5.2 km),*
Chertsey (after 18.5 km), Staines (after 24.0 km),
Egham (after 28.6 km), Windsor (Central and Riverside)

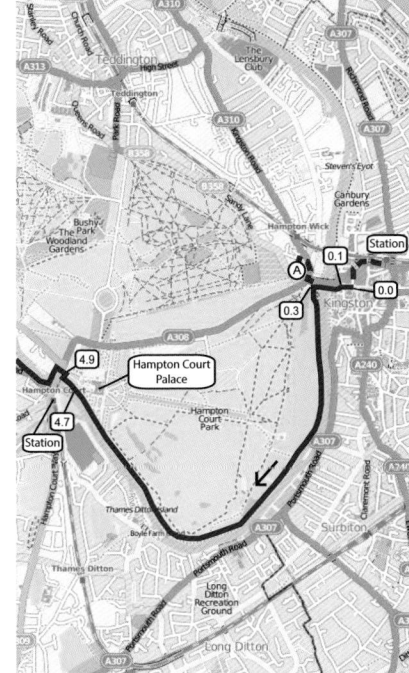

0.0 *(30.2)* At end of shopping area Kingston, onto bus lane to river
bridge (Thames Cycle Route (TCR), to Kingston Br, **4**)
0.1 Just before T-jct ↖ via 🚲 (TCR, to All Routes, **4**)
0.3 Imm after river bridge ← (TCR, to Hampton Court, **4**)
4.7 ⛨ **Hampton Court Palace** *was acquired by King Henry VIII.*
Royals have lived here more than 200 years (open daily, £17 pp).
4.9 **Dismount** at ep, → to lhts, cross rd ← via lhts
and **resume cycling** ← on pavement over bridge (to Walton, **4**)

The university town of **Kingston** is attractively located alongside the River Thames. This river proves to be the ultimate green corridor out of London. The towpath has a reasonable surface most of the way and various waterfront pubs provide perfect breaks from riding. The **Weybridge-Shepperton ferry** allows you to take your bike across the Thames, but you'll have to carry your bike down a high step onto the vessel (running daily until 5.30 pm, £3 pp). Follow route 8B to avoid the ferry and its high step. **Chertsey** has two campsites in its vicinity, the first beyond London.

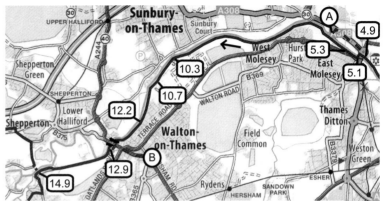

5.1   After bridge → (Riverbank, **4**)

5.2   🛏 🍴 *Hampton Court (Town: High Street on left)*

5.3   At war monument ↗ follow riverside 🚲 (**4**)

10.3   **Dismount** at Sunbury Lock, **resume cycling** beyond locks, at footbridge ↖ away from riverside (see 🚲 sign)

10.7   After 🍴 **The Weir** *(pub)* ↗ via riverside 🚲 (**4**)

12.2   🍴 **Walton on Thames** *(pub "The Anglers")*

12.9   At 🌲 **Walton Bridge** ↑ via canalside 🚲 (**4**)

14.9   At pedestrian ferry, choose **your Chertsey route**: 8A: *Ferry Route (short & scenic)* or B: *Alternative Route*

Section 8: Kingston - Windsor & Eton (42 km / 26.3 miles)

A: Chertsey Ferry Route *(2.6 km):*

14.9 Use ⛴ **Weybridge-Shepperton Ferry**, then ↗

15.0 Join 🚲 on left side of rd (TCR, to Chertsey, **4**)

15.4 At T-jct ← (TCR, to Chertsey, **4**)

15.8 Just before T-jct ↗, use crossing,
then ← via 🚲 on right side (Renfree Wy, TCR, to Chertsey, **4**)

17.0 At rndabt ↖ (to Chertsey), at end 🚲, join rd 🚗

17.5 At 🍴 🍽 **The Kingfisher** *(pub)* before bridge ↖ onto car park
(For 🏠 ⛺ 🚻 🍴 🍽 ⚓ Chertsey ↑ 🚗)

B: Chertsey Alternative Route *(4.7 km):*

14.9 At ⛴ **Weybridge-Shepperton Ferry** ↑ via riverside 🚲

15.1 Ep via car park ↗ onto rd (to Weybridge, **4**), 🚗

15.5 After 🍴 🍽 **Weybridge** *(two pubs)* 3rd rd →
(Portmore Park Rd, to Brooklands/Chertsey, **4**)

16.5 At rndabt → via narrow 🚲 on right side of rd
(Balfour Rd, to Chertsey), keep going ↑ via 🚲

18.4 Follow 🚲 ↗ onto dead end rd (to Chertsey, **4**)

18.6 1st rd → (to Chertsey Br, **4**), at school ↗ via 🚲

19.1 Ep ← via rd and imm → via 🚲 (**4**)
(For 🏠 🚻 🍴 🍽 ⚓ Chertsey ↑ via rd, only for ⛺ →)

19.3 Ep ← via 🚲 on left side of rd, **dismount** at T-jct

19.5 Walk → over bridge via footpath, → onto car park

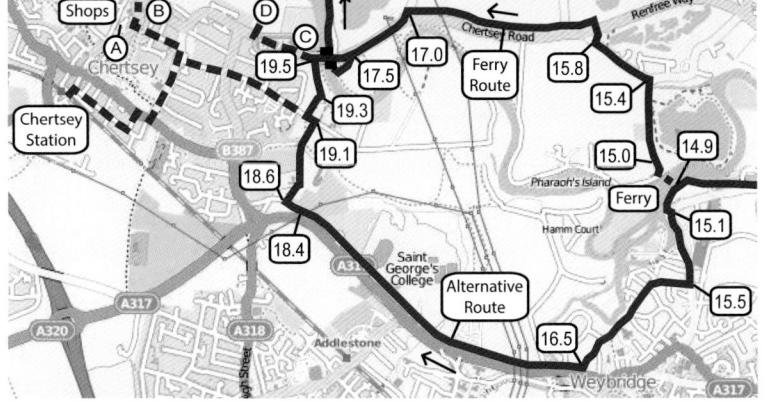

The idyllic river route gets briefly interrupted by busy **Staines** (see picture of its Town Hall below). The **Runnymede Locks** are near the site of the famous **Magna Carta** signing by King John, back in 1215 AD. The Magna Carta Historic Area is only accessible via a busy main road.

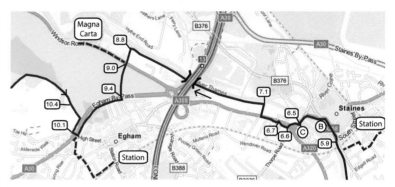

0.0 *(17.5/19.6)* On car park opposite 👉 🍴 **The Kingfisher** *(pub)*
→ via 🚲 under bridge **(4)**
0.4 Ep ⬆ join rd (under viaduct motorway M3)
2.4 In bend to right (rd moves away from river) ↖ via 🚲 **(4)**
(note: please keep to 8 m/ph (13 km/h) speed limit)
3.7 Follow riverside route via 🚻 **Penton Hook Lock**

5.9 Ep ⬆ join main rd 🚗🚗 *(optional footpath on left)*
6.5 In 🏨 🛒 👉 🍴 ⸮ **Staines** imm after river bridge ⬆ via crossing to 🚲 on right side of rd (to Egham, **4**)
6.6 At rndabt ↖ via zebra, → via 🚲 (to Egham, **4**)
6.7 Ep join main rd 🚗🚗, after 🛒 *super store* rndabt 1st rd → (River Park Av) *(Note ignore signs route 4!)*
7.1 At end of rd ← via riverside 🚲
8.8 After 👉 **Runnymede Locks** 1st rd ← (at wharf)
9.0 Cross main rd ⬆ via path (⸝ *For* **Magna Carta** → via 🚗🚗)
9.4 Ep cross main rd, → via 🚲 on left side of rd **(4)**
10.1 Before rndabt *Egham* via lhts →,
→ back via 🚲 on left side of rd, 1st rd ← (Coopers Hill Ln, **4**)
10.4 At end of rd ⬆ via steep rough track **(4)**, keep going ⬆

Section 8: Kingston - Windsor & Eton (42 km / 26.3 miles)

A short steep climb on rough gravel takes you out of the busy Thames valley into a quiet, different world. The peaceful **Runnymede Air Forces Memorial** is dedicated to more than 20,000 people who lost their lives during military service in WWII. Their bodies were never found.

Windsor Park is a striking haven of peace and quiet. Only an equestrian event will transform the park into a heaving community of horse riders and their (motorised) entourage. Don't miss the superb viewpoint opposite the statue of a young Queen Elisabeth II, mounted on her horse, overlooking **The Long Walk**, a long grass boulevard with **Windsor Castle** at its end.

11.4	⋞ **Runnymede Air Forces Memorial**
12.2	At T-jct cross rd ↑, 1st rd → (Ridgemead Rd, **4**)
12.9	At T-jct ← (Crimp Hill, **4**)
13.2	At T-jct ↗ (Bishopsgate Rd, **4**)
13.6	After 🛆 🍴 **Fox & Hounds** *(pub)* ↑ into ⋞ **Windsor Park**
13.9	At jct ← (to Cumberland Lodge)
14.6	1st rd → (to The Village Shop)
15.2	At "Chaplains Lodge" ↗ (to The Village Shop)
15.4	At next jct ↖ *(no signs at junction)*
16.0	At jct ↑, keep following this tarmac rd to end
16.4	⋞ **View Point The Long Walk** with **Queen's Statue**
18.6	Before automatic gates "The Rangers Gate" ↖ via gravel path, use lhts to cross rd, → via 🚲 (**4**)

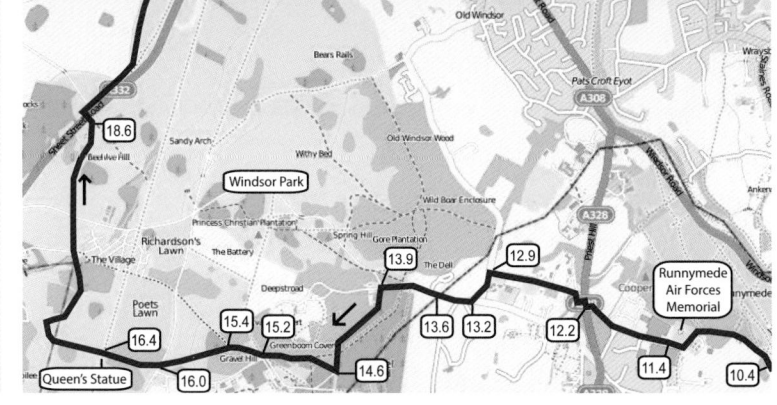

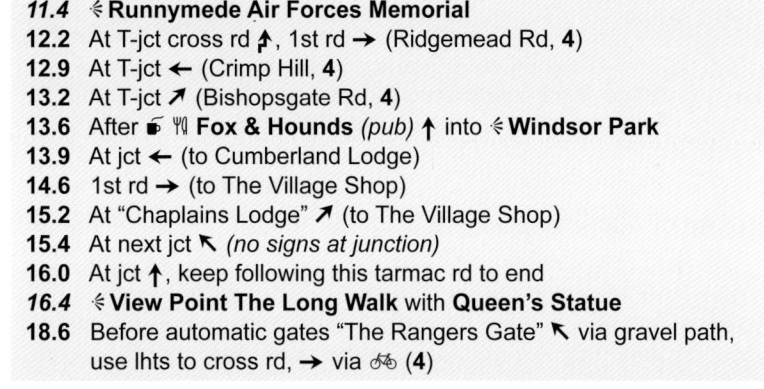

Via Windsor Park's "back door" you'll arrive in **Windsor**, an elegant and bustling town, dwarfed by **Windsor Castle**. This official residence of the British royals is the largest inhabited castle complex of the world, with its oldest foundations dating from 1070 AD (open daily, £17 pp). Also the town itself is a major tourist attraction. Expect to find crowds strolling by the **Guildhall** and the **Royal Station** (also known as Windsor & Eton Central) with its exclusive shops. The appearance of the town is further enhanced by the riverside area. The presence of many swans on the Thames (with the castle as backdrop) provides a perfect picture opportunity.

Via the historic river bridge you arrive in **Eton**. Its famous school can be found at the end of the high street, just a ten minute walk from the bridge. Back on the Windsor side, you'll find a good choice of reasonably priced independent B&Bs. You might want to stay two nights to fit in a visit to nearby **Legoland** (open daily, £45 pp); note access via a main road only.

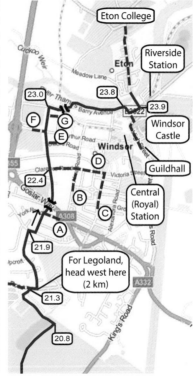

20.8 At end gravel 🚲 ← via 🚲 (**4**), ↑ via car park
21.3 At T-jct ⬆ (Bulkeley Av, to Town Centre, **4**) *(For ⚲ **Legoland** ←)*
21.9 At T-jct ⬆ (York Av, **4**), 1st 🚲 ↗ (into tunnel, **4**)
22.4 Keep going ↑ at cross rds and lhts (Van Sittart Rd)
23.0 In bend to left → (Barry Av, to Eton, **4**),
       after tunnel under railway ↟ via riverside 🚲 (**4**)
23.8 At ep → onto rd 🚗, follow bend ←
       *(bike racks in this bend on right for ⚲ 🛏 ☕ 🍴 ⚡ ℹ **Windsor**)*
23.9 At lhts ← traffic free street (to ⚲ 🛏 ☕ 🍴 **Eton**) (**4**)

Section 9: Windsor & Eton - Reading (38 km / 23.5 miles)

🚲 *18.4 km,* 🚶 *17.8 km,* 🚗 *1.6 km,* 🚗🚗 *0.1 km*
Stations: *Windsor (Central & Riverside), Maidenhead (after 10.7 km),*
Wargrave (after 27.2 km), Reading

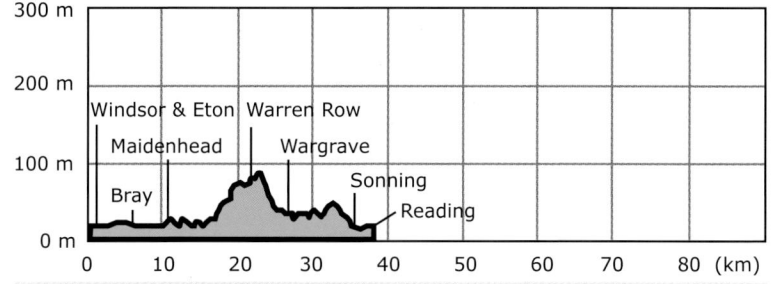

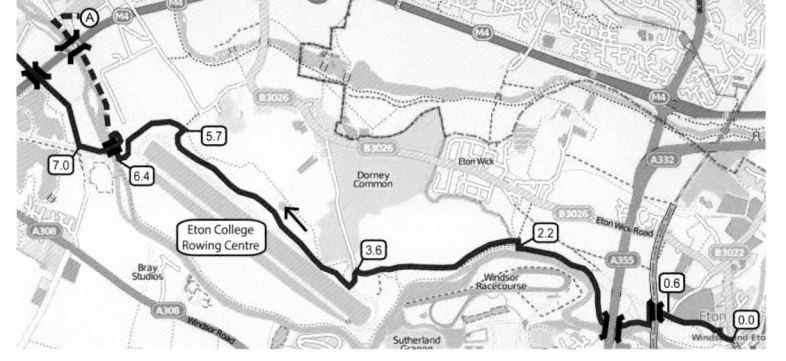

0.0 *(24.1)* On Eton side of river bridge ← (Brocas St, to Slough, **4**),
1st rd ← (Meadow Ln, to Slough, **4**)

0.6 In bend to right ↑ (to "Swan Lifeline", **4**),
after viaduct imm ← via 🚲, at river → *(ignore signs* **4***)*

2.2 Before footbridge → via tarmac 🚲, imm ← via bridge
(🚲 to Maidenhead, **4**), later join rd ↗

3.6 In bend to right ← via gravel rd (**4**), at T-jct → via tarmac rd
(ignore signs **4** *onto grass paths)*

5.7 After car pk and information "Eton College Rowing Centre"
on left side of rd ← via grass path (to Maidenhead, **4**)

6.4 Ep → via riverside path, 1st path → onto high cycle bridge (**4**)

7.0 Ep → via gravel rd (**4**), later tarmac rd

8.5 At T-jct ←, at T-jct → through 🛒 🍴 **Bray** *(pub)*

8.9 In sharp bend to right ↖ (Hibbert Road, **4**) 🚗

9.3 Just after warning sign "school" 1st 🚲 → (**4**), follow tarmac route, so ↗, then ↖, later gravel path

10.4 Ep before bridge ← via tarmac 🚲 (**4**)

10.7 Ep ← via 🚲 on right side of rd (to Station, **4**) *(For 🛒 🍴 ⚑ Maidenhead ↑ via 🚲 to Town Centre)*

11.0 Follow bend 🚲 → (to Halfords), at rndabt ← and after car park building → via 🚲 (**4**)

11.2 Ep ↑ cross via lhts (Shoppenhangers Rd, **4**)

11.5 After station, 1st rd ↗ (Ludlow Rd, **4**), later 🚲 ↗

12.2 Ep → (Brunel Rd, to Desborough Park, **4**), later 🚲

12.4 1st 🚲 ← (to Desborough Park, **4**), cross rd, 🚲 →

12.8 Ep → on rd, at T-jct ← (to Vanwall Business Pk, **4**)

13.0 At T-jct ← via 🚲 on left side (Desborough Cr, **4**)

13.2 3rd rd → (Kendall Place, to Cox Green School, **4**)

13.5 After tunnel, at ep ↖ (Cox Green Ln, to Cox Green School, **4**)

14.3 After 🛒 🍴 **Cox Green** *(pubs and shop)* at T-jct → via 🚲, 1st 🚲 ← (to Cox Green Lane, **4**)

14.4 At T-jct → via circle shaped rd (**4**), later 🚲 ↑

14.7 At T-jct → (see house no 66), 1st rd ← (**4**)

14.8 At T-jct → (see house no 24, **4**)

15.1 2nd rd ← (Lowbrook Dr, **4**), later 🚲 ↑

15.3 At T-jct ← (Bissley Dr, **4**)

15.4 At T-jct ↖ (Breadcroft Ln, **4**), later 🚲 ↑

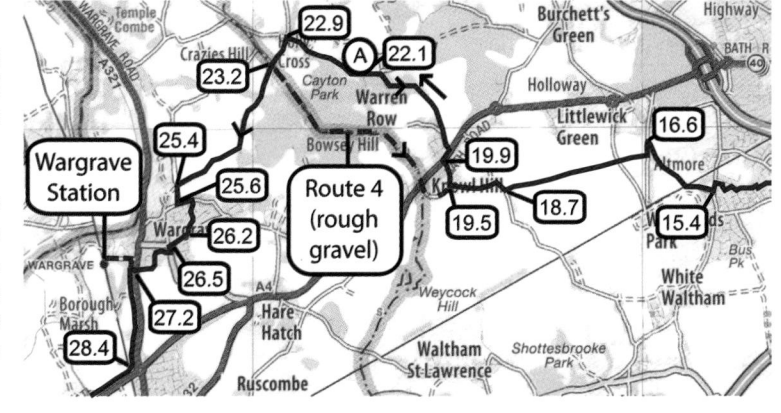

Section 9: Windsor & Eton - Reading (38 km / 23.5 miles)

Between Eton and Reading you'll experience an extreme mix of scenery; idyllic river views, pleasant rolling hills and scenic parkland, but also dull housing estates and cycle paths next to busy main roads. Whatever you encounter; it never lasts long!

On the way to **Bray** you pass the **Eton College Rowing Centre** which was used for the 2012 Olympics. **Maidenhead** is prettiest at the river bridge to Taplow, but you'll have to use the town centre route to experience this. The main route heads west via housing estates into rolling hills. In **Warren Row** you completely feel away from it all, but from **Wargrave** you start the approach to **Reading**. Although still close to London, Reading is a large urban conglomeration in its own right.

16.6	At T-jct ← (4), 1st 🚲 → (4), keep going ↑ (4)
18.7	At T-jct → and imm ← via gravel path (4), later rd
19.5	After "Knowl Hill Farm" on left side, 1st rd ↘
	(Note to ignore signs 4 here, unless using rough gravel route; in that case, follow signs 4 ↑ (see map), re-join guide route after 23.2 km)
19.9	After 🍺 **Royal Oak** *(pub)* at T-jct → 🚗🚗, 1st rd ← (Warren Row Rd, to Warren Row)
22.1	🏠🍺🍴 **Warren Row** *(pub)*
22.9	1st rd ← (to Wargrave)
23.2	At jct ↑ (to Wargrave)
	(if you used gravel route 4 you will be turning ← here)
25.4	At T jct ← (to Wargrave, 4)
25.6	At T-jct ← (Blakes Rd, 4), 1st rd → (Purfield Dr, 4)
26.2	At T-jct opposite 🏥 ***Wargrave*** *(pharmacy only)* → (4)
26.5	At T-jct ← (School Hill) 🚌, 1st rd → (Braybrooke Rd, 4), after bend to left ↑ via gravel private rd
27.2	At T-jct, cross rd via lhts, ← via 🚲 on right side (4)
28.4	At large rndabt ↗ via 🚲 on right side of main rd A4 (to Reading), later at ep ↑ via lay-by rd

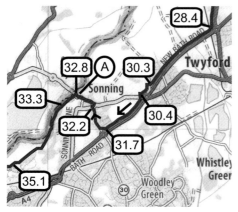

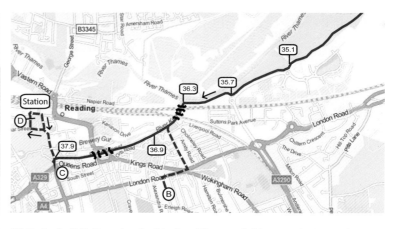

Wave farewell to the Thames River at **Sonning Lock** and its tea gardens, as you won't see it again. The **Avon & Kennet Canal towpath** takes you to Reading's town centre and will play a major role on the journey west.

30.3 At T-jct (Milestone Cr) ← via 🚲 on right side (**4**)

30.4 Ep cross rd ←, then ↑ via 🚲 through bushes, before dual carriageway A4 ↗ via 🚲 on right side (to Reading, **4**), later at ep ↑ via lay-by rd

31.7 At T-jct next to large rndabt → 🚗 *(ignore signs route 4!)*

32.2 Beyond school on left side of rd, at T-jct → 🚗, then at rndabt ← (Thames St) 🚗

32.8 In 🏨 🛒 🍴 **Sonning** just before Thames bridge ← via towpath

33.3 Beyond 🍴 🛒 🎋 **Sonning Lock Tea Garden** follow main path ↑, gradually distancing itself from river

35.1 Opposite "Health & Fitness Club" ↑ via gravel path, at ep before rndabt → via 🚲 on right side of rd

35.7 Just before next rndabt → via 🚲 down slope (**4**)

36.3 At start "Avon & Kennet Canal" follow towpath ↖ (to Reading, **4**) *(Note: don't cross the bridge across this canal!)*

36.9 🛒 🍴 **The Fisherman's Cottage** *(pub)*

37.9 Ep ← (London St, **4**), imm ↘ up ramp, before bridge ← into 🏨 🛒 🍴 🗡 ***Reading*** *(canal area with shops)*

73

Section 10: Reading - Great Bedwyn (55 km / 34 miles)

🚴 35.8 km, 🚶 18.8 km, 🚗 0.5 km, 🚗🚗 0.0 km

Stations: Theale (after 10.3 km), Aldermaston (after 16.5 km), Midgham (after 19.5 km), Thatcham (after 24.6 km), Newbury (after 31.6 km), Kintbury (after 40.4 km), Hungerford (after 46.0 km), Bedwyn

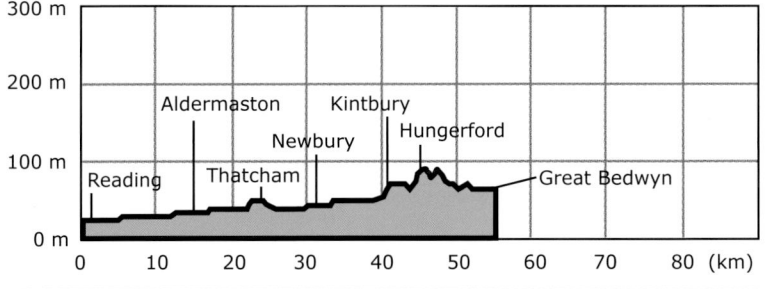

- **0.0** *(37.9)* Westbound into canal area (to Newbury, **4**)
- **0.3** Ep ←, imm cross rd ↑ onto 🚴 ↗ next to wall (to Newbury, **4**)
- **0.4** 1st 🚴 ← through tunnel, ep → (Katesgrove Ln)
- **0.7** At lhts ↑ (Elgar Rd, to Newbury, **4**)
- **1.2** Before barrier on rd →, then join gravel 🚴 ↗ (**4**)
- **2.2** Ep → via 🚴 on right side of rd (to Newbury, **4**)
- **2.3** Imm after bridge → (to Newbury, **4**), at end slope → through tunnel, follow tarmac 🚴 →
- **2.6** After next tunnel ↑ via towpath (**4**) (→ to avoid barriers; see map)

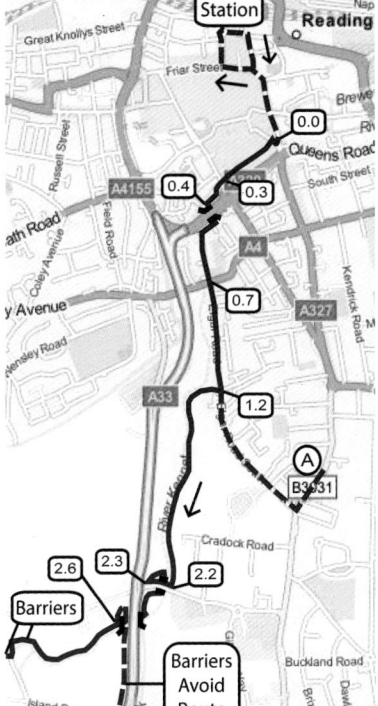

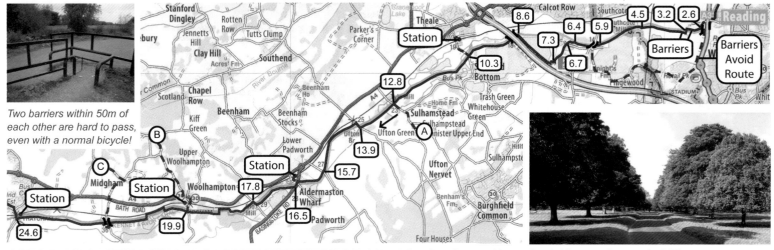

Two barriers within 50m of each other are hard to pass, even with a normal bicycle!

Two barriers at the start of the **Avon & Kennet Canal towpath** route may be difficult to pass. **Newbury** is well-known for its horse racing course. South of town, you'll find the only campsite in the area.

3.2 Cross canal ↟ to other side at lock area (**4**)

4.5 After railway viaduct, 1st bridge →, at lock area ↑ via towpath

5.9 ↑ via path under bridge; 🍴 **Cunning Man** *(pub)* on left

6.4 Just before wooden bridge over canal ↖ via gravel path (**4**)

6.7 Ep ↑ via tarmac rd ("Dewe Lane" on right side)

7.3 1st rd → and imm after bridge ← via gravel rd (**4**)

8.6 At end of gravel rd before canal bridge ← via gravel path under M4

10.3 After 🍴 **Tyle Mill** *(Theale)* at rd crossing ↑ via towpath (**4**)

12.8 Cross rd ↑ via towpath (to Aldermaston, **4**)

13.9 At rd crossing ↗ to other side of canal (**4**)

15.7 Cross rd ↑ via towpath (**4**)

16.5 At rd crossing 🍴 **Aldermaston** ↟ to other side of canal (**4**)

17.8 At rd crossing ↗ to other side of canal (**4**)

19.9 Cross rd ↑ (to Tatcham, **4**), 🍴 **The Rowbarge** on left *(Midgham)*

Section 10: Reading - Great Bedwyn (55 km / 34 miles)

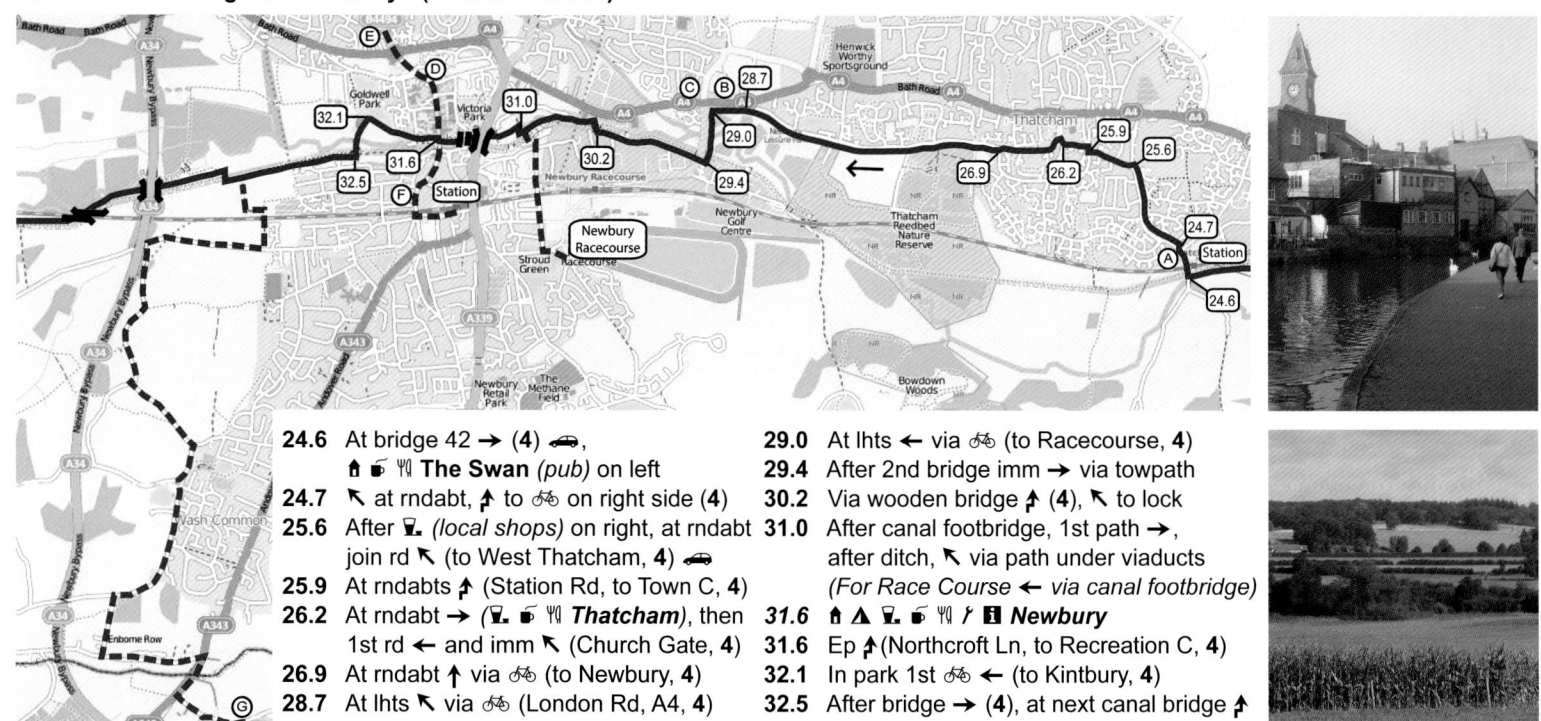

24.6 At bridge 42 → (4) 🚗,
🛏 👉 🍴 **The Swan** *(pub)* on left
24.7 ↖ at rndabt, ↟ to 🚲 on right side (4)
25.6 After 🛒 *(local shops)* on right, at rndabt
join rd ↖ (to West Thatcham, 4) 🚗
25.9 At rndabts ↟ (Station Rd, to Town C, 4)
26.2 At rndabt → (🛒 👉 🍴 *Thatcham*), then
1st rd ← and imm ↖ (Church Gate, 4)
26.9 At rndabt ↑ via 🚲 (to Newbury, 4)
28.7 At lhts ↖ via 🚲 (London Rd, A4, 4)

29.0 At lhts ← via 🚲 (to Racecourse, 4)
29.4 After 2nd bridge imm → via towpath
30.2 Via wooden bridge ↟ (4), ↖ to lock
31.0 After canal footbridge, 1st path →,
after ditch, ↖ via path under viaducts
(For Race Course ← via canal footbridge)
31.6 🛏 ⛺ 🛒 👉 🍴 ⚕ 🅸 *Newbury*
31.6 Ep ↟ (Northcroft Ln, to Recreation C, 4)
32.1 In park 1st 🚲 ← (to Kintbury, 4)
32.5 After bridge → (4), at next canal bridge ↟

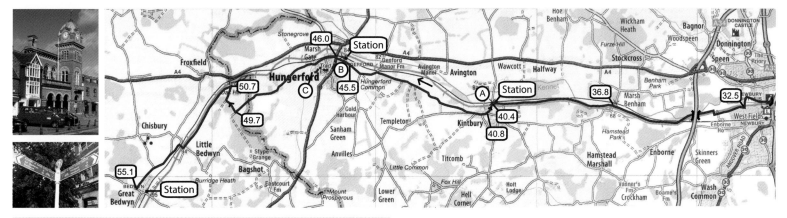

The 140 km idyllic **Avon & Kennet Canal** defines this route section. Canalisation of both Avon & Kennet Rivers dates back from 1727. It would take another 80 years before ships were able to navigate all the way between Reading and Bristol. After its opening in 1810, the canal only enjoyed 30 years of full glory. The Great Western Railway opened in 1841, reducing the importance of the canal. It then became derelict for most of its course until it was fully restored in 1990. The quiet towpath has generally an acceptable gravel surface, but there are also some short grass sections. Up to **Newbury**, you'll only find a couple of pubs on the way. **Kintbury** and **Hungerford** (see picture above) provide more opportunities for breaks, although the canal remains the main attraction.

36.8 Cross rd, ↑ via towpath (to Kintbury/Hungerford, **4**)

40.4 At 🚻 ☞ 🍴 *Kintbury* ← via rd over bridge
(ignore towpath route; very poor surface ahead!)

40.8 After climb ↑ (to Hungerford, **4**), keep going ↑

45.5 ☞ 🍴 **The Downgate** *(pub)*

46.0 At rndabt → into 🏠 🚻 ☞ 🍴 ⟂ *Hungerford*,
next rndabt ← (Church St, to Great Bedwyn, **4**), keep going ↑

49.7 Follow sharp bend → (**4**) *(Note: don't enter gravel road!)*

50.7 At T-jct ← (to Little Bedwyn, **4**), keep going ↑

55.1 🏠 🚻 ☞ 🍴 *Great Bedwyn:* choose here between
our **Avebury** route (**11A**) or the **Stonehenge** diversion (**11B**)

Section 11A: Great Bedwyn-Alton Priors via Avebury (34 km/21 miles)

🚲 9.8 km, 🚶 22.9 km, 🚐 1.4 km, 🚐🚐 0.0 km
Stations: Bedwyn

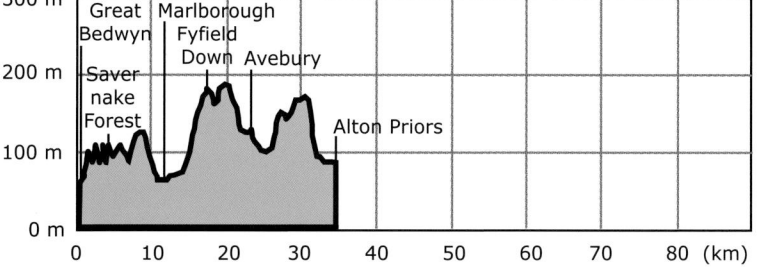

Wiltshire is famous for its **Fields of Gold**; on your bike you might get in the same frame of mind as pop star Sting when he wrote his famous song! Beyond the great empty vistas, Wiltshire is also home to two UNESCO ancient stone circles; **Avebury** and **Stonehenge**. You have the choice to visit one or the other. On the direct **Avebury route** (11A, starting on this page) cycling is best. The **Savernake Forest**, the bustling market town **Marlborough** and a great off-road route via **Fyfield Down** (an ancient glacial valley) provide a highly varied route, whereas our much longer **Stonehenge route** (11B, see page 82) is dominated by the empty **Salisbury Plains**. The book also provides **walking route suggestions** for both Avebury and Stonehenge on page 81.

After the ancient woodlands of **Savernake Forest** the hustle and bustle of **Marlborough** might come as a shock. Its rich silk history can be felt in the **Merchant's House** (open Tue/Fri/Sat, £5 pp). The route to Avebury takes you through glacial valley **Fyfield Down** via an off-road route with panoramic views. These views should make up for the uncomfortable grass and rough gravel; a tarmac alternative is provided just in case.

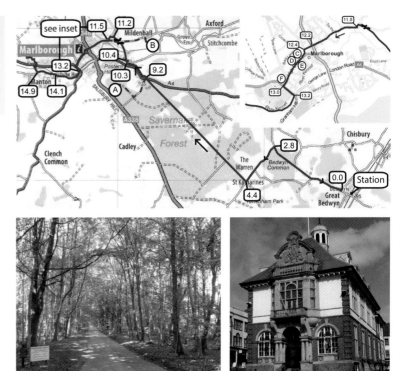

0.0 *(55.1)* At T-jct → (Forest Hill to Marlborough, **403**)

2.8 1st through rd ← (to Savernake, **4**)

4.4 Opposite iron gate on left side of rd →
(see sign "Savernake Forest, Private Property" after 10 m)

9.2 At T-jct ← via narrow path on right side of rd (**403**)

10.3 In descent 1st rd → (Choppingknife Ln),
↑ into dead end rd (Barnfield, **403**)

10.4 Opposite house "Dovecote" ↖ onto gravel ⚲ (**45**)

11.2 Just beyond road bridge over ⚲,
1st narrow path ↖ leading down *(no signs!)*, ep ← via tarmac rd

11.5 At T-jct → (Poulton Hill, sign further up road)

12.2 At cross rds ↑ *(use pedestrian lhts as needed)* ⚶

12.4 At T-jct ← and just around corner → (High St) ⚘

12.5 ⚔ ♠ ⚑ ⚐ ⚒ ⚓ ⚔ **Marlborough**

13.0 At T-jct ← (to Pewsey, A345) ⚘

13.2 At rndabt → (Granham Cl, **403**), ↑ via gravel ⚲

14.1 After tennis courts at ep ↖ via tarmac rd (**403**)

Section 11A: Great Bedwyn-Alton Priors via Avebury (34 km/21 miles)

14.9 At T-jct → (**403**)
*(Note rough gravel and grass route ahead,
not advisable in bad weather; for tarmac short-cut ← (see map),
re-join main route after 29.0 km)*

15.1 At T-jct → via 🚲 on right side (to Marlborough),
cross rd ← at lhts and ↑ via 🚲 steep up (**403**)

15.4 Ep ↑ join tarmac rd opposite house no 28 (**403**)

15.7 At T-jct "Manton Hollow" → (**403**)

17.2 Before sign "private rd" ↑ onto car park (**403**),
at end of car park → via gravel 🚲 (to Avebury, **403**)

19.5 Ep ← via gravel 🚲 (to Avebury, **403**),
follow main path through ⛰ **Fyfield Down Nature Reserve**

21.5 End grass path ↑ via gravel 🚲 (to Avebury, **403**)
(caution; steep descent on rough surface for 1.6 km!)

24.0 At cross rds ⛰ 🏠 🛏 🍴 ℹ️ **Avebury** ↖ 🚗 🚌
*(for visit ↑ to ⛰ **Keiller Museum** and walking route see map below)*

24.2 Imm after leaving historic stone circle,
in sharp bend to right ↑ via quiet rd *(no signs!)*

25.9 At T-jct ← (to Marlborough, **45**) 🚌
(use lay-by rd ahead in climb, then prepare for difficult right turn!)

26.4 1st rd → (to East Kennett, **45**)

29.0 At T-jct → (to Alton Barnes, **45**) *(tarmac short-cut rejoins route)*

34.1 After steep descent, at Alton Priors jct, 1st rd →

34.1 ⛰ **Alton Barnes White Horse** on right side of rd

WALKING at AVEBURY

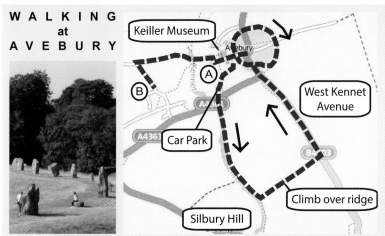

Keiller Museum

A4361

Car Park

A4361

B4003

West Kennet Avenue

Climb over ridge

Silbury Hill

Make your way to the **Keiller Museum** (open daily, £5 pp) for best bike parking options. Footpaths at Avebury **and** Stonehenge are **not suitable** for **walking bikes**. It will take half an hour to walk the Avebury ancient stone circle. From the Keiller Museum inner court gate, turn left and just walk the circle. On return, you can also walk to **Silbury Hill**, an ancient high mount south of Avebury; follow the car park signs from the museum, then cross road towards the hill (45 minute return). This walk can be extended to a one hour circular walk; keep left near Silbury Hill and climb the ridge to West Kennet Avenue with more ancient sarsen stones.

WALKING at STONEHENGE

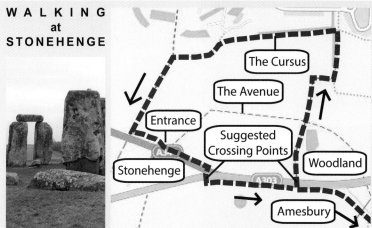

The Cursus

The Avenue

Entrance

Suggested Crossing Points

Stonehenge

Woodland

A303

Amesbury

If staying in Amesbury, walk via the Old Stonehenge Road towards Stonehenge (30 minutes one way). The best views of the stone circle are from the footpaths to the north. You'll see **The Avenue**, the ancient procession route and you'll walk on the historic **Cursus**. To get there, you'll have to cross the busy A303 just west from the point where the old Stonehenge Road joins the A303 (on the edge of the woodland on the north side of the A303). Start a one hour walk northbound here, by walking a semi-circle anti clockwise to the Visitor Centre (open daily, £8 pp). Return to Amesbury via A344/A303 footpaths.

Section 11B: Great Bedwyn-Alton Priors via Stonehenge (68 km/42 miles)

🚲 5.4 km, 🚶 58.8 km, 🚐 4.3 km, 🚐🚐 0.0 km
Stations: Bedwyn

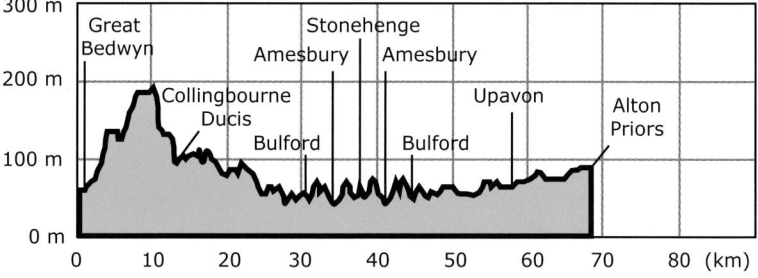

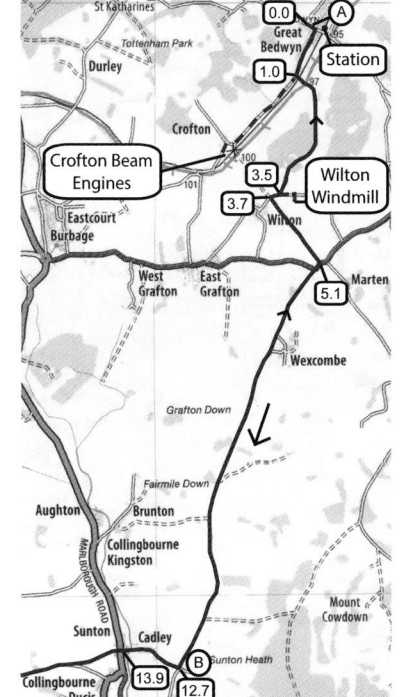

The steam powered **Crofton Beam Engines** supply the Avon & Kennet Canal with water at its highest point (open daily, £8 pp). The **Wilton Windmill** has a picnic area (tours on Sundays).

0.0 *(55.1)* At T-jct ← (to Shalbourne, **4**)
0.2 1st rd → (Church St, to Crofton, **4**)
1.0 ← over canal/railway *(For 🚲 **Crofton Beam Engines** ↑, see **4**)*
3.7 2nd rd ← (to Tidcombe) *(3.5: For 🚲 🚏 **Wilton Windmill** 1st ←)*
5.1 At T-jct → (to Salisbury), 1st rd ↖ (to Wexcombe)
12.7 At 🏠 🍴 🍽 **The Shears Inn** *(pub)* → (to Collingbourne)
13.9 In 🚏 **Collingbourne Ducis** ↗ (to Village Hall)

There are plenty of warning signs for crossing military vehicles on the empty country lanes across the vast **Salisbury Plains**, but there is only a very small chance you'll see or hear actual military action. It is more likely that your peace and quiet on this long and hilly route will be disturbed by a combine harvester doing its duty.

17.3 At T-jct → 🚗
18.0 At 🛏 🍴 **The Crown** *(pub)* 1st rd ← (to Haxton)
25.5 At cross rds ← (to Airfield Camp)
26.4 After army camp 1st rd ← (to Figheldean), keep ↑
31.8 At T-jct ↗, 2nd rd ↖ (Salisbury Rd, to Salisbury)
32.1 🛒 **Bulford** *(shop at petrol station)*
32.3 At cross rds ↑ (Salisbury Rd, to Salisbury) 🚗
(Caution; hazardous road with blind summit; no alternative)

Amesbury is the only large settlement in the area and the obvious place for an overnight stay when visiting **Stonehenge**. Amesbury's town centre has limited choice of accommodation though; book ahead if you can! It is recommended to **walk** from Amesbury to Stonehenge, rather than cycle. On foot you'll be able to escape the depressing presence of the main road A303 in the direct vicinity of Stonehenge (see page 81 for walking route suggestions). Whether by bike or on foot; be warned you'll need your wits about you to cross this very busy road. A new visitor centre and proposed closure of the A344 road might improve the situation slightly. To be able to continue our route, you'll be heading back the same way you came for some time.

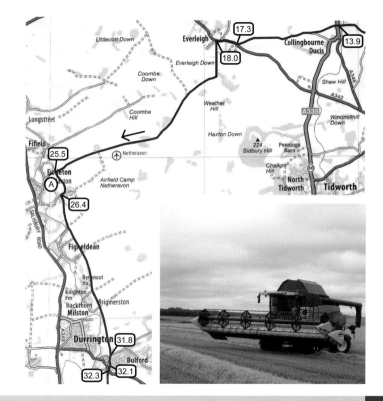

Section 11B: Great Bedwyn-Alton Priors via Stonehenge (68 km/42 miles)

33.4 Before rndabt ⬆ onto 🚲 on right side (onto viaduct over A303)

33.7 1st rd ➡ via 🚲 on left side (to Town Centre)

34.4 After rndabt 🛒 *super store* at ep ⬆ join rd

35.2 At lhts ⬆ cross rd and imm **dismount** to walk ⬆ via pavement
into 🏨 🛒 🍴 ⚡ 🅸 **Amesbury**

35.4 **Resume cycling** ⬆ where one-way restriction ends
(Church St, to Woodfords, **45**), keep going ⬆

36.3 *(For routes to Portsmouth and Poole 1st rd ⬅ (to Woodford, **45**))*

37.4 Where rd joins main rd ↖ get on path on left side

38.4 At ep ➡, somehow cross main rd *(take extreme care 🚗🚗🚗!)*,
use verges to join path ↖ on right side of A344 to Devizes
*(note this A344 is due to be closed for motorised traffic, tarmac to
be replaced by grass)*

39.0 1st driveway ➡ to ⚡🅸 **Stonehenge**,
after visit, return in same direction you came from!

39.6 Again, somehow cross main rd *(take extreme care 🚗🚗🚗!)*,
join the path ⬅ on right side of main rd

40.6 1st rd, ↗ rejoin main carriageway

42.6 In 🏨 🛒 🍴 ⚡ 🅸 **Amesbury** ⬆ (High St)

0.0 *(42.8)* At lhts ⬆ (London Rd, to Sports Centre)

0.8 Just before rndabt 🛒 *super store* ⬆ join 🚲 on right side

1.4 Before next rndabt ⬅ via 🚲 on left side (onto viaduct over A303)

1.8 Ep ⬆ via rd (to Bulford, A3028) 🚗
(Caution; hazardous road with blind summit; no alternative)

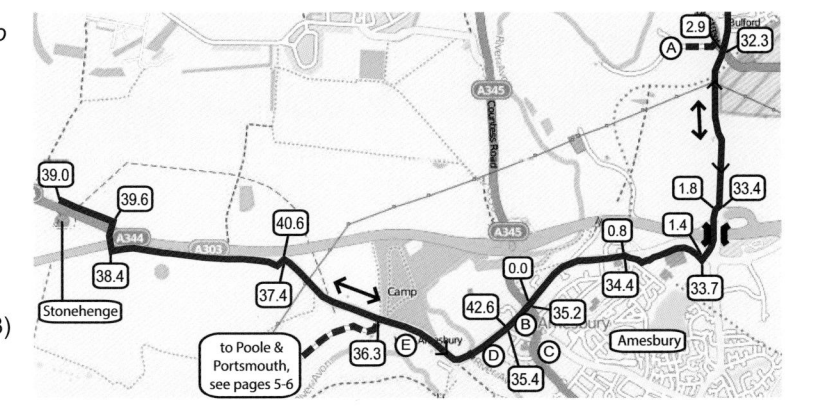

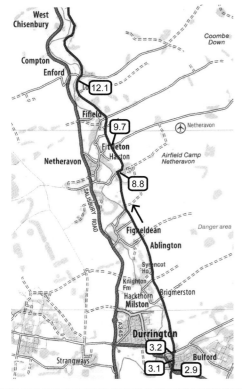

2.9 At cross rds ↑ (Salisbury Rd, to Milston)
3.1 🍺 Bulford *(shop at petrol station)*
3.2 At T-jct ↗, 1st rd ↖ (Milston Rd, to Milston), keep ↑
8.8 At T-jct → (pass army camp)
9.7 At cross rds ↑ (to Coombe)
12.1 🍺 **The Swan** *(pub)*
15.2 At T-jct ↑ (to Upavon, A342) 🚗
16.4 After bridge 1st rd → (High St, to Marlborough)
16.5 🍺🍴 **Upavon**
18.5 At rndabt ⚠ 🍺🍴 **Woodbridge Inn** *(pub)* ↑ (to Woodborough), keep going ↑
24.8 ⚠ 🍺🍴 **Barge Inn** *(pub)*
25.7 At Alton Priors jct, 1st rd ← (to Devizes)
25.7 ⚐ **Alton Barnes White Horse** on right side of rd

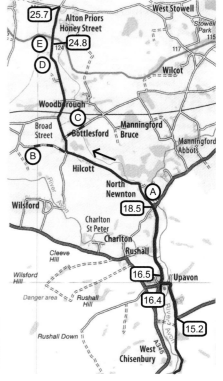

Section 12: Alton Priors - Bath (52 km / 32 miles)

🚲 37.8 km, 🚶 7.0 km, 🚌 7.3 km, 🚌🚌 0.0 km
Stations: Bradford on Avon (after 32.8 km) , Avoncliff (after 35.1 km),
Bath Spa

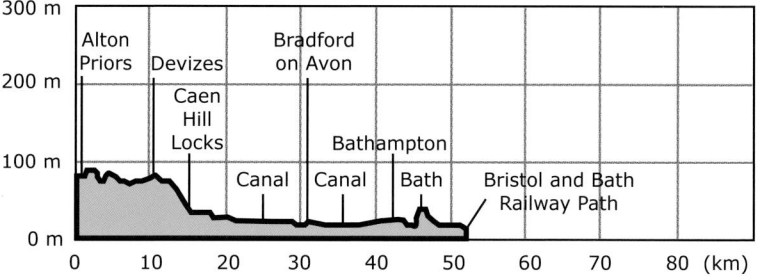

Beautiful scenery and some of southern England's most spectacular landmarks await you on this section. The route starts with views over **Alton Barnes White Horse** on **Milk Hill**, Wiltshire's highest point. The chalk depiction of a white horse dates from 1812 and is one of England's largest. The road westbound runs parallel with the **Wansdyke Ridge** to the north, providing panoramic vistas. Unfortunately there is some fast moving traffic here; use the alternative traffic-calmed route as needed. Just before arriving in **Devizes** you can spot another White Horse on the horizon. Market town Devizes with its many historic buildings used to be an important stop for stagecoaches travelling between London and Bristol.

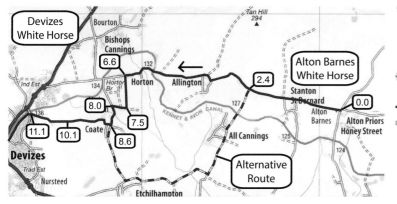

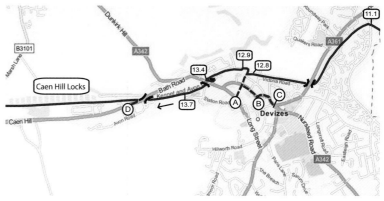

0.0   *(34.1/25.7)* At Alton Priors jct westbound (to Devizes) 🚗
      (⊰**Alton Barnes White Horse** *on right side of rd*)

2.4   *(To escape occasional fast moving traffic on this scenic rd, you can*
      use a longer traffic-calmed alternative route; take 3rd rd ←
      (to All Cannings), then 3rd rd → (to Etchilhampton), follow signs 4
      to Coate to rejoin route after 8.6 km (turn ← here), see map)

6.6   In Horton 2nd rd ← (see sign trucks limit 7.5T)

7.5   At jct with electricity grid mast →

8.0   At T-jct ← (Spaniels Bridge Rd, sign further on rd)

8.6   1st rd → (Puddles Ln, to Devizes, **4**)

10.1 ⊰**Devizes White Horse** *(on horizon on right)*

11.1 At T-jct → via path on left side of rd, imm ←via towpath route (**4**)

12.8 Before 4th canal bridge (bridge no 140) ↖ up ramp,
       ep → via bridge

12.8 *(For 🏠 🛏 ⛽ 🍴 ℹ🅷 **Devizes** at end of ramp at ep ←,*
       *then 1st rd ↗ (to Market Place), **dismount** and walk ↑)*

12.9 After bridge in front of cemetery ↙ via towpath
       (to Bradford on Avon, **4**)

13.4 Ep ← via bridge path and imm ← via 🚲 into subway
       (to Caen Hill Locks), continue towpath route

13.7 ⊰**Caen Hill Locks** *(first lock of flight of locks)*

Section 12: Alton Priors - Bath (52 km / 32 miles)

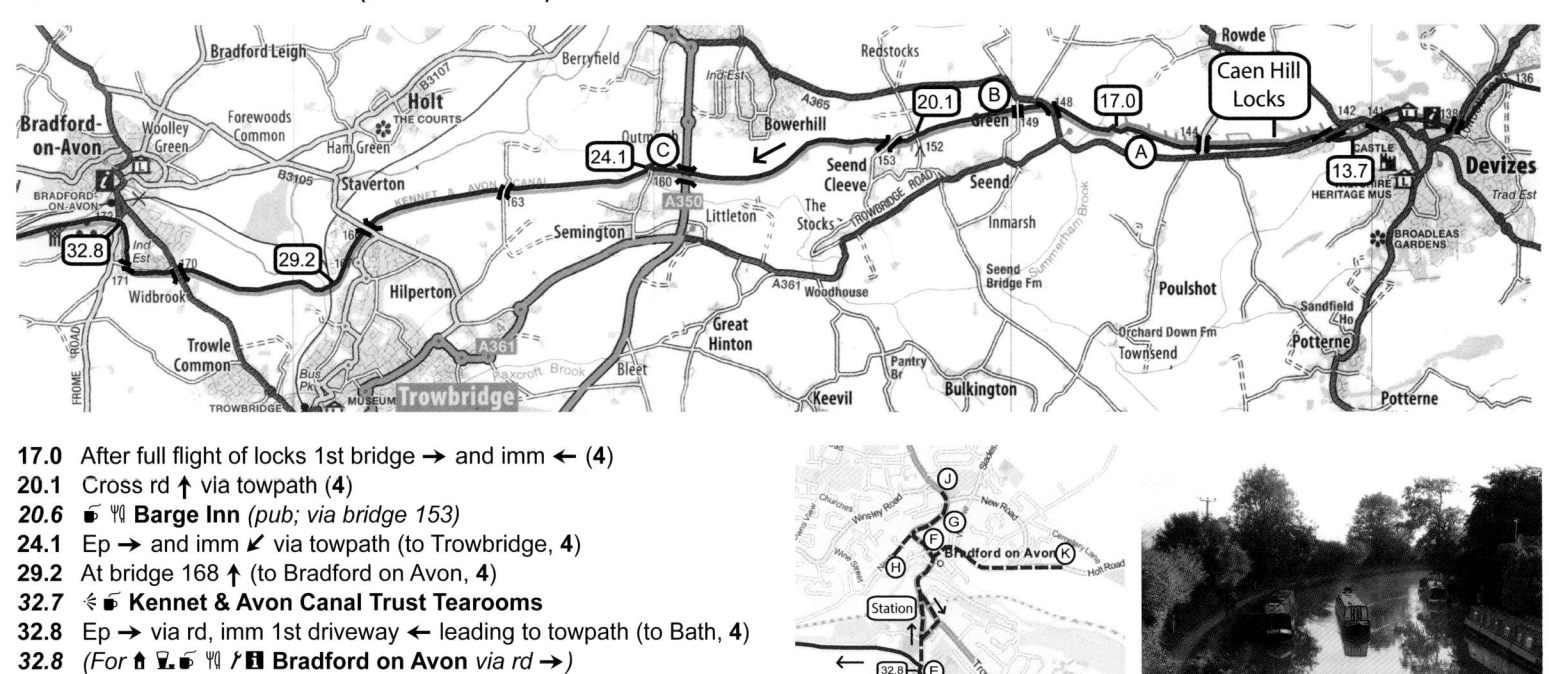

17.0 After full flight of locks 1st bridge → and imm ← (**4**)

20.1 Cross rd ↑ via towpath (**4**)

20.6 🍴 **Barge Inn** *(pub; via bridge 153)*

24.1 Ep → and imm ↙ via towpath (to Trowbridge, **4**)

29.2 At bridge 168 ↑ (to Bradford on Avon, **4**)

32.7 ⮪ **Kennet & Avon Canal Trust Tearooms**

32.8 Ep → via rd, imm 1st driveway ← leading to towpath (to Bath, **4**)

32.8 *(For 🏠 🅿️ 🍴 ⚕ 🚉 Bradford on Avon via rd →)*

At Devizes, the route rejoins the **Avon & Kennet Canal** towpath. Just west of town you'll pass the spectacular **Caen Hill Locks**, a flight of 29 locks bridging a height of 72 metres. It takes 5 hours to travel the locks by boat.

If you are a camping cyclist you might like to use the campsites just west from Caen Hill. Besides one pricy campsite near Bath, there are no other campsites until you hit Clevedon on the Bristol Channel. Beyond Caen Hill, the surface of the towpath temporarily degrades, but once the canal hits the **Cotswolds** hills, you are in for a spectacular journey. The now well-surfaced towpath provides a flat route through a stunning valley. **Bradford on Avon** with its many historic buildings is well worth a stop.

On the way to Bath you'll cycle the **Avoncliff and Dundas Aqueducts**, both dating from 1801. These aqueducts fell in serious disrepair from 1954, with the canal bed standing dry until its full restoration in 1984.

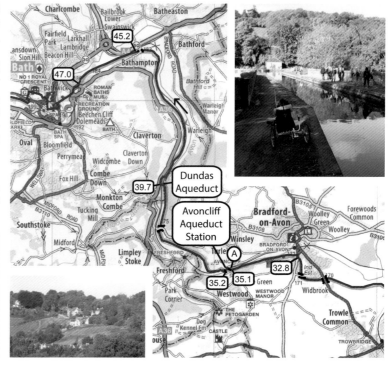

35.1 After sharp bend to right imm → via tarmac rd
(to Dundas, **4**, 🛏 🍴 **Cross Guns** *(pub)* on right)
(For Avoncliff station ↑ across aqueduct)

35.2 Follow rd under aqueduct, then ↙ via steep climb up,
then ← via towpath ⟨ **Avoncliff Aqueduct** (**4**)

39.7 After ⟨ **Dundas Aqueduct** ↑ over bridge of side canal,
then → via towpath (to Bath, **4**), after next bridge ← (**4**)

45.2 🍴 🍴 **Bathampton** *(pub on canal side on right)*

Section 12: Alton Priors - Bath (52 km / 32 miles)

Bath became one of the very first UNESCO world heritage sites in 1987 and is one of England's most beautiful cities. The Georgian architecture (1714-1830) has defined its character, but the **Roman Baths** are the major attraction of the city. A full exploration of these historic baths can take up to three hours. In July and August, the baths are open until 9pm, a great way to avoid the day-time queues (open daily, £13 pp). Next door, you might want to visit the beautiful **Bath Abbey** (open daily, £3 pp, church services free).

Another major attraction in Bath is the **Jane Austen Museum** (open daily, £8 pp). The famous novelist lived in Bath during the Georgian era, a stone's throw from another Bath marvel; the **Royal Crescent**. This impressive semicircle of terraced houses stands on a high hill overlooking the valley. At the **No 1 Museum** you can get a glimpse on how the houses look on the inside, decorated in Georgian style (open Tue-Sun, £6 pp).

Also worth a mention is your arrival in Bath via **Pulteney Bridge**. This 1773 bridge is lined with small shops on both sides, so you won't notice the river Avon until you are cycling on the Grand Parade.

Bath is well worth one or two overnight stays, but make reservations in advance, especially for budget accommodations, like the YHA, YMCA and the popular campsite on the west end of town.

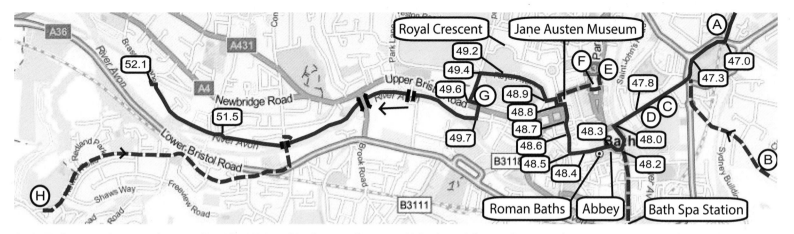

Royal Crescent

Jane Austen Museum

Roman Baths

Abbey

Bath Spa Station

47.0 Before canal tunnel ↗, ep → (Beckford Rd, to City Centre, **4**) 🚗

47.3 At lhts ↖ (**4**) 🚗, 2nd rd → (Great Pulteney St, **4**)

47.8 At rndabt with fountain ↑ onto ⧊ **Pulteney Bridge**

48.0 At lhts ← (Grand Parade, **4**) 🚗

48.2 Move to right lane to turn → on square with obelisk → (**4**) 🚗

48.3 At lhts ↑ via narrow one way rd (Cheap St, **4**)

48.4 ↑ at Union St *(main shopping street* ⧊ ⌂ ⌂ ▲ ▯ ☞ 🍽 ℐ ℹ *Bath)*

48.5 Follow sharp bend → *(Note: ignore signs route* **4***!)*

48.6 After climb, on square ↑ (to Jane Austen Centre)

48.7 **Dismount** in sharp bend, walk ↑ (to ⧊ **Jane Austen Centre**)

48.8 At end Queen Sq, cross ↑ onto pavement on left side of main rd (Gay St), **resume cycling** on 1st rd ← (Queen's Parade Pl)

48.9 At war monument 1st rd → via gate (Royal Av)

49.2 ⧊ **The Royal Crescent** *(behind bushes on right)*

49.4 At T-jct ← (Marlborough Ln)

49.6 **Dismount** at T-jct, ← on pavement, after B&Bs on left side →, cross rd into narrow alleyway, **resume cycling** ↑

49.7 At T-jct →, at end ↑ via 🚲 (to Saltford/Bristol, **4**)

51.5 At ☞ 🍽 **Dolphin** *(pub)* ⚲ onto tarmac rd (**4**)

52.1 1st rd ↖ to 🚲 (Bristol and Bath Railway Path, **4**)

91

Section 13: Bath - Bristol (22 km / 14 miles)

🚲 *21.3 km,* 🚶 *0.8 km,* 🚗 *0.0 km,* 🚗🚗 *0.0 km*
Stations: *Bath Spa, Bristol Temple Meads*

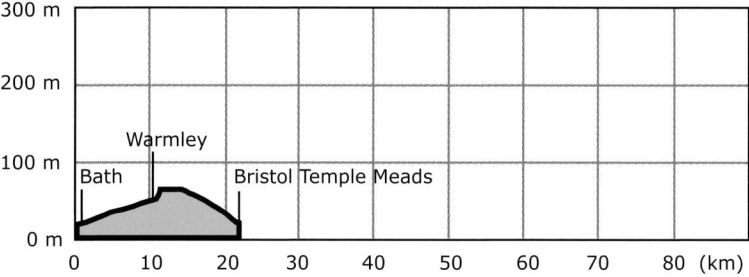

This section takes you onto historic grounds for cycling in England. The
Bristol & Bath Railway Path was the first traffic-free route in the country!

0.0 *(52.1)* Join 🚲 Bristol and Bath Railway Path (**4**)
4.4 🚲 🍴 **Bird in Hand** *(pub, on left side of path after 100m)*
7.8 Ep ↑ across car park ↙🚲 **Avon Valley Railway** (to Bristol, **4**)
10.2 At crossing "Victoria Rd" ↑ via 🚲 (to Bristol, **4**)
11.5 At crossing 🏠 🚉 🚲 🍴 ⚡ **Warmley** ↑ via 🚲 (to Bristol, **4**),
pass 🚲 **Warmley Waiting Room** *(cafe)*
12.2 Imm after cattle grid ↗ at split jct, follow right path
12.6 After short climb ← via 🚲 viaduct over main rd,
follow 🚲 ↗ (Bristol and Bath Railway Path, to Bristol, **4**)

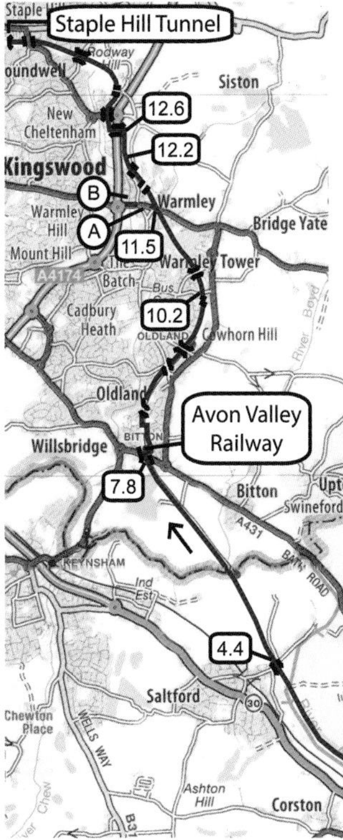

The history of the Bristol and Bath Railway Path dates back to 1869 when the **Midland Railway** company opened its own link between Bristol and Bath. It allowed passengers from the Midlands to travel to Bath without having to use the Great Western Railway, running parallel on the same route. Obviously, the nationalisation of the railways didn't allow the operation of two parallel railway lines and the longer Midland Railway link between Bath and Bristol was closed in 1971.

The disused railway bed became an easy "prey" for environmental campaigners from Bristol. From 1979, dedicated volunteers started to make the track suitable for cycling. In 1983 the group founded the **Sustrans** "sustainable transport" charity and in 1986 the route was entirely open. Thirty years on, Sustrans keeps developing its **National Cycle Network** and this book wouldn't have been possible without it. The Bristol and Bath railway path offers both rural and urban cycling and takes you truly from one city to the other without having to worry about traffic. The well-lit **Staple Hill Tunnel** is its most spectacular feature.

17.1 🍴 ☕ ⛱ **Fishponds** *(super store and picnic area)*
21.1 Ep ↑ (St Philips Rd, to Bristol Bridge & Centre, **4**)
21.4 At T-jct ↗ (Horton St, to Bristol Temple Meads, **4**),
    follow rd ↑ to end *(Note: ignore signs route **4** to the right!)*
21.7 At T-jct ← *(Note ignore signs to Bristol Temple Meads!)*
21.9 At lhts, 1st 🚲 → via canal bridge, ↑ onto car park
22.1 **Dismount** *(for Bristol Temple Meads station walk ↖)*

Section 14: Bristol - Cheddar (59 km / 36 miles)

🚲 28.4 km, 🚶 27.8 km, 🚗 1.9 km, 🚗🚗 0.7 km
Stations: Bristol Temple Meads, Yatton (after 41.1 km)

Elevation profile with labels: Bristol, Avon Gorge, Pill, Gordano Valley, Clevedon, Yatton, Strawberry Line, Axbridge, Cheddar. Horizontal axis 0–80 (km), vertical axis 0 m–300 m.

Bristol is one of Britain's trendiest cities. The **Floating Harbour** used to be a rundown dock area, but has been reshaped as a place where people live, work, dine, drink and enjoy! Modern design meets impressive heritage, especially at the **M Shed**, Bristol's City Museum with its four iconic four cranes (open Tue-Sun, free entry). The harbour is also home to the first ever iron ship of the world, the **SS Great Britain** (open daily, £13 pp). If you make your way there, you'll also pass **Aardman Studios**, famous for its **Wallace and Gromit** animations. The **YHA** provides great budget accommodation at one of the most pleasant quays of the city. From here, it is only a stone's throw to the impressive **Cathedral** (open daily, free entry); walk/cycle up "College Green" from the central square.

You'll leave Bristol through **Avon Gorge**, the treacherous spectacular waterway that connects Bristol with the sea. The difference between high and low water is 15 metres! You'll cycle under the amazing **Clifton Suspension Bridge**, a masterpiece of the famous engineer Isambard Kingdom Brunel, completed in 1864.

0.0 *(22.1)* Leave Bristol Temple Meads station via exit "Temple Quay" and walk ↑ onto "The Square"
(if you did section 13, walk → onto The Square)

0.1 At end of "The Square" ← **resume cycling** via rd (to City Centre)

0.2 At lhts ↑ across main rd (Temple Back)

0.5 At T-jct ← (Counterslip)

0.6 At T-jct with lhts → (Victoria St) 🚗🚗

0.9 At lhts after bridge ←, keep going ↑ 🚗🚗 *(Note: ignore signs 4!)*

1.3 **Dismount** on arrival at ⛵🏠🏛🚻📷🍴ℹ️ *Bristol City square*, ↖ join pavement and use lhts to cross rd ↑ onto central pedestrian area, then walk ← along fountains, at end of square keep ↖, **resume cycling** ↑ via cobbled quay rd *(canal on right hand side)*

1.8 After sharp bend to left, at end of cobbled quay rd → via bridge (Wapping Rd, sign at other side bridge)

2.1 At rndabt → via path on left side of rd (Cumberland Rd), official 🚲 ↑ (**41**) starts after 100 m

2.6 Follow lower 🚲 ↖ close to riverside (**41**)
*(For ⛵**SS Great Britain** ↟ join main rd, 1st rd →)*

3.9 2nd 🚲 bridge ← (old railway bridge, to Pill, **41**), after bridge imm → (to Pill/Portishead, **41**), keep ↑ via riverside 🚲

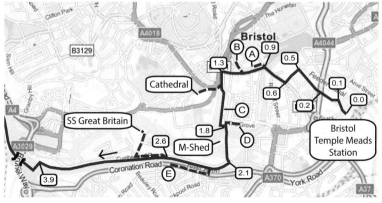

Section 14: Bristol - Cheddar (59 km / 36 miles)

5.2 ⚓ **Clifton Suspension Bridge & Avon Gorge**

10.8 Ep ↑ via tarmac rd

11.4 After short climb at T-jct ↗, at next jct ↑ via ᚒᚒ (to Pill, **41**)

11.7 Ep ⬆ via ᚒᚒ (**41**), then ↗ via tarmac ᚒᚒ (**41**)

12.3 Ep ←, at T-jct → (**41**) *(shops 🛒📷🍴* **Pill** *on left, behind field)*

13.0 Via "Underbanks" to end of "Marine Pd", at T-jct → (Avon Rd, **41**)

13.2 2nd rd ← (**41**), before tunnel → via ᚒᚒ (**41**)

13.7 Before steep slope ↖ via ᚒᚒ (to Portishead, **26**)

13.9 After tunnel under M5 ↖ via tarmac rd (**26**)

14.2 1st ᚒᚒ ↖ (**26**), follow main gravel route parallel to railway line

15.5 Cross dead end tarmac rd ↑, follow gravel ᚒᚒ (**26**)

16.4 Ep ← via tarmac rd *(Note: ignore signs route* **26***!)*

16.9 Just before T-jct ↖ cross motorway M5 via ᚒᚒ bridge

17.4 After 📷🍴 **The Priory** in sharp bend → (Caswell Ln, to Clapton)

20.0 At T-jct ↗ (Naish Hill), 2nd rd ← (Clevedon Ln, to Clapton Wick)

26.8 At T-jct ↘ (Walton Rd, to Walton) 🚗

27.2 1st rd ← (Holly Ln, later Castle Rd)

Pill used to be home to river pilot boats and marks the end of the Avon Gorge route. A new cycle route takes you through the industrial **Royal Portbury Docks** into the rural **Gordano Valley.** This valley takes you to the seaside town of **Clevedon.** The Victorian **Grand Pier** has great views over the Bristol Channel (open daily, £2 pp). As the beach is mostly rocky the seaside is best enjoyed from the pleasant **promenade.** If you cycled from Dover or Harwich, Clevedon could serve as a "coast-to-coast" destination. **Yatton** station is nearby. This is where the **Strawberry Line** starts, another great cycle path on a former railway line. It runs through fruit orchard country (try some local apple cider!) towards Cheddar.

28.5 ⬿ ⅌ *Benches with panoramic sea views on right side of rd*
29.2 After Walton Park and Highcliffe Hotels 1st rd ↗ (Marine Pd)
*(At this junction great views down over the ⬿ **Grand Pier**)*
29.5 ⬿ ⌂ 🛏 ⅋ ⚓ **Clevedon** *(Entrance ⬿ **Grand Pier**)*
29.8 At T-jct → (Elton Rd) 🚗
30.2 (⚓ *For alternative promenade route (walking only)* ↗ *onto pavement of promenade, at end ← via car park and playground, join rd →, continue reading at 30.9 km)*
30.5 1st rd → (Old Church Rd, to Portishead) 🚗
30.9 2nd rd → (Church Rd, to St Andrews Church)
31.3 At end of rd ↑ via tarmac path, after sharp bend ←, join gravel path ↗ on sea defences
31.9 Ep at pumping station ← via wide gravel path
32.8 1st tarmac rd →, at next jct ↗ (New Cut Bow)
35.1 At T-jct ← (Back Ln)

Section 14: Bristol - Cheddar (59 km / 36 miles)

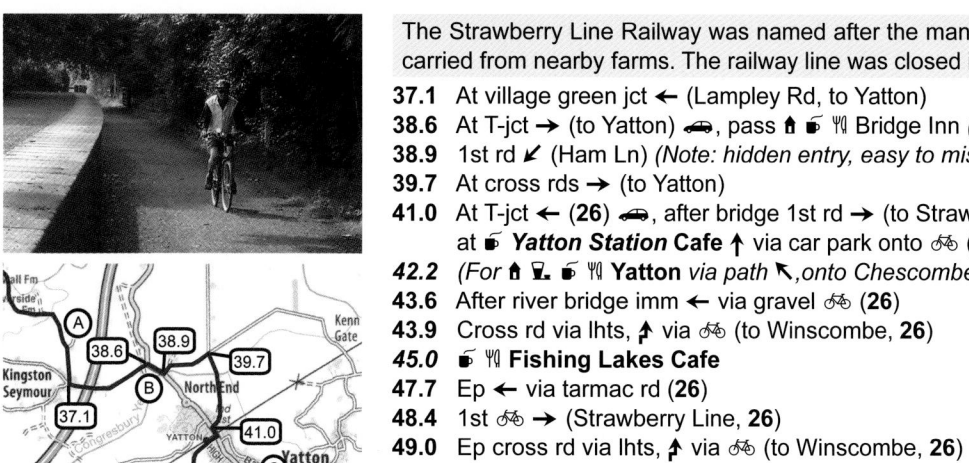

The Strawberry Line Railway was named after the many strawberries it carried from nearby farms. The railway line was closed in 1963.

37.1 At village green jct ← (Lampley Rd, to Yatton)

38.6 At T-jct → (to Yatton) 🚗, pass 🏠 🛏 🍴 Bridge Inn *(hotel)*

38.9 1st rd ↙ (Ham Ln) *(Note: hidden entry, easy to miss!)*

39.7 At cross rds → (to Yatton)

41.0 At T-jct ← (**26**) 🚗, after bridge 1st rd → (to Strawberry Line, **26**), at 🛏 *Yatton Station* Cafe ↑ via car park onto 🚲 (Strawberry Line)

42.2 *(For 🏠 🚻 🛏 🍴 Yatton via path ↖, onto Chescombe Rd, keep ↑)*

43.6 After river bridge imm ← via gravel 🚲 (**26**)

43.9 Cross rd via lhts, ↑ via 🚲 (to Winscombe, **26**)

45.0 🛏 🍴 **Fishing Lakes Cafe**

47.7 Ep ← via tarmac rd (**26**)

48.4 1st 🚲 → (Strawberry Line, **26**)

49.0 Ep cross rd via lhts, ↑ via 🚲 (to Winscombe, **26**)

51.1 🚏 🛏 🍴 **Winscombe** (🛏 🍴 *via 🚲 just beyond former station)*

51.8 Keep going ↑ (Strawberry Line, to Axbridge, **26**)

53.6 Ep cross rd ↑ onto 🚲 (Strawberry Line, **26**)

54.1 Ep → via rd (to Axbridge, **26**)

54.4 At T-jct ← via 🚲, at ep use crossing points onto rd ↗ (West St, into Axbridge, **26**)

55.0 🏠 🚻 🛏 🍴 **Axbridge**

55.9 At T-jct ↗ via 🚲 on right side of main rd (to Cheddar, **26**), then 1st 🚲 → (Strawberry Line, to Cheddar, **26**)

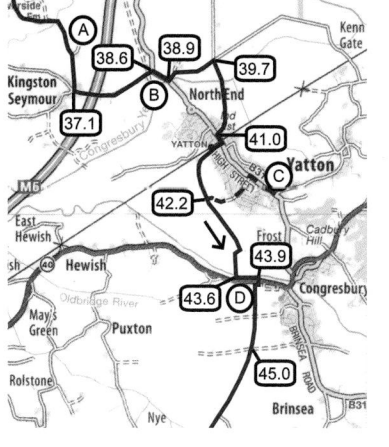

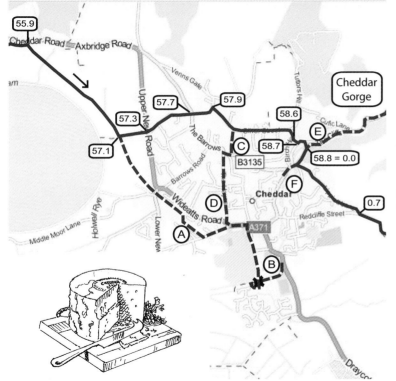

The **Shute Shelve Tunnel** takes you through the Mendip Hills to pleasant **Axbridge**. **Cheddar** is famous for its cheese and its gorge. At the **Original Cheddar Cheese Company** you can learn everything about it. It is located at the start of the dramatic **Cheddar Gorge**. The limestone cliffs make for good **abseiling** and you can also do some **caving** here. It is also worth cycling up and down the gorge to escape the touristy high street.

57.1 *Pay attention;* after concrete bridge over ditch ← (Holwell Ln, see info sign) *(Note: leave Strawberry Line here!)*

57.3 At cross rds ↑ (Pound Oak Rd)

57.7 At cross rds ↑ (Hannay Rd)

57.9 1st rd → (Kent St), keep ↑ (Silver St)

58.6 After sharp bend to right, at house "Wayside Cottage" ↖ via narrow path down steep slope

58.7 Ep ←, follow tarmac rd with bend to ↗

58.8 ⛸ 🏠 🏕 🛒 🚲 🍴 ℹ **Cheddar** (for Cheddar Gorge ←)

Section 15: Cheddar - Taunton (60 km / 37 miles)

🚲 24.4 km, 🚶 35.4 km, 🚗 0.7 km, 🚗🚗 0.0 km
Stations: *Bridgewater (after 39.6 km), Taunton*

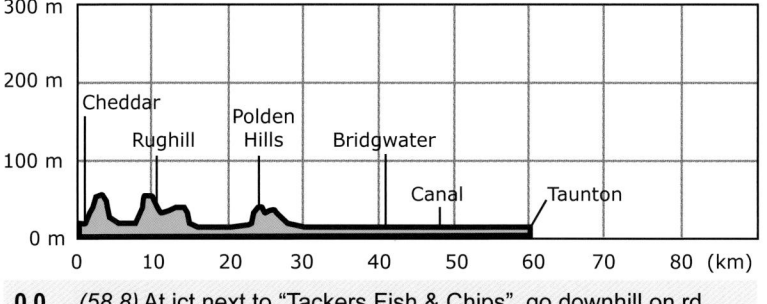

Elevation profile labels: Cheddar, Rughill, Polden Hills, Bridgwater, Canal, Taunton

0.0 *(58.8)* At jct next to "Tackers Fish & Chips", go downhill on rd (away from Cheddar Gorge), take 1st ← (The Lippiatt, steep hill)

0.7 At T-jct ↖

2.9 1st rd → ("Strawberry Farm" around corner)

3.0 At cross rds ↑ (Latches Ln, to Nyland)

6.9 At T-jct → (to Cheddar/Wedmore)

8.2 At T-jct → (to Cheddar) 🚗, imm 1st rd ↖ (Rughill, to Stoughton)

10.0 At T-jct ↖ (to Blackford)

12.4 3rd rd ← *(Note; after sharp bend to right at "Lavender Cottage")*

12.8 At cross rds ↑ (Wells Way)

13.3 1st rd → (Hozzard Ln)

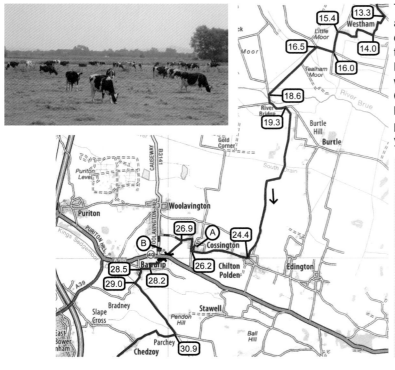

The **Somerset Levels** is a low lying peat-based plain, artificially drained and used for cattle grazing. Much of the original reedswamps have disappeared. As the swamps were historically subject to winter flooding, the area remains remarkably thinly populated. Most farms can be found on higher ridges like **Rughill** and **Polden Hills**, rising from the plain. Cyclists will note the total lack of pubs and shops on the way, even in villages like **Cossington**, **Bawdrip** and **Chedzoy**. Buy some food and drinks before leaving Cheddar! The area is great for bird watching and naturally provides pleasant cycling on empty lanes. There is plenty of choice of farm B&B's if you are after an overnight stay away from it all.

14.0	At T-jct →
15.4	At T-jct "Laurel Farm" ←
16.0	1st rd → (to Mark)
16.5	1st rd ↖
18.6	At T-jct ← (to Bridgwater), ↑ follow bends
19.3	2nd rd → (see sign "rd liable to subsidence")
24.4	At T-jct opposite "The Grange" → (Broadway)
26.2	In sharp bend to left ↗ (to Woolavington, **3**)
26.9	Imm after bridge over disused railway bed, 1st ⬲ ↖ (**3**)
28.2	Ep → via tarmac rd (to Chedzoy, **3**)
28.5	At T-jct ← (Church Rd, **3**), follow through route
29.0	Imm after canal bridge 1st ⬲ ← (to Chedzoy, **3**)
30.9	Ep → via tarmac rd (to Chedzoy, **3**), keep going ↑

Section 15: Cheddar - Taunton (60 km / 37 miles)

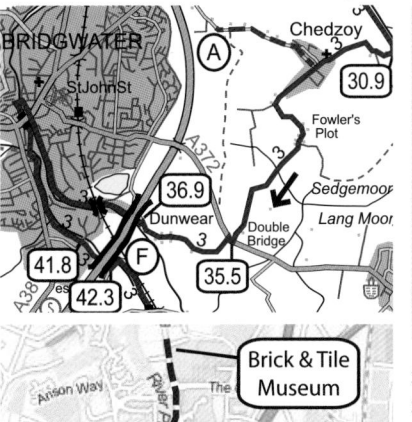

To be able to cross the River Parrett, you have to make your way into **Bridgwater.** The first river bridge crossing in Bridgwater dates from 1200 AD and you'll make the river crossing exactly at this spot. The town provides plenty of shopping opportunities and is a good place to stock up on provisions. You might want to visit the **Somerset Brick and Tile Museum** (open Tue-Thurs, free entry). This industry flourished due to the abundance of coastal clay deposits in the area, but is now very much a thing of the past. The Somerset coast lacks continous cycling-friendly options, which makes an inland route south via the Taunton and Bridgwater Canal the obvious choice. From Taunton, we'll resume heading west!

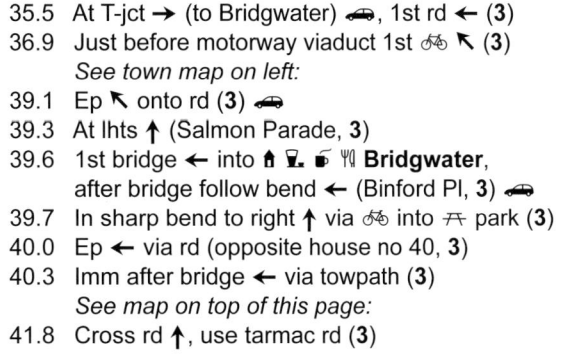

35.5 At T-jct → (to Bridgwater) 🚗, 1st rd ← (3)
36.9 Just before motorway viaduct 1st 🚲 ↖ (3)
      See town map on left:
39.1 Ep ↖ onto rd (3) 🚗
39.3 At lhts ↑ (Salmon Parade, 3)
39.6 1st bridge ← into 🏠 🛒 🍴 **Bridgwater**,
      after bridge follow bend ← (Binford Pl, 3) 🚗
39.7 In sharp bend to right ↑ via 🚲 into 🌳 park (3)
40.0 Ep ← via rd (opposite house no 40, 3)
40.3 Imm after bridge ← via towpath (3)
      See map on top of this page:
41.8 Cross rd ↑, use tarmac rd (3)

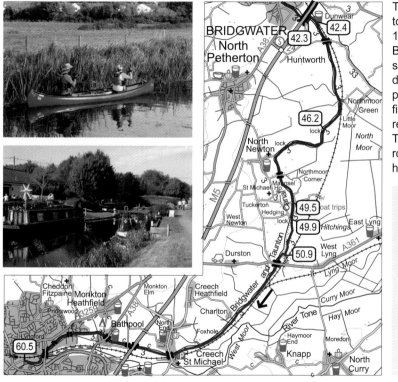

The **Taunton and Bridgwater Canal** provides a pleasant continuous towpath route with a reasonably good surface. This canal dates from 1827 and was designed to be part of the Grand Western Canal between Bristol and Exeter, an inland waterway which would make it possible to short cut the treacherous sea journey around Devon and Cornwall. The development of this canal was plagued by problems. The Devon hills proved to be an engineering nightmare and the arrival of the railways meant financial backing for the canal dried up. The Taunton and Bridgwater Canal remained a "dead end", only providing a water link between the two towns. The number of canal boats is still very small, making the canal popular for rowing and kayaking. The **Lower Maunsel Canal Centre** halfway along has a pleasant cafe.

42.3 In sharp bend to right ← over bridge,
imm → via towpath (3), keep going ↑ via towpath (3)

42.4 ⌂ 🛏 🍴 **Boat and Anchor Inn** *(pub)*

46.2 ⛩ **Locks Green**

49.5 🛏 **Lower Maunsel Canal Centre** *(via bridge)*

49.9 Ep ↑ via rd (3)

50.9 At house "Greenway" ↗ back to towpath (3),
keep to towpath on left side of canal into Taunton (3)

60.5 At bridge no 37, the towpath crosses canal ↗ and ends;
* For Taunton station ↑ via dead end rd
* For next route section after bridge imm ←
(see lock area with benches on left, continue on page 105)

Section 16: Taunton - Dulverton (51 km / 31 miles)

🚲 2.2 km, 🚶 43.8 km, 🚐 4.6 km, 🚗🚗 0.0 km
Stations: *Taunton*

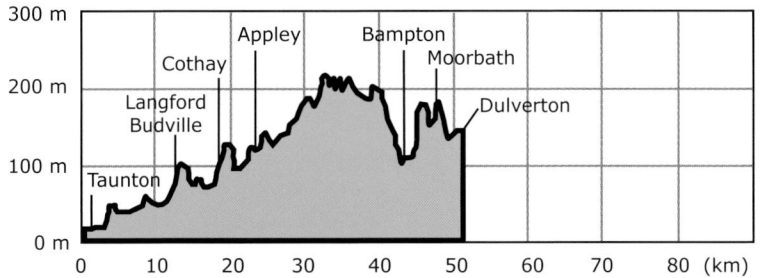

Taunton marks the end of a reasonably easy ride from the east. From Taunton you enter a different world; a **remote landscape** with nearly continuous **climbing** or **descending**. From now on, every kilometer cycled feels like two! Those who found the Wiltshire hills hard going should be warned. This doesn't mean the route to Dulverton is impossible to do. As long as you are prepared to walk some short climbs and allow plenty of time, you'll get there in the end. **Splendid views** will be your reward! Alternatively, those who also love **walking** might like to take up the author's offer to do a demanding four day-walk on the stunning **South West Coast Path** across Exmoor National Park, whilst he transfers and stores your bikes and luggage. With this "Devon & Somerset Explorer Tour" you'll skip route sections 16 and 17, see www.eoscycling.com.

Busy **Taunton** has plenty to offer to visitors; what about a Roman mosaic in the **Museum of Somerset** (open Tue-Sat, free entry) or the **Cricket Museum** (open Tue-Fri, £2 pp)? Shoppers shouldn't miss the pleasant **Old Market Centre**.

Beyond Taunton, the scenic **Cothay Manor Gardens** (open Tue-Thu and Sun, £7 pp) is pretty much the only attraction on the way. **Gamlins Farm** is the last campsite before hilly Exmoor and is beautifully located; don't miss it! **Bampton** is a small town in a scenic valley with some local services, as is Dulverton. In **Dulverton** you'll also find the excellent **Exmoor National Park Centre** with plenty of information to extend your stay beyond the obvious cycling.

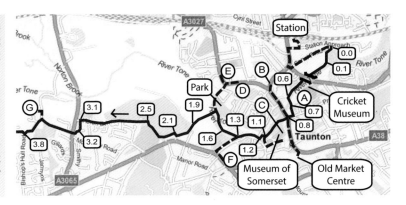

0.0 *(60.5)* At bridge no 37 westbound via riverside gravel path (**3**) *(see lock area with benches on left)*

0.1 At next footbridge over river ↑ (**3**)

0.6 **Dismount** to cross bridge ← (to Town Centre, **3**)

0.7 **Resume cycling** on car park, ↑ via rd (see Nicky's Flower Studio), at jct → against traffic flow (**3**)

0.8 ⬥🏨🍴📷🍽🛈 *Taunton*

0.8 Cross main rd ↟ via lhts onto 🚲 (**3**), ↗ to riverside path

1.1 2nd bridge → (**3**), ep ← via 🚲 on left side (**3**)

1.2 At jct → via lhts onto 🚲 on right side of rd (Tangier Wy, to SCAT, **3**)

1.3 In bend ↖ (rd crossing with lhts), ↗ via 🚲 (to Staplegrove Rd, **3**)

1.6 At entrance 🍴 *super store* on left side ↑, then **dismount** to cross "French Weir", 1st path ←, **resume cycling** after next bridge (**3**)

1.9 At "crossroads" of cycle paths ↑ (**3**)

2.1 After building "Arts & Design" ↗ via 🚲 (at "Graduate Hair Academy", **3**), ep ↗ via school rd (**3**)

2.5 At rndabt ↑ (rd with football fields on right side)

3.1 Just before end rd ← (Robin Cl, **3**), 1st 🚲 ↗ (**3**)

3.2 At lhts cross main rd → (Bishops Hull Hill, **3**)

3.8 At end of climb 🍴 📷 **Bishops Hull** *(pub and shop)* in bend to left ↗ (Shutewater Hill, **3**), keep going ↑

Section 16: Taunton - Dulverton (51 km / 31 miles)

5.8	After ⚡ electrity grid masts, 1st rd → (to Allerford, **3**)
6.5	After ⚤ **Allerford Inn** *(restaurant)* and railway crossing at T-jct ← (to Hillfarrance, **3**), then 1st rd ← (**3**)
8.8	After ♠ ☞ ⚤ **The Anchor Inn** *(pub)* at T-jct ← (to Bradford, **3**), then imm 1st rd → (Broom Ln, **3**)
10.2	At T-jct ← (to Nynehead, **3**), keep going ↑
15.4	At T-jct ↗ and imm ↖ (to Langford Budville, **3**)
16.4	In ☞ ⚤ **Langford Budville** *(pub)* at cross rds on climb → (to Greenham, **3**), at next cross rds ↑ (**3**)

19.1	At T-jct ← (to Greenham, **3**), follow through rd
20.6	⚞☞ **Cothay Manor Gardens** *(main entrance)*
21.8	At T-jct → (to Greenham, **3**)
22.6	At T-jct → (to Greenham, Bampton Alt Route **344**) *(For △ **Gamlins** ↖ 700m)*
24.1	1st rd → (to Stawley, **344**) *(For ⚑ **Appley** (shop) ↑ 20m)*
24.5	1st rd ← (to Stawley, **344**) *(For ☞ ⚤ **Globe Inn** (pub) ↑ 30m)*
26.0	1st rd ← (to Ashbrittle, **344**)
26.5	After bridge, imm 1st rd ↗ (to Clayhanger, **344**)

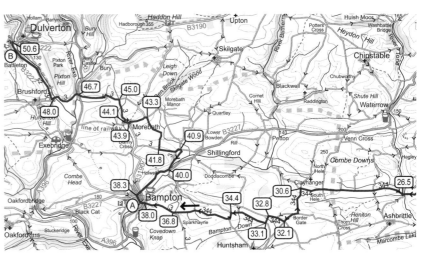

30.6 At 3rd cross rds ← (to Huntsham, **344**)
32.1 At T-jct ↗ (to Bampton, **344**)
32.8 Follow sharp bend ← (to Huntsham, **344**)
33.1 At jct → via tarmac rd (to Bampton, **344**)
34.4 *Pay attention:* In steep descent 1st rd ← (**344**)
36.8 At T-jct ↗ (**3**)
38.0 ↑ (Briton St, **3**) 🚗 into 🏠 🍴 🛒 🍽 **Bampton**
38.3 At T-jct → (to Wiveliscombe, **3**) 🚗
40.0 Before "Hukeley Bridge" ← (to Loyton, **3**)

40.9 At cross rds ← (to Moorbath, **3**)
41.8 1st rd → (Firway, to Keens, **3**)
43.3 At T-jct ← (**3**), at next jct ↑ (to Moorbath, **3**)
43.9 In Moorbath in bend to left 1st rd → (**3**)
44.1 At house "Fern" 1st rd ↗ (**3**)
45.0 At T-jct ← (to Dulverton, **3**)
46.7 At cross rds ↑ (to Dulverton, **3**)
48.0 At T-jct → (to Dulverton, **3**) 🚗
50.6 River bridge ⚓ 🏠 🍴 🛒 🍽 ℹ **Dulverton**

Section 17: Dulverton - Barnstaple (55 km / 34 miles)

17A: 🚲 6.4 km, 🚶 48.4 km, 🚗 2.1 km, 🚗🚗 0.0 km
17B: 🚲 6.4 km, 🚶 46.6 km, 🚗 0.0 km, 🚗🚗 0.0 km
Stations: *Barnstaple*

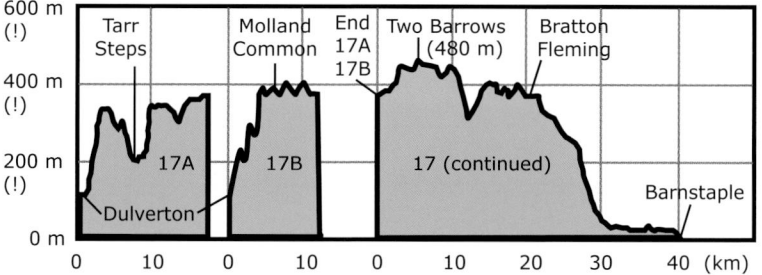

Extreme climbing is required to take you out of Dulverton onto **Exmoor**. Our route via the prehistoric **Tarr Steps** river bridge is spectacular, but hard. Only slightly easier is the **Official Route 3** via spacious **Molland Common**. Beyond these two route options, the climb continues to **Two Barrows**, at 480m above sea level the highest point of our route. Stock up on provisions in Dulverton, because there is not much out there until you descent to **Barnstaple**. Its historic **Pannier Market** (open Mon-Sat, free entry) is worth a visit. Barnstaple is also the official "home" to this London-Land's End cycle route. We hope to welcome you at our own special leisure cycling hub in the future; check our website for the latest news!

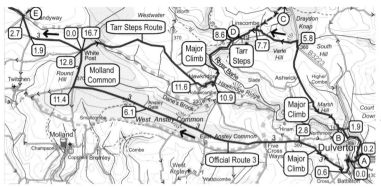

*The **Tarr Steps***

17A: Tarr Steps Route (16.7 km):

0.0 *(50.6)* At river, cross bridge to town centre 🚗

0.2 After Exmoor National Park Centre, 1st rd ←
(Lady St, becomes Northmoor Rd, B3223) 🚗

1.9 After leaving Dulverton 1st rd ← (to Hawkridge),
then 1st rd → (to Ashwick), start **major climb**

5.8 At T-jct ← 🚗, 1st rd ← (to Tarr Steps)

7.7 At jct ↖ (to Tarr Steps)

8.6 After 🏠 ☕ 🍴 **Tarr Farm Inn** *(pub)* **dismount** at end of rd,
walk ↑ via ⛲ **Tarr Steps**, then **resume cycling** ↑

10.9 After **major climb** at church →, keep ↑ (to Dulverton)

11.6 At T-jct → (to North Molton)

16.7 In sharp bend to left → via cattle grid, **end route**

17B: Official Route 3 via Molland Common (12.8 km):

0.0 *(50.6)* Just before river bridge Dulverton ← into Oldberry Ln **(3)**,
follow sharp bend ←, start **major climb**

0.6 At T-jct opposite house "Barnfield" ↗ **(3)**,
then 1st rd → (to Hawkridge, **3**)

2.8 At T-jct ↖ (to East Anstey), keep going ↑

6.1 ⛲ **Molland Common** *(cattle grid)*

11.4 At "Ridgeway" cross rds → **(3)**

12.8 At jct ← via cattle grid, **end route**

0.0 **BOTH ROUTES REJOINED:** *(16.7/12.8)* ↗ (to Sandyway, **3**)

1.9 At cross rds → (to Sandyway, **3**)

2.7 At T-jct → (to Withypool), imm 1st rd ← (to Simonsbath, **3**)
*(For 🏠 ☕ 🍴 **Sportsman Inn** ↑100m)*

Section 17: Dulverton - Barnstaple (55 km / 34 miles)

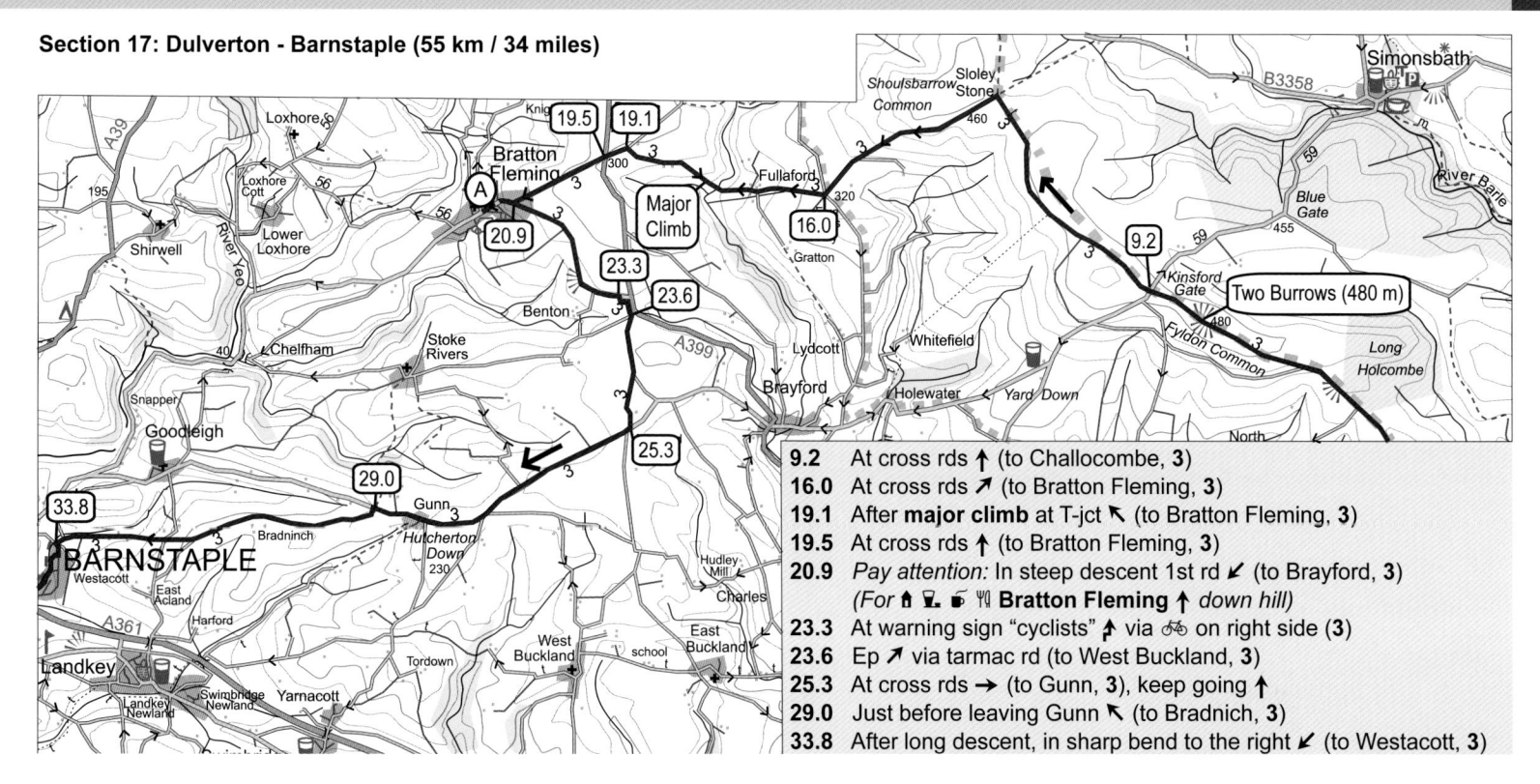

9.2 At cross rds ↑ (to Challocombe, **3**)

16.0 At cross rds ↗ (to Bratton Fleming, **3**)

19.1 After **major climb** at T-jct ↖ (to Bratton Fleming, **3**)

19.5 At cross rds ↑ (to Bratton Fleming, **3**)

20.9 *Pay attention:* In steep descent 1st rd ↙ (to Brayford, **3**)
(For 🏠 🛏 🛒 🍴 **Bratton Fleming** ↑ *down hill)*

23.3 At warning sign "cyclists" ↑ via 🚲 on right side (**3**)

23.6 Ep ↗ via tarmac rd (to West Buckland, **3**)

25.3 At cross rds → (to Gunn, **3**), keep going ↑

29.0 Just before leaving Gunn ↖ (to Bradnich, **3**)

33.8 After long descent, in sharp bend to the right ↙ (to Westacott, **3**)

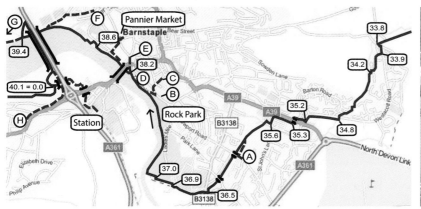

33.8 After left turn to Westacott (see previous page) imm ↗ via ♻ (**3**)

33.9 Ep 1st rd → (Larkspur Gdns, **3**)

34.2 At jct ♻ ↖ ("Whiddon Valley Woods", **3**)

34.8 Ep → via ♻ on left side of rd (**3**)

35.2 At ep before rndabt, cross rd → onto ♻ leading to tunnel (**3**), ↖ into tunnel (**3**)

35.3 Imm after tunnel before 🛒 *super store* →, stay close to building and follow ♻ around car park (**3**)

35.6 Ep at rndabt → via ♻ on right side of rd (to "Wickes", **3**), then 1st ♻ ← (cross rd, **3**), keep going ↑

36.5 Ep cross rd ↑ via lhts, join ♻ ↑ (to Rock Park, **3**)

36.9 At end of steep descent ↑ via ♻ (to Leisure Centre, **3**)

37.0 At split of paths ↗, keep on ♻ with football fields on right, follow sharp bend → (riverside ♻, **27**) *(Note: ignore signs 3!)*

38.2 At ⛵ 🏠 ⛺ 🚆 ⛽ 🍴 ℹ 🏛 ***Barnstaple*** "The Square" (clock tower) ↖ via riverside ♻ (to Braunton, **27**), ↑ through narrow tunnel

38.6 Ep at slipway → and imm ↖ via ♻ on left side of rd (**27**), after bend imm ← (riverside ♻, **27**)

39.4 After passing under high bridge 1st ♻ → (to Bideford, **27**), ep → onto high bridge; use ♻ (to Bideford, **27**)

40.1 After high bridge 1st ♻ → (to Bideford, **27**), after slope down at next ♻ junction: ↑ *for Barnstaple station*, → *for main route*

Section 18: Barnstaple - Sheepwash (42 km / 26 miles)

18A: 🚲 36.8 km, 🚶 16.2 km, 🚗 1.4 km, 🚗🚗 0.0 km
18B: 🚲 34.1 km, 🚶 7.1 km, 🚗 0.9 km, 🚗🚗 0.0 km
Stations: *Barnstaple*

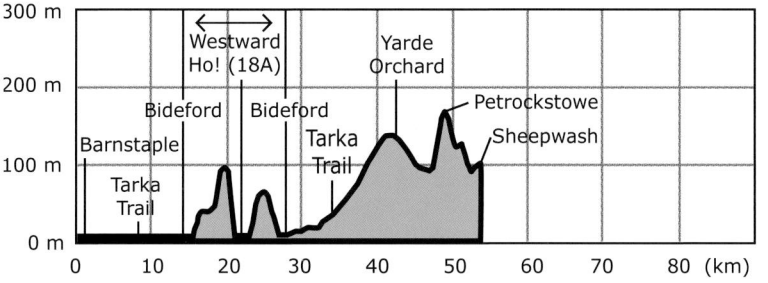

0.0	*(40.2)* At jct of cyclepaths at south side of high bridge, join Tarka Trail (to Bideford, **3/27**)
4.1	At 🚶🏠🍴🚻 **Fremington Quay** ↑ via 🚲
7.5	At rd crossing ↑ via 🚲
8.8	At row of houses on right side of path ↑ via "MOD" gate onto gravel rd *(note: leave Tarka Trail!)*, at end → via tarmac rd 🚗
9.4	🚶🏠🚆🚲🍴⚓ **Instow**
10.1	At former railway crossing rejoin Tarka Trail ↗ **(3)**
14.5	🚶🏠🚆🚲🍴⚕ **ℹ Bideford** *(former railway station)*

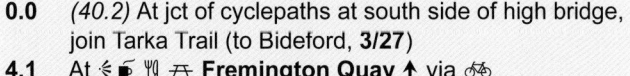

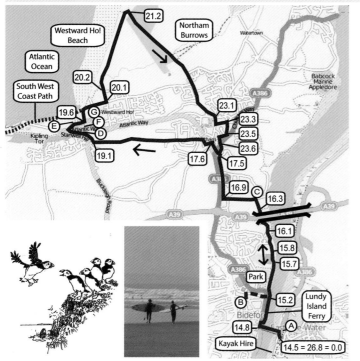

14.5 Walk ↘ via ramp, resume cycling ↑ at rndabt onto bridge 🚗

14.8 After river bridge → at rndabt and imm **dismount**; use lhts to cross rd ↟ onto quay 🚲, **resume cycling**, keep ↗

15.2 At end quay route 1st rd ↗ (Riverbank Car Park)

15.7 At end car park rd **dismount**; walk ↑ via footpath

15.8 **Resume cycling** on "Riverbank House" rd, at sharp bend to left ↑ via path (Coast Path), ↗ onto rd

16.1 At rndabt ↑ (Riverside Cl), at T-jct → (Chircoombe Ln), at end of tarmac ↖ via gravel rd

16.3 At end of gravel rd ↑ via tarmac rd, at T-jct ←

16.9 At T-jct → via 🚲 on right side of rd

17.5 Ep ← (Cleveland Pk), **dismount** at T-jct, cross "Churchill Way" and walk ↑ via pavement to bus stop

17.6 Cross main rd ↟, **resume cycling** on 1st rd ↖ (Bay View Rd)

19.1 Just before "Stop"-sign → (Fosketh Hill), down hill, at end T-jct ↗

19.6 In 🏠 🏛 🍴 ☕ 🍽 ⚓ **Westward Ho!** ← to seafront (Golf Links Rd)

20.1 After cricket field on left side of rd 1st rd ← (Pebble Ridge Rd)

20.2 ⚓ **Northam Burrows Country Park** (↑ via gravel rd)

21.2 At ⚓ **Sandymere Beach Access** → via tarmac rd, keep going ↑

23.1 In 🍴 **Northam** ↑ on square, 1st rd ← (Cross St)

23.3 1st rd → (Burrough Rd)

23.5 At T-jct →, 1st rd ← (Castle St, dead end rd), **dismount** at end

23.6 ↗ via footpath, cross main rd and walk → on pavement, keep ↖, **resume cycling**, ↑ onto 🚲, *same route back, see map!*

Section 18: Barnstaple - Sheepwash (42 km / 26 miles)

The **Tarka Trail** is one of England's best cycle routes. Views over the River Taw are best at **Fremington Quay.** We get off the trail at **Instow** to be able to enjoy its sheltered beach and charming views over **Appledore**.

The trail then continues next to the River Torridge to the "little white town" of **Bideford**. You can board a ship at its busy quay to remote **Lundy Island** (day trip £35 pp, check www.lundyisland.co.uk for time tables). You shouldn't miss out on the spectacular **Westward Ho!** Atlantic Beach, so make the effort to do our **Atlantic Beach route** (route 18A, see page 113) before heading further south on theTarka Trail (route 18B, see page 115).

From **Bideford Kayak Hire** you can enjoy the Torridge River upstream, just like **Tarka the Otter** from the 1927 novel. The narrowing Torridge valley is stunning. You'll cross the river several times and there is also a tunnel, taking you close to **Torrington**. This town lies on the top of a hill, so it is easier to stay on the Tarka Trail. Those who make the effort to do the climb into town will find the tiny **Pannier Market** charming. Learn about the English Civil War in the **Torrington 1646 Museum** (open Tue-Thu, £8 pp) or learn about glass making at **Dartington Crystal** (open Mon-Fri, £8 pp).

Via **Tarka Country Park** a steady climb starts to the **Yarde Orchard Cafe** with great budget accommodation. Hilly lanes take you to tiny **Sheepwash** where you either go towards Plymouth or Land's End.

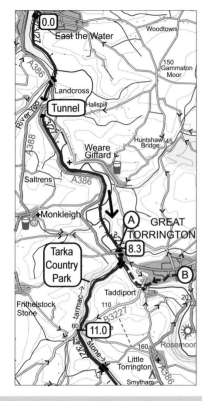

0.0 *(14.5/26.8)* ↑ via 🚲 (to Torrington, **3/27**)

8.3 At 🚲 🔧 **Torrington Cycle Hire/Puffing Billy café** ↑ via 🚲 (**3/27**) into 🌲 **Tarka Country Park**

8.4 *(For 🌲 🏠 🛏 🚲 🍴 ℹ️ Great Torrington (2km): after bridge over path → through gate (to Taddiport), imm ← via gravel path, keep ↑ through factory, ep ↖ start climb "Mill St", keep ↑ to town centre)*

11.0 Ep → and imm ← onto car park, ↑ via 🚲 (**3/27**)

13.6 Cross rd, ↑ via 🚲 (**3/27**)

15.6 Ep ↗ via 🚲 (to Meeth, **3/27**), 🏠 ⛺ 🚲 🍴 **Yarde Orchard** on left

20.9 At 3rd rd crossing beyond Yarde Orchard ↗ onto rd (to Petrockstowe, **3/27**) *(note: ignore Tarka Trail to Meeth!)*

22.0 At jct ↑ (to Sheepwash, **3/27**) *(For 🚲 🍴 pub ←, 200m)*

24.7 At T-jct ← (to Sheepwash, **3/27**), follow through rd

27.6 🏠 🛏 🚲 🍴 **Sheepwash** *(pub and small shop)*

Don't miss out on the unique "away from it all" vibe at Yarde Orchard; a small-scale eco-accommodation with bunkhouse, yurts and campsite right on the trail.

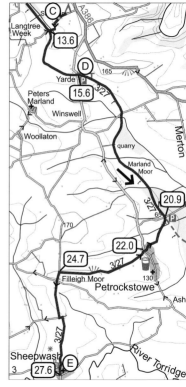

Section 19: Sheepwash - Plymouth (86 km / 53 miles)

🚴 *37.1 km,* 🚶 *48.2 km,* 🚗 *0.2 km,* 🚗🚗 *0.6 km*
Stations: Okehampton (after 21.7 km, limited services only), Plymouth

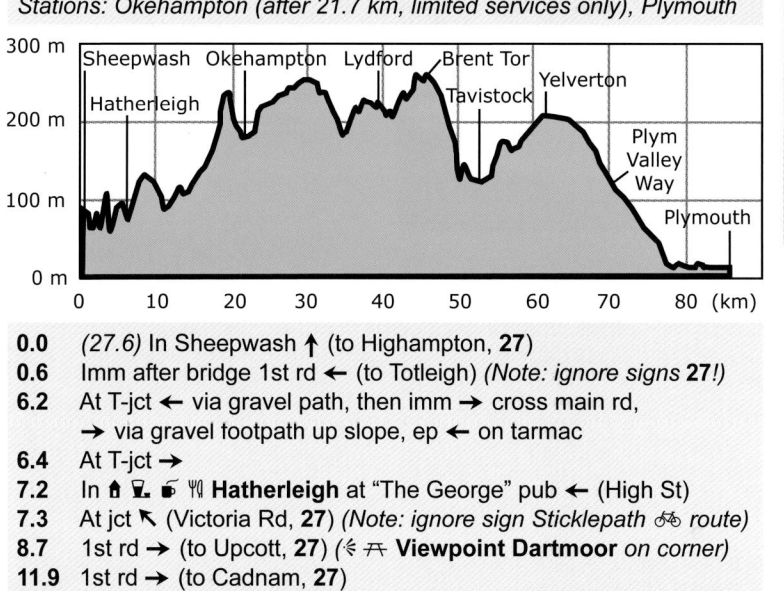

0.0	*(27.6)* In Sheepwash ↑ (to Highampton, **27**)
0.6	Imm after bridge 1st rd ← (to Totleigh) *(Note: ignore signs **27**!)*
6.2	At T-jct ← via gravel path, then imm → cross main rd, → via gravel footpath up slope, ep ← on tarmac
6.4	At T-jct →
7.2	In 🏠 🚉 📷 🍴 **Hatherleigh** at "The George" pub ← (High St)
7.3	At jct ↖ (Victoria Rd, **27**) *(Note: ignore sign Sticklepath 🚴 route)*
8.7	1st rd → (to Upcott, **27**) (← 🏞 **Viewpoint Dartmoor** *on corner*)
11.9	1st rd → (to Cadnam, **27**)
13.6	At T-jct ← (to Woodhall, **27**) 🚗, 1st rd → (to Okehampton, **27**), then imm 1st rd ← (**27**)

Those who choose the route to Plymouth won't be disappointed. The **Devon Coast to Coast Route** (27) southbound features some of the very best cycling of this route book. Excellent railway paths provide spectacular views over Dartmoor, including **ten stunning high viaducts** and two fun former railway tunnels. In many ways, this route is actually better than the journey to Land's End. The climbing to Plymouth is generally much lighter then on the Cornwall route, although up to the small town **Hatherleigh** the climbs are hard-going. Note the official route 27 has various route options, keep to the guidebook route for the smoothest experience.

More climbing is needed to get to **Okehampton**, a popular base for those ready to explore **Dartmoor**. The **YHA youth hostel** next to the scenic railway station runs various tours and activities into the National Park. The **Castle ruins** are slightly away from the route, but worth a visit (open daily, £4 pp, English Heritage members and Overseas Visitor Pass holders free).

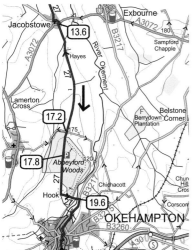

17.2 At cross rds ↑ (to Hook, **27**)

17.8 ≶ ⊼ **Abbeyford Woods** *(via car park on left)*

19.6 At T-jct → (to Okehampton, **27**), keep going ↑

20.8 At T-jct → 🚌🚗 into 🏠 🏨 🖼 🍴 ⚕ ℹ️ *Okehampton*, over bridge imm ←, beyond church ↑ via rd (**27**)

21.0 At square ↖ (Station Rd, **27**)

21.5 1st rd ↖ (Station Rd, **27**)

21.7 At station entrance 1st rd ↘ (to Lydford, **27**), imm 1st 🚲 ↙ (to Lydford, Granite Way, **27**)

Section 19: Sheepwash - Plymouth (86 km / 53 miles)

Once you have taken the hard climb out of Okehampton onto the **Granite Way** the fun gets really going. You cycle high over deep valleys on the **Meldon** and **Lake Viaducts**, both masterpieces of Victorian engineering. These viaducts provide superb views over Dartmoor. The railway line on these viaducts closed in 1968. Heritage specials on the short remaining section between Okehampton and Meldon quarry remind us of the old days. Work is on its way to make the Granite Cycle Way continous all the way to Lydford, but at the time of publishing this book, you still need to make the country lane detour via the peaceful village of **Bridestowe**. It is hard to believe its narrow High Street was once part of the main driving route to Cornwall; ask older locals for their traffic horror stories!

25.2 ≼ 🖻 **Meldon Viaduct & Railway Buffet Car**
      (Note: irregular opening times!)
27.9 Cross rd, ↑ via 🚲 (**27**)
30.4 After ≼ 🚏 **Lake Viaduct** ↖ via 🚲 *(Note; leave Granite Way!)*,
      via zigzag to base of viaduct, then ← (to Bearslake Inn, **27**)
31.2 At 🖻 🍽 **Bearslake Inn** *(pub)* cross main rd ↑ (**27**)
31.4 At T-jct ↖ (**27**)
32.8 In 🏠 🛏 🖻 🍽 **Bridestowe** *(pub & shop)* at T-jct ←
      (to Tavistock, **27**)
35.5 Imm after bridge over former railway 1st 🚲 ↘ (to Lydford, **27**)
37.5 After 🏠 🖻 **Lydford Country House** *(tearooms)* at ep → (**27**)
38.3 ≼ 🖻 🍽 **Lydford** *(castle ruins and pub)*

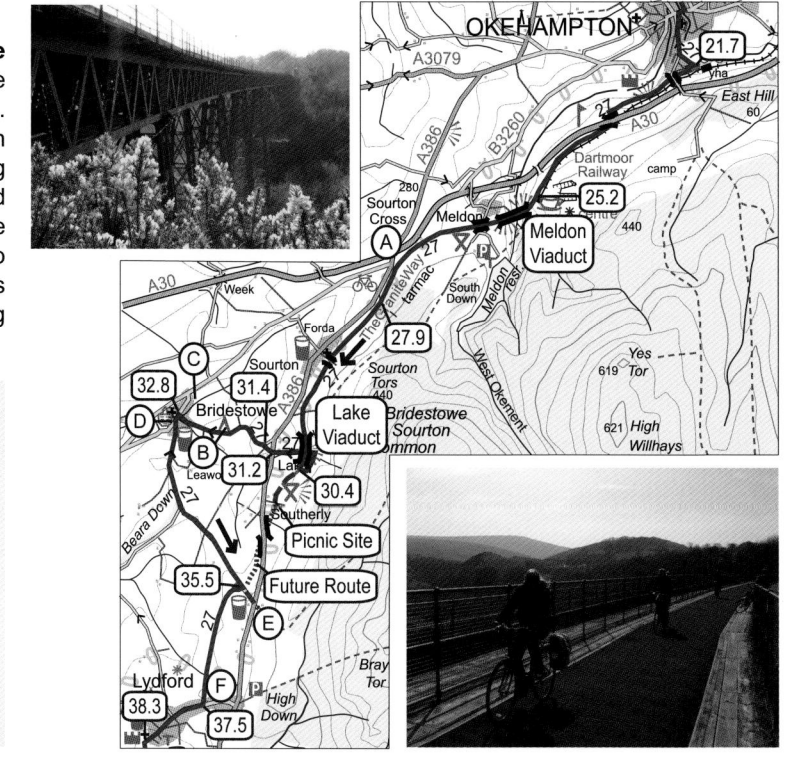

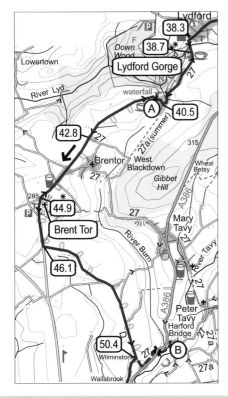

Lydford is another peaceful village on the edge of Dartmoor, featuring a notorious medieval prison, the small **Lydford Castle** (free access). Just down the road, you can go for a spectacular walk in **Lydford Gorge**, the deepest valley in Southwest England. The demanding wooded walk features various waterfalls (open daily, £7 pp). Just as spectacular is the free walk onto exposed **Brent Tor**, a weathered volcano, topped by a 13th century church. You must make the effort to park your bike and make the five minute walk to the top as the views are just amazing!

A long descent will take you into lively **Tavistock**. This small town is popular for shopping, especially because of its historic **Pannier Market**. Its most famous son is **Sir Francis Drake**, second in command when defeating the Spanish Armada in 1588. The next cycle path on the Devon Coast to Coast Route, the **Drake Trail**, is named after him.

38.7 ⇇ 🚶 **Lydford Gorge** *(Visitor Centre and Walks)*

40.5 Follow rd with bend to → over narrow bridge (**27**)
*(Note: ignore signs "Summer Route **27**" to the left!)*

42.8 Keep ↑ *(Note: ignore signs route **27** to North Brentor to the left!)*

44.9 ⇇ **Brent Tor**
(park your bikes at the car park on the right side of the road, using the "cut through" opposite the footpath gate to Brent Tor, see also the church sign with information)

46.1 In descent, imm after rd to left to "South Brentor", 2nd rd ↖
(Note: no signs!), keep going ↑

50.4 Just before viaduct over rd → (**27**)

Section 19: Sheepwash - Plymouth (86 km / 53 miles)

51.1 After viaduct over rd, 2nd path ↗ (**27**)

51.6 After ⬳ ⛱ **Wallabrook Viaduct** at ep ← via rd

52.3 Keep going ↑ under viaduct *(Note: ignore signs* **27** *to the left)*,
then in descent 1st rd ↙ (Barley Market St)

> ***52.3** (If you'd like to bypass Tavistock town centre, you can do so
> by turning ↙ onto the 🚲 before the viaduct (**27**), see the map)*

52.8 At T-jct ← into ⬳ 🏠 🏨 🍷 📷 🍴 ✈ 🛈 **Tavistock**,
then 1st rd → (Market Rd)

53.0 **Dismount** at T-jct, cross main rd via lhts, walk ← on pavement,
after river bridge imm → **resume cycling** on 🚲 (St Johns Av, **27**)

53.3 At car park ↗ via narrow path (to Meadowlands Pool)

53.5 Ep → via narrow bridge, then imm ← (**27**)

53.6 After playground ↗ via wide path (**27**), leading to tunnel,
keep ↑ via 🚲 (**27**)

54.7 Cross rd, ↑ via 🚲 (**27**)

54.9 Ep ↟ (West Devon Business Park, **27**)

55.0 At end of rd via 🚲 ramp ↗ to rndabt, cross 🍷 *super store* rd ↖
onto 🚲 on right side of main rd (**27**)

55.1 Cross main rd ↟ via lhts, continue via 🚲 (**27**)

55.3 Ep ↟ (Hazel Rd, **27**), at end of rd ↑ via 🚲 (**27**)

55.5 Ep →, 1st rd ↖, at end 🚲 ← via rd (**27**)

55.9 At T-jct ← (**27**), imm ↗ via 🚲 (to Plymouth, **27**)

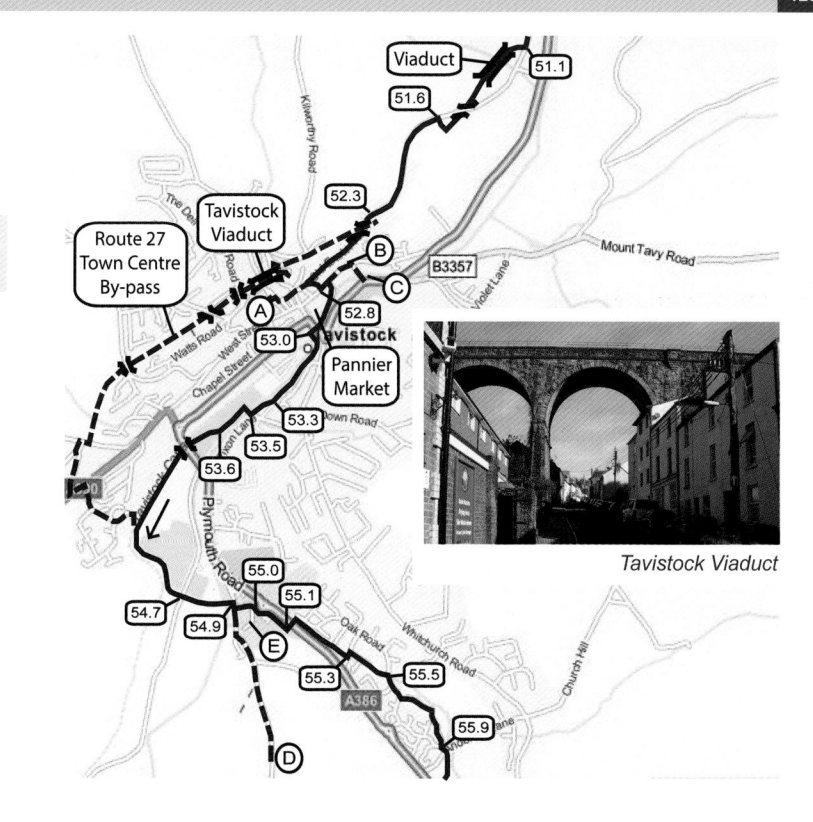

Tavistock Viaduct

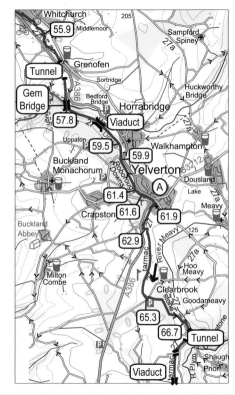

Leaving Tavistock, you'll cycle through the long spooky **Grenofen Tunnel** onto **Gem Bridge**, allowing you to cycle traffic-free through rugged wooded country without too much climbing. The monumental Gem Bridge opened in 2012, embodying the revival of sustainable transport. The bridge lies on the course of the Walkham railway viaduct, which was blown up by the army as an exercise in 1965. A steep climb is required to take you onto **Harrowbeer Common**, site of a former RAF airfield. Note **Yelverton** is the last place to buy food and drinks before starting the long descent to Plymouth; do so to have a great picnic on the heights just south of Yelverton! The superb **Plym Valley Cycle Way** is the grand finale to your ride, taking you through another long tunnel and another four high viaducts with splendid views over a beautiful wooded valley. Cycling paradise it is!

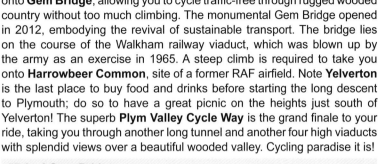

57.8 ⇐ **Gem Bridge**

59.5 Ep ↑ via residential rd

59.9 At T-jct ↑ via 🚲 (**27**)

61.4 ⇐ **Harrowbeer Common**

61.6 Cross rd ↑ via 🚲 (**27**), (🍺 ☕ 🍴 *pub and shop on left*), cross car park ↑, continue via 🚲 (**27**)

61.9 Cross main rd 🏠 🍺 ☕ 🍴 **Yelverton**, → via 🚲, imm ↑ onto lay-by rd (**27**), becomes 🚲 (**27**)

62.9 Ep ← via bridge, imm → (Clearbrook, **27**), keep ↑

65.3 Ep ← via bridge, imm → (to Goodameavy) *(Note: ignore signs* **27***!)*

66.7 At end of descent, just beyond side rd from left, ↑ onto 🚲 (Plym Valley Cycle Way, **27**), keep going ↑

Section 19: Sheepwash - Plymouth (86 km / 53 miles)

The cycle route avoids Plymouth's suburban wilderness by following the Laira estuary through the **Saltram House Estate**; house and gardens are open to the public (open daily, £10 pp).

You arrive in Plymouth's City Centre via the historic **Barbican** port from where the **Mayflower** left for the New World. The area is now dominated by cafés and restaurants. The **National Marine Aquarium** is based here (open daily, £12 pp). The **Citadel** is a stronghold overlooking Plymouth Harbour (guided tours £5 pp). **The Hoe** is Plymouth's seafront promenade. Its landmark lighthouse, **Smeaton's Tower**, dates from 1759 (open Tue-Sat, £3 pp). Route 27 ends at the international ferry terminal, but our guidebook will take you via quiet roads all the way to Plymouth station.

73.1 Ep cross car park ↗ to continue ⚲ (**27**)

75.0 Ep ↑ via rd, at T-jct ↖ via narrow ⚲
*(Note not to cross the railway; ignore signs **27**!)*

75.4 Ep → via ⚲ on left side of rd (to City Centre, **27**)

75.5 1st ⚲ ← (to Plympton, **27**), keep ↑ (to Hoe, **27**)

76.5 In park, 1st gravel path → (**27**), keep going ↑ via riverside path
*(For ⚲ 🏛 **Saltram House Estate** ↑)*

77.9 Ep ↗ via tarmac rd (**27**)

78.7 Just before T-jct ↗ via ⚲ (to Plymouth Hoe, **27**)

79.2 At lhts → via ⚲ on left side of rd onto estuary bridge
(to Hoe, **27**)

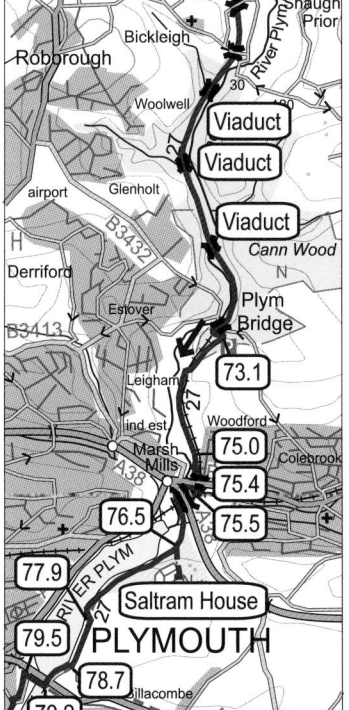

79.5 After estuary bridge 1st rd ← via 🚲 on right side of rd
(to Cattedown Wharf, **27**) *(Note: ignore signs to City Centre)*

80.0 At rndabt ← onto rd (Maxwell Rd, **27**)

80.3 At T-jct ← (Cattedown Rd, **27**), follow sharp bend to →

80.8 At end of rd ↑ via 🚲 (South West Coast Path, **27**)

81.5 Ep ↖, at T-jct ← 🚗, in bend ↖ (to Lock Gates, **27**)

81.9 Keep ↑, **dismount** to walk through lock area,
after locks ← (**27**) **resume cycling** *(For ⚓ 🏨 ☕ 🍴 ℹ Barbican →)*

82.4 At T-jct ↖ (Madeira Rd, to Hoe, **27**)

83.0 At rndabt ↖ (to "Boat Trips", **27**) *(For ⚓ The Hoe ↑)*

83.5 At rdabt ↑, keep following coastal rd, keep going ↑

84.5 At rndabt ↙ (to Continental Ferry Port) 🚗🚗

84.8 For **Continental Ferry Port** at rndabt ← *(end of route)*
For **Plymouth Station** at rndabt → (to Exeter) 🚗🚗

85.0 At rndabt cross main rd ↑ (Octagon St, to "R.C. Cathedral")

85.2 At mini rndabt ↑, at top of hill via bend →, keep ↑

85.7 **Dismount** at house no 3 on Archer Pl,
walk ↑ with park on right side, then **resume cycling** → 🚗

85.9 1st rd ↖ (Bayswater Rd)

86.1 **Dismount** at end of rd, walk ↗ to bus stop,
cross main rd via footbridge to 🚉 ☕ *Plymouth Station*

To cycle in France from **Roscoff** back to **Dover** for a **full circle** around the **English Channel**, look into using the **Voies Vertes**, the French greenways; see http://www.af3v.org/CarteAF3V/carte-detaillee.html. Still fancying **Land's End**? Take bikes on the train to Newquay or Truro!

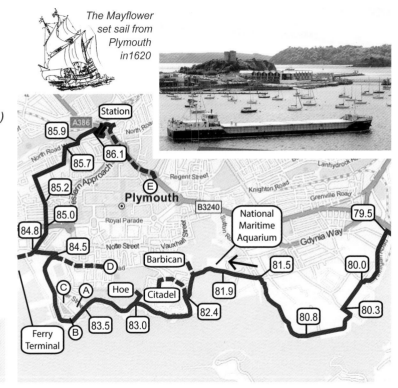

The Mayflower set sail from Plymouth in1620

Section 20: Sheepwash - Crackington Jct (47 km / 29 miles)

🚲 4.2 km, 🚶 37.0 km, 🚐 6.0 km, 🚐🚐 0.0 km
Stations: None

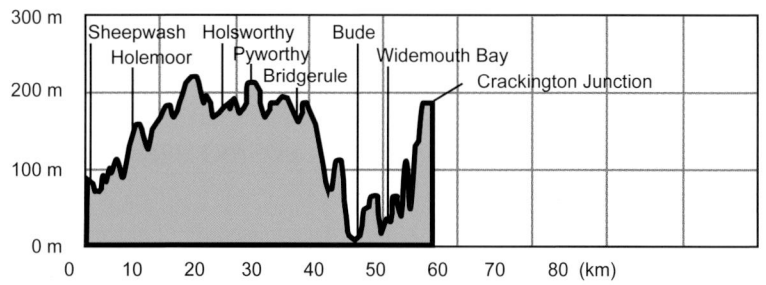

This section has two distinct feels. About two-thirds of the ride takes place in **Ruby County**, a very rural part of Devon. The main enjoyment comes from the peace and quiet of the empty lanes and the surrounding farms and fields. The Cornish section of the ride, beyond Bude, takes you via a spectacular coast line.

Progress can be slow on the first stretch between Sheepwash and Holsworthy, due to a fair number of short steep climbs. **Holsworthy** has a town square with various eateries and a small museum (open Mon-Fri, free entry). A high former railway viaduct takes you out of town. The ride via lively villages **Pyworthy**, **Bridgerule** and **Marhamchurch** is definitely easier going, with less climbing involved; hurrah!

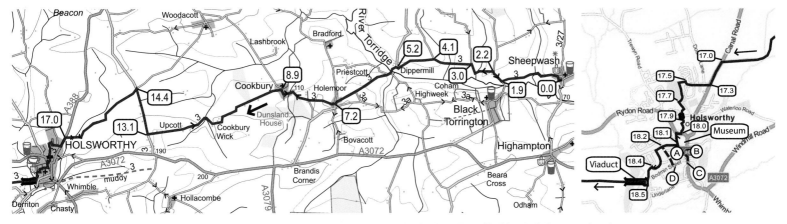

0.0 (27.6) In Sheepwash → (to Blk Torrington, **3**)	**17.3** 1st rd → (Dobles Ln), keep going ↑
1.9 At T-jct → (to Shebbaer, **3**)	**17.5** After bend to right 1st rd ← (**3**), at end ← via path through park
2.2 1st rd ← (to New Inn, **3**)	
3.0 1st rd ← (to Libbaer, **3**)	**17.7** ↟ onto path on right side of playground, via bend → to bridge
4.1 At next jct ← (to Dipper Mill, **3**)	
5.2 At T-jct ⚙**Waterwheel** ← (to Cookbury, **3**)	**17.9** After bridge, follow path around car park, via narrow path ↖ onto dead end rd with police station on left
7.2 In Holemoor village, 2nd rd ↗ (to Village Hall, **3**)	
8.9 Before house "High Park" ← (to Anvil Corner, **3**)	**18.0** At T-jct → 🚗 , 1st rd ← (**3**), keep ↑ up hill via narrow 🚲 lane
13.1 At T-jct → (to Holsworthy Beacon) *(Note: ignore signs 3!)*	**18.1** At end of 🚲 lane imm → (Glebe Ln, **3**)
	*(For 🏠 🛏 ☕ 🍴 ℹ **Holsworthy** walk ↑ to Square, 30m)*
14.4 In descent 1st rd ← (Blagdonmoor Jct)	**18.2** At cross rds ↑ (**3**), 1st rd ← (Deer Valley Rd, **3**)
17.0 At T-jct ← (to Holsworthy) 🚗	**18.4** On steep slope down 1st 🚲 ← (**3**)
	18.5 Via 🚲 ↖ up onto high viaduct (to Bude, **3**)

125

Section 20: Sheepwash - Crackington Jct (47 km / 29 miles)

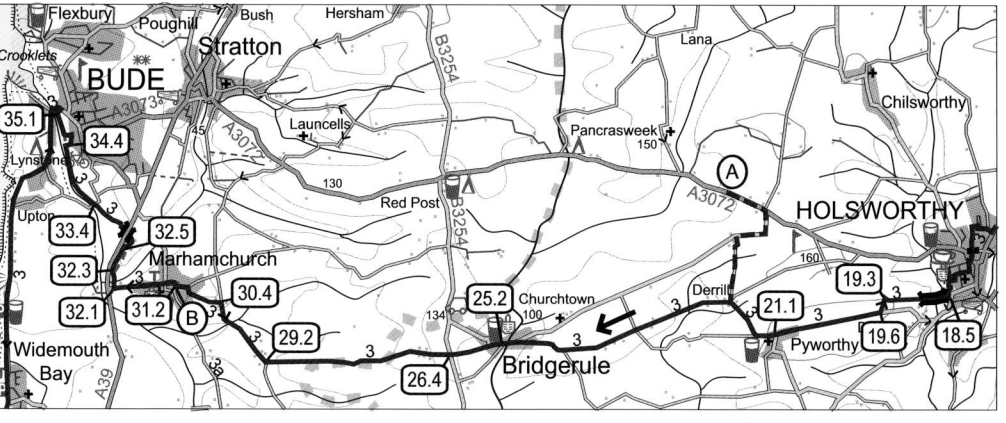

19.3 At end railway path ← via concrete rd (**3**)
19.6 At T-jct → (**3**)
21.1 At T-jct ↗ (to Derril, **3**), ☞ ⊮ **Pyworthy** *(pub on left)*
25.2 Keep ↑ through ⛾ ☞ **Bridgerule** *(pub & shop)* (**3**)
26.4 At cross rds ↑ (Borough Cross, **3**)
29.2 At T-jct → (to Marhamchurch, **3**)
30.4 1st rd ← (Hilton Rd, **3**)
31.1 At T-jct ← (**3**), at next T-jct → (to Bude, **3**), keep ↑
31.2 ⌂ ⛾ ☞ ⊮ **Marhamchurch** *(hotel, pub and shop)*
32.1 Just before T-jct → (Hele Rd, **3**)

32.3 After two bridges imm ↖ through gate onto ⚲ (**3**)
32.5 1st ⚲ ↗ to underpass (**3**), ep ← (**3**), becomes ⚲
33.4 At rd crossing ↑ (**3**), keep following ⚲
34.4 Ep ← via rd and imm ← via ⚲ (**3**)
35.1 → onto car park, keep ↑ to exit, at T-jct ← (**3**) 🚗
(For ⌂ ⛾ ☞ ⊮ ⼁ ⛰ ⓘ **Bude** *at T-jct → 🚗, at rndabt ← 🚗)*

You arrive in Bude alongside its canal at the visitor centre car park. Kayaks and canoes are available for rent from the canal basin at the other side of the bridge; just follow the footpath.

The main attraction of **Bude** is its striking coast. Naturally, the beach close to the town centre is popular with surfers and the bucket and spade brigade, but the dramatic cliffs heading north and south give the place its special character. Take some time to walk the **South West Coast Path** south towards Widemouth Bay. There is easy direct access from the town centre beach and, if camping, from the **Upper Lynstone campsite** with its fabulous views. Various bus services operate on the coastal road nearby.

It is this same road you'll use to cycle south to **Widemouth Bay**, a very small settlement overlooking a popular surf beach. Beyond it, the main flow of tourists moves inland, leaving you on a spectacular lane following the coast, but with some severe climbing.

Depending on your experiences on this very hard section, you'll have to decide whether you cycle the next section via the legendary Tintagel Castle (with much more extreme climbing, route 21A) or the slightly more "gentle" official route 3 via inland Bodmin Moor (21B).

39.2 🍺 🛒 🍴 ⛺ **Widemouth Bay** *(pub, cafe and shop)*
40.8 After Widemouth Bay in bend to left ↗ (**3**),
see sign "unsuitable for long vehicles", **major climb** ahead!
47.2 **Dismount** at 1st jct after house "Canberra" (on right side of rd). The rd bends here to the left, with the first through rd to the right. Note: There are no signs at this, what we call, "Crackington Junction", except a route **3** sign. Choose now between **Tintagel route** (21A) or **Bodmin Moor route 3** (21B), see page 128.

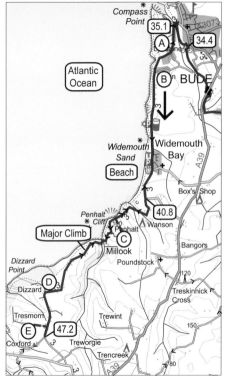

Section 21A: Crackington Jct - Blisland via Tintagel (38 km/23 miles)

🚲 0.0 km, 🚶 35.8 km, 🚗 1.9 km, 🚗🚗 0.1 km
Stations: None

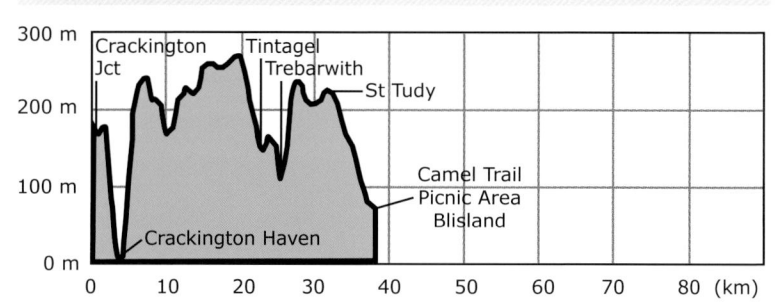

The highest point of all routes in this guidebook is on Exmoor, but this section is the **real challenge** for those who wish to be a worthy wearer of a "king of the mountains" jersey! **Four extreme climbs** can be found on this section, all on a par with the climb out of Widemouth Bay in section 20 and the climbs out of Dulverton/Tarr Steps in section 17. "It is easier to cycle across the Alps than to cycle via Tintagel" some Dutch touring cyclists have told the author, so yes; it is hilly! **Stunning coastal scenery** and the impressive ruins of legendary **Tintagel Castle** are your reward. Alternative route 21B via Bodmin Moor is by no means flat, but with gradual gradients and with less up and down, it is much easier to accomplish, see pages 131 and 132 for more information.

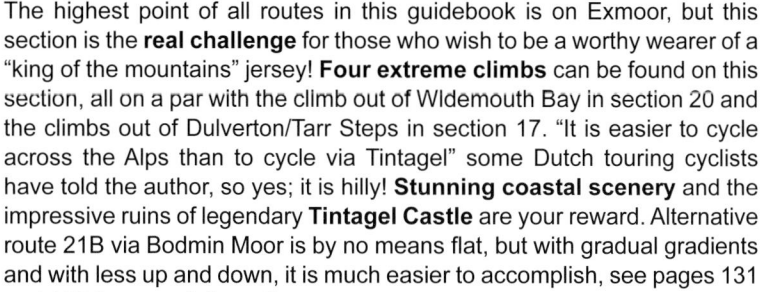

Crackington Haven is a small village at sea level with a tiny sandy beach. As is the situation with many Cornish coastal villages, it sits at the mouth of a narrow stream, only to be accessed by road via extremely steep roads up and down the surrounding high hills. These villages are very hard for cycling, so Crackington Haven is the only village of this type to be included in this routebook. The route heads inland to make its way around the next one, **Boscastle**. In this area, the heights of **Bodmin Moor** dramatically drop down to reach sea level, making an exposed and remote route section. Famous **Tintagel** lies high up the cliffs where, from nowhere, you'll suddenly find crowds of tourists browsing the high street.

The real attraction of Tintagel can be found on the headland at the end of town, the legendary **Tintagel Castle**, built by Earl Richard of Cornwall in 1233. The legends of **King Arthur** were already around when the castle was built and Tintagel was thought to be the birth place of this largely mythical figure. So, although Arthur never actually ruled from Tintagel Castle, it is not difficult for your imagination to be sparked when visiting the dramatic location (open daily, £6 pp, English Heritage members and Overseas Visitor Pass holders free). Note the South West Coast Path offers plenty of great (free) views over the castle ruins. The Tintagel YHA and campsite both offer fantastic budget overnight stays within walking distance.

Section 21A: Crackington Jct - Blisland via Tintagel (38 km/23 miles)

From Tintagel the route continues via remote **Treknow** to **Trebarwith**. Its small beach (Trebarwith Strand) is fantastic, but by going down to the beach, you add another extreme climb to your itinerary. From here, the route heads inland, taking you via the quiet villages of **St. Teath** and **St. Tudy** to the start of the **Camel Trail**. The next section on this flat trail will bring a long awaited relief from all the climbing!

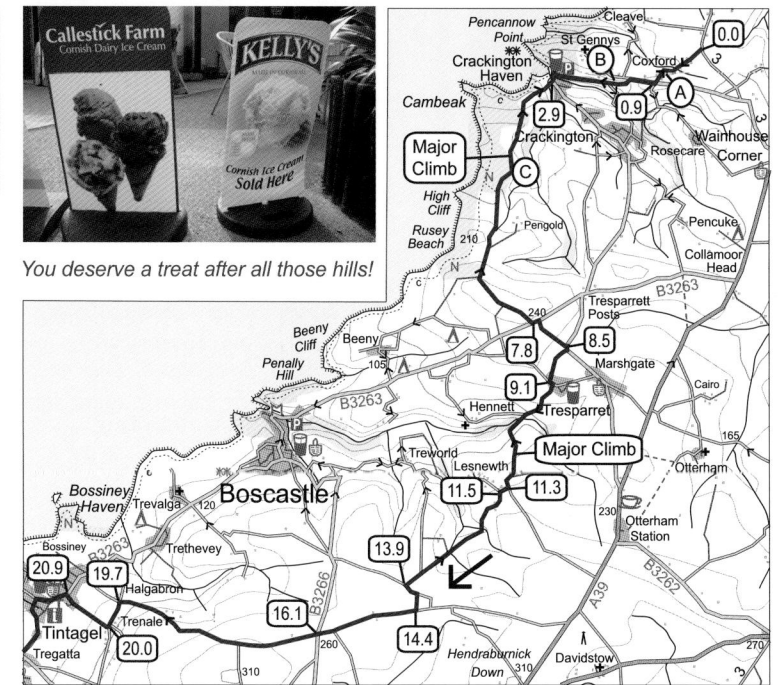

You deserve a treat after all those hills!

0.0 *(47.2)* At "Crackington Junction" ↗ via narrow rd *(Ignore signs* **3***!)*
0.9 At cross rds → (to Crackington Haven)
2.8 🏠 ⛽ 🚻 🍴 ⚓ **Crackington Haven**
2.9 1st rd → (to Trevigue), **major climb** ahead!
7.8 At T-jct ←, imm 1st rd → (to Marshgate)
8.5 At T-jct →, imm 1st rd ↗ (to Tresparett)
9.1 At T-jct ↟ (to Lesnewth), **major climb** ahead!
11.3 At end climb 1st rd → (to Lesnewth)
11.5 1st rd ← (see sign "ford ½ mile")
13.9 At T-jct ← (to Davidstow), 1st rd →
14.4 At T-jct →
16.1 At cross rds ↑ (to Tintagel)
19.7 *Pay attention:* in descent, 2nd rd ← (to Trenale)
20.0 1st rd → (at "Jasmin Cottage" and "Lilic Cottage")
20.9 At T-jct ← 🚌 into ⚑ 🏠 🏨 ⛺ 🚻 ⛽ 🍴 ℹ **Tintagel**

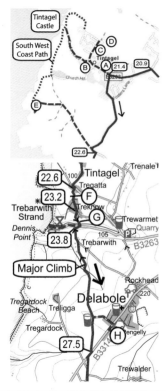

21.4 At rndabt ← (Molesworth St, to Camelford) 🚗
*(For ⚓ **Tintagel Castle** ↑)*
22.6 After sharp bend to left imm 1st rd → (to Treknow)
23.2 In 🏠 ☕ 🍴 **Treknow** *(pub)* ↑ (to Trebarwith)
23.8 At cross rds ↑ (to Trebarwith Village), **major climb** ahead!
*(For ⚓ **Trebarwith Strand** →)*
26.5 ☕ 🍴 **Poldark Inn** *(pub)*
27.5 At T-jct → (to St. Teath) 🚗, 1st rd ↖ (to St. Teath)
30.0 In 🏠 🛒 **St .Teath** *(shop)* at clock tower → (The Square)
30.2 1st rd ← (Trehannick Rd, to Trehannick)
31.8 At T-jct → 🚗🚗, imm ↖ before parking bay,
keep ↑ over old bridge, **major climb** ahead!
33.6 At cross rds ↑ (to St .Tudy)
34.7 At T-jct ↖ into 🛒 ☕ **St.Tudy** *(pub and shop)*
34.8 At T-jct ← (Chapel Ln, to Bodmin), keep ↑
35.7 At cross rds ↑
36.3 At cross rds ↑ (to Blisland) *(Note: ignore sign "Camel Trail")*
37.8 1st 🚲 ↗ to 🍴 **Camel Trail picnic area Blisland**

Those who wish to stay away from all the extreme climbing via Tintagel can use the offical route 3 via **Bodmin Moor**, see route 21B on the next pages. This inland route offers an entirely different experience. Most of its charm lies in the remote feel, especially on the heights near Camelford. Note **Wainhouse Corner**, **Hallworthy** and **St. Breward** have limited facilities. **Camelford** is a proper sized town, but slightly off-route.

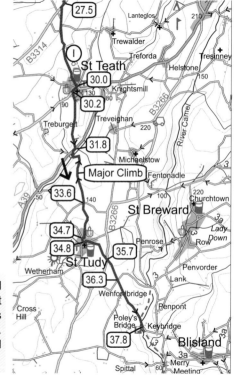

Section 21B: Crackington Jct - Blisland via Bodmin Moor (34 km/21 miles)

🚲 1.0 km, 🚶 33.1 km, 🚗 0.1 km, 🚗🚗 0.0 km
Stations: None

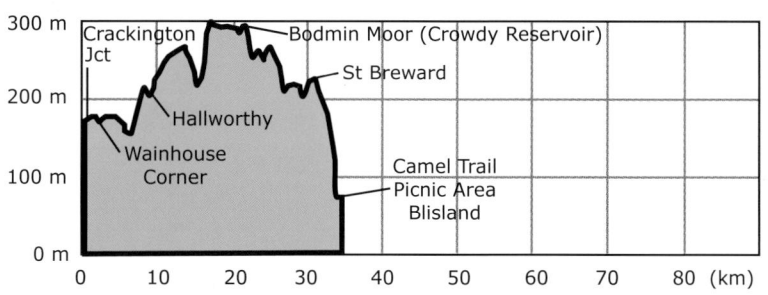

Read information on the previous page before starting this route section!

0.0	*(47.2)* At "Crackington Junction" follow road ↖ **(3)**
1.1	At T-jct ↖ (to Wainhouse Corner, **3**)
2.3	At 🏠 🚇 🛍 🍴 **Wainhouse Corner** ↑ (to Canworthy Water, **3**)
4.0	Opposite church 1st rd → (to Trengune, **3**)
4.9	At T-jct ← (to Hallworthy, **3**)
8.4	At cross rds ↑ (to Hallworthy, **3**)
8.8	At T-jct ← **(3)**
9.0	At T-jct → (to Bodmin, **3**)
11.1	At T-jct 🏠 🛍 🍴 **Hallworthy** → 🚗 *(for hotel ←)*, imm 1st rd ↖ **(3)**

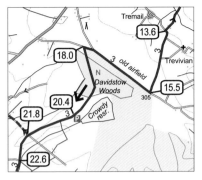

13.6 At T-jct ← (3)
15.5 On ⛰ **Bodmin Moor** at jct → (to Camelford, 3)
18.0 1st tarmac rd ↙ (to Crowdy Reservoir, 3)
20.4 (For ⛰ Crowdy Reservoir ←)
21.8 At cross rds ↑ (to Advent Church, 3)
  *(For 🏠 🛏 📷 🍴 **Camelford** →, at T-jct ← 🚗🚗)*
22.6 Via bend ↖ over weak bridge, then → (3), keep ↑
25.4 At T-jct ← (3)
25.7 1st rd → (3), imm at T-jct ↗ (3)
27.6 1st through rd ← (3)
28.2 Follow sharp bend → (3), follow through rd ↑ (3)
30.6 At jct ↑ to 🛏 📷 🍴 **St. Breward** (3)
  (Note: ignore sign alternative route 3 to left!)
30.8 At T-jct ↖ onto main rd (to St Tudy, 3) *(for pub ↘)*
33.2 At end of long descent ← (to The Camel Trail, 3),
  imm ↗ via car park onto Camel Trail 🚲
34.2 Ep ← via 🚲 to ⛱ **Camel Trail picnic area Blisland**

This route section is at its prettiest after completing the gradual climb up to **Bodmin Moor**. You cycle on a road across a former airfield and through a pretty pine forest. The lakeside area of **Crowdy Reservoir** is ideal for picnics and is also good for bird watching. Beyond the turn for **Camelford** you follow narrow bendy lanes through a deserted barren landscape. In remote **St. Breward** you start to descent to the **Camel Trail**.

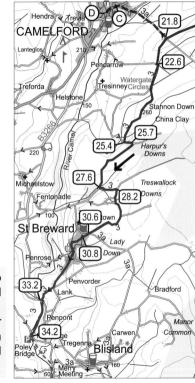

Section 22: Blisland - Newquay (69 km / 42 miles)

🚲 27.0 km, 🚶 33.8 km, 🚗 6.4 km, 🚗🚗 1.7 km
Stations: Newquay

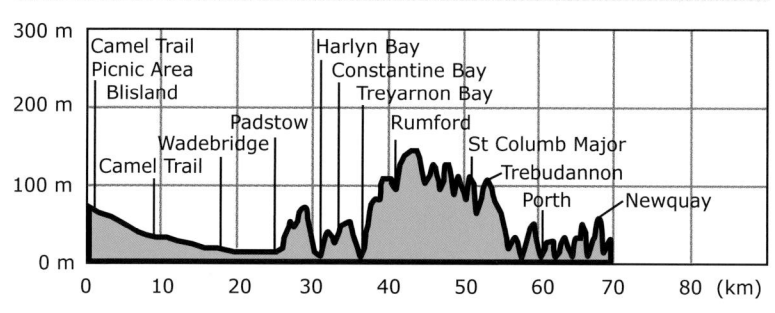

The gravel **Camel Trail** may well be England's most famous and well-loved cycle route. The section from **Blisland** to **Bodmin** is a haven of peace and quiet, taking you through a deep, forested valley. There is a side branch to local services of nearby Bodmin. The **Bodmin & Wenford Steam Railway** has a station on the Camel Trail and can also take you to Bodmin (open daily, £12 pp return, bicycles free). The **John Betjeman Centre** in the old station of busy **Wadebridge** provides more railway nostalgia. From here, the valley of the River Camel widens and are you entering the most popular section of the Camel Trail. The wide estuary provides great views all the way to posh **Padstow** with its scenic harbour and the famous seafood restaurants of TV chef **Rick Stein**.

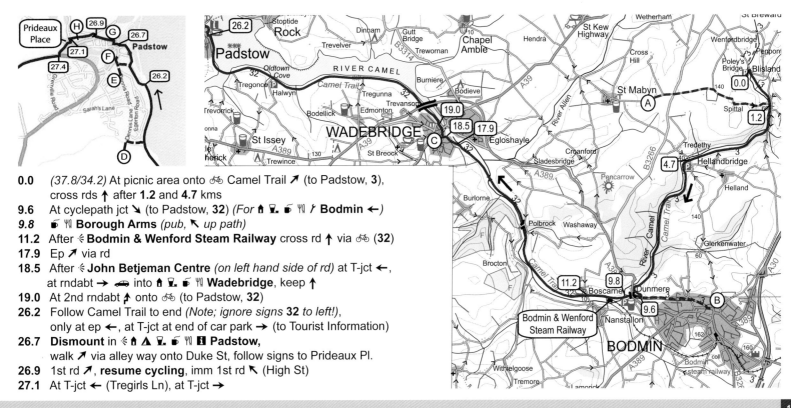

0.0 *(37.8/34.2)* At picnic area onto 🚲 Camel Trail ↗ (to Padstow, **3**), cross rds ↑ after **1.2** and **4.7** kms

9.6 At cyclepath jct ↘ (to Padstow, **32**) *(For* 🛏 🍽 ☕ 🍴 ⚓ **Bodmin** ←*)*

9.8 ☕ 🍽 **Borough Arms** *(pub,* ↖ *up path)*

11.2 After ⚙ **Bodmin & Wenford Steam Railway** cross rd ↑ via 🚲 (**32**)

17.9 Ep ↗ via rd

18.5 After ⚙ **John Betjeman Centre** *(on left hand side of rd)* at T-jct ←, at rndabt → 🚌 into 🛏 🍽 ☕ 🍽 **Wadebridge**, keep ↑

19.0 At 2nd rndabt ↑ onto 🚲 (to Padstow, **32**)

26.2 Follow Camel Trail to end *(Note; ignore signs* **32** *to left!)*, only at ep ←, at T-jct at end of car park → (to Tourist Information)

26.7 **Dismount** in ⚙ 🛏 ⛺ ⛽ ☕ 🍽 ℹ **Padstow**, walk ↗ via alley way onto Duke St, follow signs to Prideaux Pl.

26.9 1st rd ↗, **resume cycling**, imm 1st rd ↖ (High St)

27.1 At T-jct ← (Tregirls Ln), at T-jct →

Section 22: Blisland - Newquay (69 km / 42 miles)

Just before leaving Padstow you'll pass the stately home **Prideaux Place** (open daily, £8 pp for house & grounds, £4 pp for gardens only). From here, the route returns to the Atlantic coast. At **Harlyn Bay** the route has direct beach access. Taking a surfing lesson at the **Padstow Surf School** at this beach is a great break from the cycling (£30 pp for 2½ hr session). **Constantine Bay** and **Treyarnon Bay** with its campsite and hostel have great beaches too, but these are slightly off-route. Pleasant rolling hills take you inland to **St. Columb Major**.

27.4 After ⬦ **Prideaux Place** (on corner on right) at T-jct → **(32)** 🚗

28.1 At T-jct ↗ (to Newquay, **32**) 🚗
(Caution: hazardous winding road; no alternative)

29.9 2nd rd → (to Harlyn Bay, **32**)

31.1 ⬦ 🏠 📷 🍴 ⛵ **Harlyn Bay & Padstow Surf School**

31.6 In sharp bend to the left 1st rd → (to Trevose Head, **32**)

32.9 At T-jct ↗ **(32)** to 🏖 **Constantine Bay** (For ⛵ 1st rd →)

34.0 Keep ↑ (For 🏨 ⛺ 🏖 ⛵ **Treyarnon Bay** 2nd rd →)

34.4 In sharp bend to right 1st rd ← **(32)**

35.2 At T-jct → (to Porthcothan, **32**) 🚗

35.6 1st rd ← (to Rumford, **32**)

37.2 At T-jct → (to Rumford, **32**), follow sharp bend ←

39.3 At cross rds → (to Rumford, **32**)

40.7 At T-jct ← (to St. Columb, **32**)

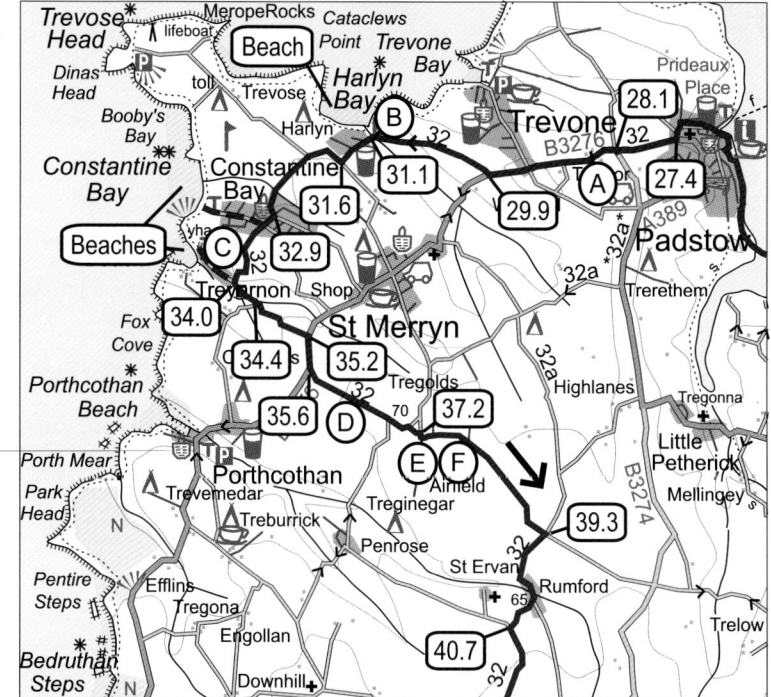

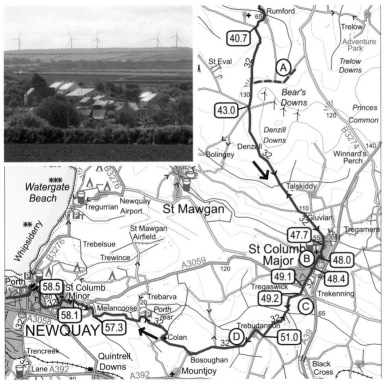

43.0 At T-jct ← (to St Columb Major, **32**), keep ↑
47.7 At T-jct ↗ into 🏠 🍺 🛍 🍴 **St. Columb Major** (**32**)
48.0 At T-jct ← (at "Red Lion" pub)
48.4 1st rd →, imm ← (Trekenning Rd, **32**)
49.1 At T-jct ↑ via 🚲 (to Newquay, **32**), ep ↑ via rd
49.2 At T-jct → (see "weak bridge ½ mile", **32**)
51.0 1st rd → (to Trebudannon, **32**), keep ↑
57.3 Keep ↗ onto 🚲 on right side of main rd (**32**),
      bit further, cross rd ↑ onto 🚲 with steep climb (**32**)
58.1 Ep ← via rd (**32**) into 🛍 🍴 **St. Columb Minor** (*pub*)

Harlyn Bay

Section 22: Bliisland - Newquay (69 km / 42 miles)

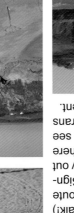

It's a sharp contrast to arrive from the backwater of **St. Columb Major** and **Trebudannon** in the hustle and bustle of **Newquay**. This is Britain's premier surf resort, home to about 100,000 people during the summer months. Allow two hours to enjoy all the sights by bicycle. Note multiple dismounting is required on our devised route. This route takes you to **Porth Beach** at the north end of town (picture top right), ideal for those wishing to camp overnight. Don't miss the view down on **Lusty Glaze Beach**, on three sides enclosed by high cliffs (picture bottom right). From here you follow the busy boulevard road to the town centre. It is worth walking your bike via the cliff path, overlooking the beaches.

From the noisy town centre, a route via some more quiet back streets takes you to **Fistral Beach**, Britain's internationally renowned surfing beach overlooked by the spectacular, but pricy **Headland Hotel**. More affordable accommodation can be found on **Mount Wise**, still at walking distance from the beaches. To be able to leave town, busy roads (feel free to walk!) can't be avoided, reason for the Sustrans route makers to bypass Newquay all together. Sign-posted official route 32 keeps you completely out of town and away from the fantastic coast. There is some fast moving traffic on this "bypass", see the map. This map also shows some Sustrans routes into town which are under development.

58.5 After pub, 1st rd → (Stanways Rd, **32**)

58.7 At end of rd ↑ via 🚲 (**32**)

59.1 Ep → (**32**), at next junction ↑
*(Ignore signs **32** to left, unless you wish to use "bypass" route **32**)*

59.3 Where rd bends to the right ↖ (Lewarne Rd, see sign height 12'9")

60.0 After 📷 ⌂ **Porth** at T-jct ↗ (Porth Beach Rd) 🚗

60.1 **Dismount** at Porth Veor Manor Hotel,
walk → into driveway of hotel, ↑ via gate onto public footpath

60.2 Ep **resume cycling** ↑ (Manewas Wy), at rndabt ↑

61.0 After ⌂ ⌂ **Lusty Glaze Beach** *(walk via grass)* at T-jct → 🚗🚗

61.7 At station ⌂ ⌂ ⌂ △ ⌂ 📷 🍴 ℹ️ ⚡ ⌂ **Newquay** ↑ 🚗🚗

62.0 **Dismount** at lhts and get on pavement on left of the rd,
then cross main rd ↗ via lhts (to ℹ️ and bus station)
(For short-cut 2x at lights ↖ 🚗🚗, see map)

62.1 1st rd → (next to post office), **resume cycling**

62.2 At T-jct ← (Trebarwith Cr)

62.4 In sharp bend to left **dismount**, ↑ via footpath

62.5 Ep → and **resume cycling** via rd steep down

62.7 At T-jct ← and **dismount** to take 1st alleyway ↗ via steep climb

62.8 1st rd ↘ and **resume cycling** (to Fistral Beach), keep ↑

63.2 At rndabt ↑ (Beacon Rd, to Fistral Beach)

63.4 1st rd ↖ (to Fistral Beach Surf Hire)

64.1 ⌂ 📷 ⌂ **Fistral Beach**, do u-turn and head back to resume route

64.8 At cross rds →

65.0 At rndabt ↗ via through rd (Tower Rd) 🚗

65.6 At rndabt ← (to "P" Mount Wise) 🚗

66.6 At 2nd jct with lhts → (Trenance Rd) 🚗🚗

67.2 At double rndabt ↑ (Treninnick Hill) 🚗

67.6 At rndabts ↑ (Treloggan Rd) 🚗 *(Note: ignore signs **32**!)*

68.5 At ⌂ *super store* rndabt ↟ onto path on left side of rd,
← at next rndabt via path on left side of rd

68.9 Beyond 📷 🍴 **Kings Head Inn** *(pub)* 1st rd →, cross main rd

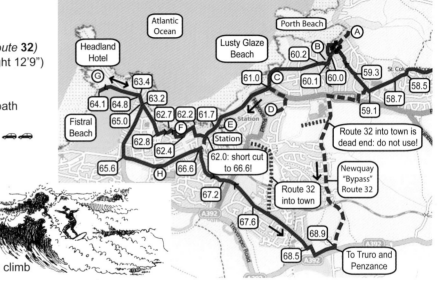

139

Section 23: Newquay - Penzance (71 km / 44 miles)

🚲 12.7 km, 🚶 55.0 km, 🚗 3.1 km, 🚗🚗 0.7 km
Stations: Newquay, Truro (after 20.8 km), Redruth (after 38.2 km),
Camborne (after 44.7 km), Hayle (after 57.2 km), Penzance

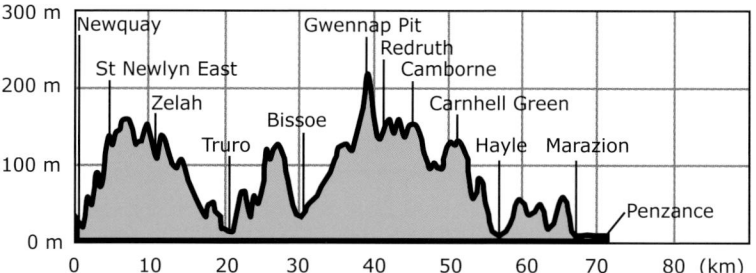

Away from Newquay's surfing beaches, it is a bit of a shock to be back in the remote Cornish countryside. **Trerice House** is a beautiful Elizabethan manor with a tea garden (open daily, £8 pp), hidden away in the hills. The villages of **St. Newlyn East** and **Zelah** have both pubs and are good places for a break. Via the sheltered valley of the River Allen and **Idless Wood** it is a pleasant ride to **Truro**. The pretty cathedral, cobbled streets, Georgian architecture and small town feel define the look of Cornwall's only city. The **Royal Cornwall Museum** displays Cornish art, regional archaeology, social history and flora and fauna (open Mon-Sat, £5 pp).

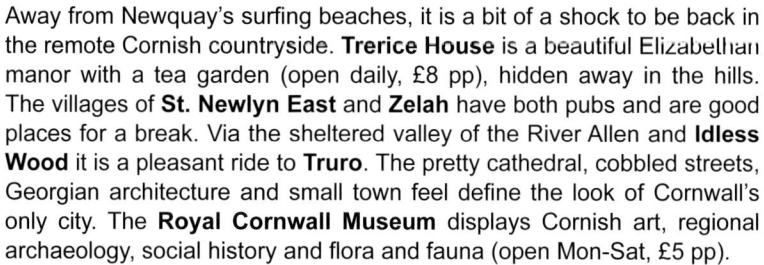

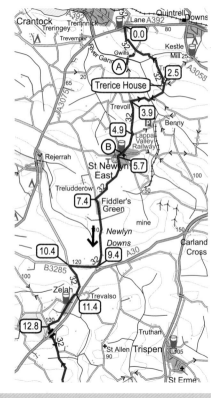

0.0	*(68.9)* Join rd southbound (to Gwills/Legonna, **32**)
2.5	At T-jct → (**32**), ⬅ ☕ **Trerice House** on right side
3.9	At cross rds ← (to Newlyn East, **32**)
4.9	At T-jct ↗ (**32**)
5.7	At cross rds ☕ ☕ ⚇ **St. Newlyn East** *(pub and shop)* ↑ (**32**)
7.4	At T-jct ↖ (to A30, **32**)
9.4	At cross rds ↗ (to Perranporth, **32**)
10.4	1st rd ↙ (**32,** see sign "unsuitable for heavy good vehicles")
11.4	1st rd ↗ (**32**) into ☕ ⚇ **Zelah** *(pub)*
12.8	After climb, 1st rd ← (to Redruth, **32**), keep ↑ 🚗
15.1	In descent, 1st through rd ← (**32**)
15.7	1st rd → (**32**), keep ↑
17.4	⬅ 🌲 **Idless Wood** *(after 50 m, turn ←)*
18.2	After hamlet (some houses), look out for rd ↖ leading down (**32**)
20.1	At T-jct → (**32**)
20.5	At T-jct ← (**32**) 🚗🚗, 1st rd → (Union Pl, **32**)
20.7	At T-jct ← (King St, **32**), at church ↗
20.8	**Dismount** at T-jct ⬅ ♿ ☕ ☕ ⚇ ℹ ⚡ *Truro*, cross ↑ via zebra, then → 🚗 **resume cycling** *(Note; ignore signs routes* **3** *&* **32***!)*
21.3	Keep ↑ and at T-jct ↗ (Kenwyn St, **3**) 🚗, then 1st rd ↖ (Chapel Hill, to Redruth, **3**)
22.0	Cross main rd ↑ (to Penweathers, **3**)

Beyond Truro, at **Bissoe**, you'll hit the **Mining Trail** which takes you into a surreal landscape of disused copper and tin mines. The first **Methodists** used the **Gwennap Pit** for their open-air preaching (free entry).

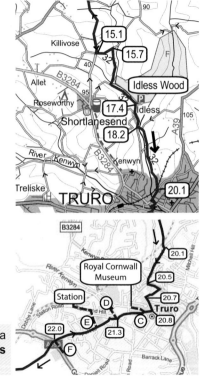

Section 23: Newquay - Penzance (71 km / 44 miles)

25.2 At T-jct → (to Chacewater, **3**)
25.8 1st rd ↖ (**3**)
26.6 At T-jct ← (**3**), keep to surfaced rd with bends
27.7 At T-jct → (**3**)
28.2 At T-jct → via 🚲 on left side of rd (to Bissoe, **3**)
28.3 1st rd ← (**3**), 1st 🚲 → (to Redruth, **3**)
29.2 Ep ↑ onto car park 🛈 ⸕ **Bissoe Bike Hire & Cafe**
29.4 At end car park → via 🚲 on steep hill, follow main path
30.4 Ep → via rd (**3**)
30.7 1st path ← (Mining Trail, to Carharrack, **3**),
after short climb → (Mining Trail, **3**), keep ↑ via 🚲
32.7 Cross rd ↑ via 🚲 (Mining Trail, **3**)
33.2 Ep → via rd (**3**)
33.4 At T-jct ↖ (Consols Rd), imm next T-jct → (**3**)
33.7 At cross rds ↑ (**3**), follow through rd
34.8 At T-jct 🛈 ⸕ **The Star Inn** *(pub)* ← (**3**) 🚗,
then 1st rd ↖ (to Gwennap Pit, **3**), keep going ↑ (**3**)
36.0 ⸙ **Gwennap Pit** *(1st rd ←, after 50 m → via gate)*
37.2 At T-jct → via 🚲 on left side of rd (**3**)
37.4 Follow 🚲 ↑ onto housing estate rd (**3**), then bend to ←

The **Cornish Mines and Engines Museum** between mining towns **Redruth** and **Camborne** features displays of the 18th century mining boom. It also has impressive working machinery (open Tue-Sat, £7 pp).

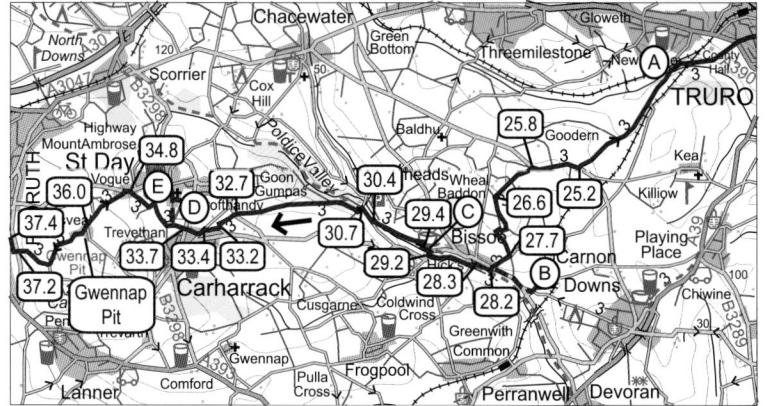

Hill top **Carn Brea** has ruins of a settlement, dating from 3500 BC!

37.8 In descent at 2nd cross rds → (**3**)
38.1 In bend to right ← (Heanton Tc, **3**)
38.2 At cross rds ↑ (**3**) *(For* 🏠 🛏 📷 🍽 ℹ *Redruth* →*)*
38.4 At T-jct → 🚲, before high viaduct 1st rd ← (**3**)
39.0 At T-jct ↖ (Trevingly Rd, **3**), keep going ↑ onto 🚲 (**3**)
40.8 At split of cycle paths keep ↖ on tarmac 🚲
         (For ⚒ *Cornish Mines and Engines Museum* → *via bridge
         over railway, keep* ↑*, at lhts* ← 🚲🚲*, 2nd rd* →*)*

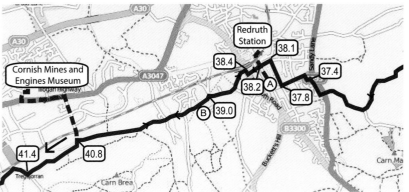

41.4 Ep ↗ via rd (to Great Flat Lode, **3**), at T-jct ↖ (**3**)
41.7 At T-jct ↗ 🚲, imm 1st rd ↖ (to Brea Inn, **3**)
42.5 After 📷 🍽 **Brea Inn** *(pub)* 2nd rd ← (Chapel Hill, **3**),
         at T-jct ← (**3**), imm 1st rd → (**3**)
42.8 In climb 1st 🚲 ↗ (**3**)
43.1 At rd crossing → (**3**) and ↟ into housing estate (**3**)
43.3 At T-jct ← (**3**), 2nd rd → (Stray Park Wy, **3**)
43.7 At T-jct → (**3**), 1st rd ← (Park Ln, **3**), keep going ↑
44.5 At T-jct → (Trevu Rd, **3**) 🚲
44.7 Before railway crossing, 1st rd ← (Mount Pleasant Rd)
         (Note; ignore signs **3***!) (For* 🏠 🛏 📷 🍽 *Camborne* ↑*)*
45.0 1st rd ↗ (Killivose Rd)

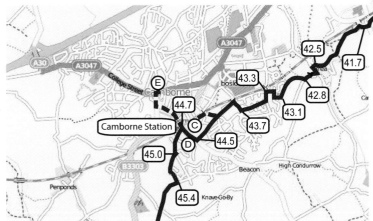

Section 23: Newquay - Penzance (71 km / 44 miles)

Hayle used to be an important port shipping out coal and copper and now marks the end of the old mining area of Cornwall. Its inland estuary (see left picture) is now great for bird watching. It is worth making the detour to **Towans Beach**, an unspoilt swathe of sands and sand dunes. There is a B&B and campsite overlooking this beach.

45.4 At T-jct with bench →, at cross rds ↑
46.2 At T-jct ←, 1st rd → (Ramsgate, to Barripper)
47.2 At T-jct → (to Penponds), at T-jct with church ↙
49.3 🍺 🛒 🍴 **Carnhell Green** (pub and shop)
49.6 After pub, 1st rd → (to Gwinear, Gwinear Ln, **3**)
54.1 At T-jct → (to Hayle, **3**)
54.3 In descent 1st rd ← (Ventonleague Hill, **3**)
54.6 1st rd → (Ventonleague Row, **3**)
54.8 At T-jct → and imm ↙ before pedestrian lhts, then 1st 🚲 ← (**3**)
55.1 Ep ↑ via dead end rd, leading onto gravel 🚲 (**3**)
55.5 Ep ← (King George V Memorial Walk, **3**)
      (For ⛺ 🏠 ⛺ ⛵ **Towans Beach** ↑, at T-jct ↑, at next T-jct ←)
56.5 At T-jct ← (**3**), at T-jct → (**3**) 🚗🚗
57.2 At rndabt 🏠 🍺 🛒 🍴 ⚡ **Hayle** (after passing under high railway viaduct) ↗ (to Penzance, **3**), go again under high viaduct, but now imm ↖ onto car park, at end car park ↟ via 🚲 (**3**)
58.3 Ep ← via rd (**3**), keep ↑ via through rd (through St Erth)

We leave route 3 to take in **St. Michael's Mount**. This special island with its castle can be accessed on foot at low tide or via ferry when the tide is in (castle open Sun-Fri, £8 pp). Bikes will have to be parked in **Marazion**.

64.3 At T-jct ↖ (**3**), after tunnel keep ↖ *(Note; ignore signs 3!)*

65.9 After Marazion Community Center 1st rd → (School Ln)

66.1 At T-jct →, ↑ through ⚶ ♙ 🍺 📷 🍴 ⛴ **Marazion**

66.5 *(For ⚶ ⛱ **Viewpoint St. Michael's Mount** opposite house no 10 Penmeneth ← (Leys Ln), follow signs to Top Tieb Landing)*

66.9 ⚶ **St. Michael's Mount Castle** (via causeway/ferry)

68.0 Before 📷 **Jordan's Cafe** ↖ via car park onto 🚲 (**3**), follow coastal route to end of path at main car park Penzance

71.5 ⚶ ♙ 🏛 ⛺ 🍺 📷 🍴 ⚡ ℹ *Penzance*

(For station →, for circular route to Land's End ↑, see next page)

Section 24: Land's End Round Trip (51 km / 32 miles)

🚲 *5.4 km,* 🚶 *32.6 km,* 🚌 *11.6 km,* 🚗🚗 *1.5 km*
Stations: *Penzance*

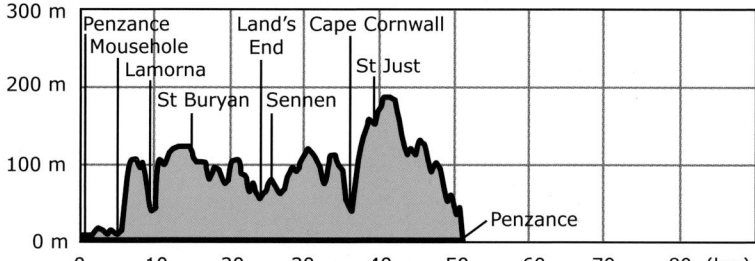

Penzance has England's most westerly train station. Join us on a circular ride to Land's End, also via Cape Cornwall. **Newlyn** and **Mousehole** (see picture next page) have scenic harbours, popular with the crowds. Penwith Peninsula is empty though and in the deep green valley of Lamorna you'll once again feel away from it all. **Sennen Cove** has a beautiful beach (see picture next page), but a climb back up is required to rejoin the route.

0.0 *(71.5)* At end of coastal 🚲 from Marazion ↑ via car park, at end ← via rd (**3**) 🚗🚗
1.5 At rndabt ↑ (to Mousehole, **3**) 🚌
2.3 At lhts ← via 🚲 (**3**), ep → via rd, keep ↖
2.6 At T-jct ← via through rd (**3**) 🚌

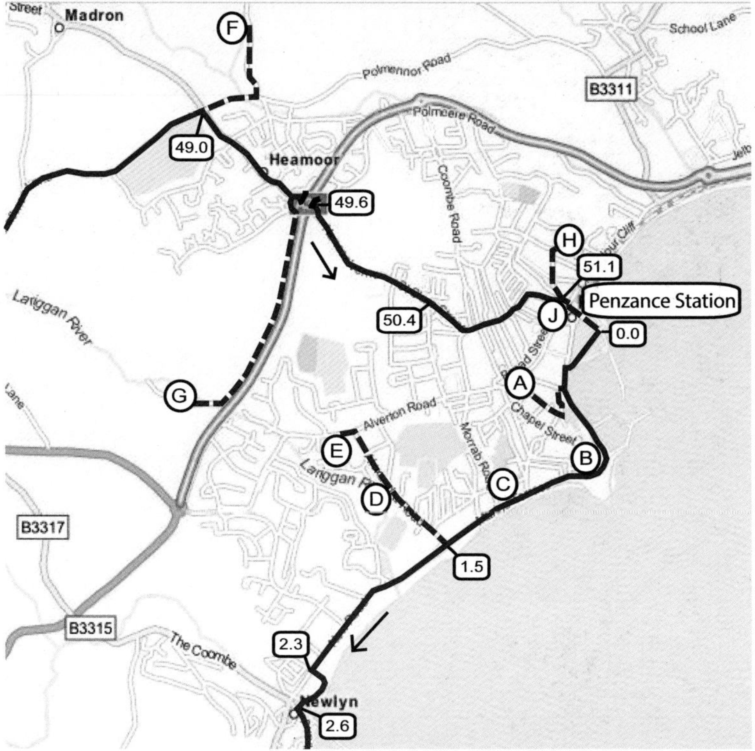

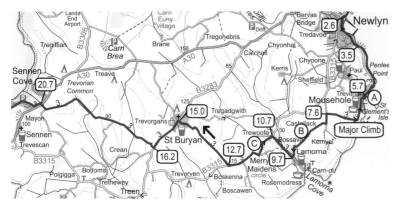

3.5   At end ⟨ 🚲 🍴 **Newlyn Harbour** ↑ via coastal 🚲 (**3**), ep ↑
5.7   In ⟨ 🏠 🚏 🚲 🍴 **Mousehole** ↑ via harbour rd (**3**)
7.6   After **major climb** at T-jct ← (to Castallack, **3**),
      at next jct follow through rd to → (to Castallack, **3**)
9.7   In 🚲 🍴 **Lamorna** *(pubs)* at T-jct ↘ (see sign "Through Traffic", **3**)
10.7   At T-jct ← (to Land's End, **3**)
12.7   1st rd → (to St Buryan, **3**)
15.0   At T-jct 🚏 🚲 🍴 **St Buryan** *(pub and shop)* ← (to Logan Rock, **3**)
16.2   After leaving St Buryan, in descent, 1st rd → (**3**)

Views from the cape of **Land's End** are splendid, but the developments on the cape are a bit ugly. You might prefer unspoiled **Cape Cornwall**, which was considered England's most western point for a long time.

Section 24: Land's End Round Trip (51 km / 32 miles)

20.7 At T-jct ← via 🚲 on right side of rd (to Land's End, **3**), follow 🚲 to → towards 🚻 📷 🍴 ⛵ **Sennen Cove**

21.4 After car park, in descent, 1st rd ↖ (Maria's Ln, **3**)

22.1 In bend to left ↑ via gravel 🚲 (to Land's End, **3**)

23.7 Ep ↘ and use main entrance (**3**), end car park ↟ around buildings, **dismount** at end of tarmac, ↗ to viewpoint

24.4 ↞ 🚻 📷 🍴 **Land's End**, → walk via shops to exit, **resume cycling** at car park, join rd ↑ 🚗 (or rejoin route **3** for same way back)

Note our route back to Penzance via Cape Cornwall is spectacular, but has some sections on main roads and paths with rocky/muddy surface!

26.3 🚻 📷 🍴 **Sennen** (pub and shop)

27.2 At rndabt ↑ (to Penzance) 🚗 (or rejoin route **3** via 1st rd →)

29.1 1st through rd ↖ (to St Just, B3306) 🚗

31.2 (For short-cut to Penzance; after 📷 **Land's End Airport** 1st rd ↘, follow bendy rd and at T-jct ↘ to rejoin route after 40.4 km)

32.3 In descent, at "Cot Manor", ↖ (dead end rd to YHA), keep ↗

33.3 **Dismount** at end of rd, keep ↑ via narrow footpath (poor surface)

33.4 *Don't despair!* Ep **resume cycling** ↗ via tarmac rd

34.3 On arrival in village, 1st path ← (Pleasant Tc) (keep speed low!)

34.4 Ep ← via rd, 1st rd ↖ (to Carn Gloose), keep going ↑

36.1 **Dismount** on gravel path at start of steep descent (take care!)

36.3 Ep at car park ↞ **Cape Cornwall** → **resume cycling** via tarmac rd

38.2 At T-jct → into 🏨 🚻 📷 🍴 **St. Just**, keep going ↑ 🚗

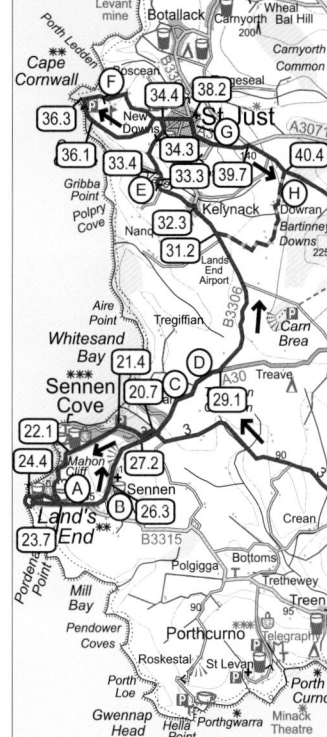

St. Just has a square with a nice atmosphere. You might want to stay here before heading for the train station in Penzance. On the way back, you'll also pass two campsites and a youth hostel. There are some B&Bs next to the station too. See the map of Penzance on page 146.

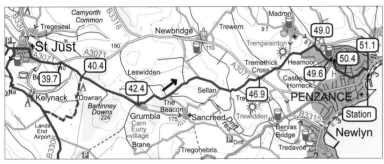

Land's End

39.7	After leaving St Just, in descent ↗ (to Numphra)
42.4	1st rd ← (to Tremethick Cross)
46.9	At T-jct ↑ (to Madron/Heamoor)
49.0	At cross rds → (to Penzance)
49.6	Just before rndabt ↖ via 🚲 tunnel, ep ↖ 🚗
50.4	At rndabt ↑, then in bend to right ← (Taraveor Rd)
51.1	Dismount at T-jct, walk ↑ to Penzance station

Congratulations on your achievement! We hope you enjoyed the ride!

Cape Cornwall

Facility Listings

These listings should by no means be regarded as a full overview of Bed & Breakfasts, guesthouses, hotels, hostels, campsites and bike repair shops on the route. Venues requiring a minimum stay of two nights are not listed. Most facilities haven't been visited by us in person, but they appear to be generally suitable. If you find other suitable accommodations or if you find listed facilities shut down, renamed or unsuitable, please let us know via Twitter @LondonLandsEnd or via our website www.london-landsendcycleroutebook.com. We publish all important changes on the route updates page. Note the UK international dialling code is 00 44.

Pricing indication for ♠ B&Bs/Hotels and ♠♠ Hostels/bunkhouses:
£   £60 or less per night for a shared room with 2 people
££   between £60 and £80 per night for a shared room for 2 people
£££   more than £80 per night for a shared room for 2 people
Note: Solo travellers pay up to 80% of prices above for a single room; hostels and bunkhouses provide more value for money for solo cyclists!

Pricing indication for ▲ campsites:
£   £10 or less per night for one person
££   more than £10 per night per pitch for one person
Note: the "expensive" rate can be good value for two, as the price per pitch often sleeps two!
🗡   Accommodation located in reasonably quiet and peaceful surroundings
🔊   Accommodation located near railways or roads with noisy traffic or street noise (people)

Rte	Km	Page	Ref	Town	Info	Name, address and postcode	Phone	Internet	Distance to route & extra instructions
B	3.2	21	A	London (Connections)	♠♠ 🗡 £	YHA London Central, 104 Bolsover St, W1W 5NU	0845 3719154	ww.yha.org.uk	- (1st rd ←)
1	0.5	25	A	Dover	🗡	Cyclelife Dover, 15 Bench St, CT16 1JW	01304 207582	www.cyclelife.com	0.5 km (see station route)
1	0.5	25	B	Dover	♠♠ 🔊 £	Hostel Alma, 37 Folkestone Rd, CT17 9RZ	01304 241762	www.almadover.com	1.0 km (see station route)
1	0.9	25	C	Dover	♠ 🗡 ££	Victoria Guest House, 1 Laureston Pl, CT16 1QX	01304 205140	www.guest-house.fsbusiness.co.uk	-
1	0.9	25	C	Dover	♠ 🗡 ££	Cleveland Guest House, 2 Laureston Pl, CT16 1QX	01304 204622	-	-
1	0.9	25	C	Dover	♠ 🗡 ££	Churchill House, 6 Castle Hill Rd, CT16 1QN	01304 208365	www.toastofdover.com	-
1	0.9	25	C	Dover	♠ 🗡 ££	Castle Guest House, 10 Castle Hill Rd, CT16 1QW	01304 201656	www.castle-guesthouse.co.uk	-
1	0.9	25	C	Dover	♠ 🗡 £££	Hubert House, 9 Castle Hill Rd, CT16 1QW	01304 202253	www.huberthouse.co.uk	-
1	7.0	26	A	St Margaret's at Cliffe	♠ 🗡 £££	The White Cliffs Hotel, High Street, CT15 6AT	01304 852220	www.thewhitecliffs.com	- (←, after 50 m)
1	7.0	26	B	St Margaret's at Cliffe	▲ 🔊 🗡 £	Hawthorn Farm Park, Station Rd, Martin Mill, CT15 5LA	01304 852658	www.keatfarm.co.uk	2.5 km (←, at A258 🗡, 1st ←)
1	11.8	26	C	Kingsdown	▲ ♠♠ 🗡 £	Kingsdown Int Camping Centre, The Avenue, CT14 8DU	01304 373713	www.kingsdowncamping.co.uk	0.8 km (← climb Upper St, in bend ←)
1	12.0	26	D	Kingsdown	♠ 🗡 ££	Hardicot House, Kingsdown Rd, Walmer, CT14 8AW	01304 373867	www.hardicot-guest-house.co.uk	-
1	15.6	26	E	Deal	♠ 🔊 ££	Malvern Guest House, 5-7 Ranelagh Rd, CT14 7BG	01304 372944	www.themalvernguesthouse.com	0.1 km (← Ranelagh Rd)
1	15.9	26	F	Deal	♠ 🔊 ££	Beachbrow Hotel, 29 Beach St, CT14 6HY	01304 374338	www.beachbrow-hotel.co.uk	-
1	15.9	26	F	Deal	♠ 🔊 £££	Dunkerleys Hotel, 19 Beach St, CT14 7AH	01304 375016	www.dunkerleys.co.uk	-
1	15.9	26	F	Deal	♠ 🔊 £££	Clarendon Hotel, 51-53 Beach St, CT14 6HY	01304 374748	www.clarendondeal.co.uk	-
1	15.9	26	F	Deal	♠ 🔊 £££	The Royal Hotel, Beach St, CT14 6JD	01304 375555	www.theroyalhotel.com/	-
1	16.3	26	G	Deal	🗡	Curwens Cycle Repairs, 194 High St, CT14 6 BL	01304 365823	-	0.2 km (← Griffin St, at T-jct →)
1	24.0	27	A	Sandwich	♠ 🗡 £££	White Rose Lodge, 88 St Georges Rd, CT13 9LE	01304 620406	www.whiteroselodge.co.uk	0.4 km (see station route)
1	24.5	27	B	Sandwich	🗡	Atman, 9 Gilliard St, CT13 9BG	01304 611621	www.atman.uk.com	0.3 km (not right into footpath, but ↑)

Rte	Km	Page	Ref	Town	Info	Name, address and postcode	Phone	Internet	Distance to route & extra instructions
1	24.5	27	C	Sandwich	♠ ⚘ £	Kings Arms Hotel, Strand St, CT13 9HN	01304 617330	www.kingsarms-sandwich.co.uk	-
1	24.6	27	D	Sandwich	♠ ⚘ ££	St Peters B&B, 36 St Peters St, CT13 9BS	01304 617644	http://saintpetersbandb.co.uk	-
1	24.6	27	E	Sandwich	♠ ⚘ ££	The New Inn, 2 Delf St, CT13 9ES	01304 612335	www.newinn-sandwich.co.uk	-
1	25.2	27	F	Sandwich	▲ ⌂ ££	Sandwich Leisure Park, Woodnesborough Rd, CT13 0AA	01304 612681	www.sandwich-leisurepark.co.uk	0.8 km (← The Butts, ↑ to end, ep →)
1	32.8	28	A	Preston	▲ ⚘ £	Westmarsh Farm Park, Wass Drove Farm, CT3 2LT	01304 813222	-	-
1	41.9	28	B	Stodmarsh	♠ ⚘ £££	Gate Lodge Cottage B&B, Grove Rd, CT3 1SD	01227 728305	www.gatelodgecottage.co.uk	1.0 km (↑ at Stodmarsh jct)
1	47.6	28	C	Fordwich	▲ ⚘ £	Canterbury Camping Club, Bekesbourne Ln, CT3 4AB	01227 463217	www.campingandcaravanningclub.co.uk	1.2 km (↑, at T-jct → on A257, 1st ←)
2	0.1	31	A	Canterbury	♠ ⚘ £££	Cathedral Lodge, The Precincts, CT1 2EH	01227 865350	www.canterburycathedrallodge.org	-
2	0.3	31	B	Canterbury	♠ ⚘ ££	The Coach House, 34 Watling St, CT1 2UD	01227 784324	www.coachhouse-canterbury.co.uk	0.4 km (↑ to East Station, at T-jct ←)
2	0.3	31	C	Canterbury	⌂ ⚘ £	Kipps Hostel, 40 Nunnery Fields, CT1 3JT	01227 786121	www.kipps-hostel.com	1.4 km (via East Station & ⚲ Oxford Rd)
2	0.6	31	D	Canterbury	♠ ⚘ ££	Peregrine House, 18 Hawk's Ln, CT1 2NU	01227 761897	www.theperegrinehouse.co.uk	0.3 km (← Stour St, ← Hawk's Ln)
2	0.6	31	E	Canterbury	⚘	Canterbury Cycle Centre, 22-24 Stour St, CT1 2NZ	01227 787880	-	0.1 km (← Stour St, beyond Heritage M)
2	0.6	31	F	Canterbury	♠ ⚘ ££	Tudor House, 6 Best Ln, CT1 2JB	01227 765650	www.tudorhousecanterbury.co.uk	0.1 km (→ Best Ln)
2	1.6	31	G	Canterbury	⌂ ⚘ ££	Acacia Lodge/Tanglewood, 39 London Rd, CT2 8LF	01227 769955	www.acacialodge.co.uk	0.2 km (→ London Rd)
2	3.0	31	H	Canterbury	▲ ⚘ ££	Neals Place Farm, CT2 8HX	01227 765632	-	- (Note: end of ⚲ imm ↙)
2	5.2	32	A	Blean	♠ ☏ ££	Amadis B&B, 53 Blean Common, CT2 9EX	01227 786928	www.amadis53.co.uk	0.7 km (←, at T-jct →)
2	12.1	32	B	Whitstable	▲ ☏ ££	Primrose Cottage Caravan Pk, Golden Hill, CT5 3AR	01227 273694	-	-
2	10.8	32	C	Whitstable	⚘	Herberts Cycles, 103-105 High St, CT5 1AY	01227 272072	www.herbertscycles.co.uk	3.0 km (↑ cross station via footbridge, ←)
2	26.5	33	A	Faversham	⚘ ☏ £££	Gladstone House B&B, 60 Newton Rd, ME13 8DZ	01795 532341	www.bandbinfaversham.co.uk	0.6 km (↑ via main rd to station)
2	26.5	33	B	Faversham	♠ ☏ ££	The Sun Inn, 10 West St, ME13 7JE	01795 535098	www.sunfaversham.co.uk	0.3 km (↑ to cobbled centre, →)
2	26.5	33	C	Faversham	⚘	Bike Warehouse, 30-32 Preston St, ME13 8PE	01795 539439	www.the-bike-warehouse.com	0.5 km (↑ to cobbled centre, ←, →)
2	26.6	33	D	Faversham	♠ ☏ ££	Swan & Harlequin B&B, Conduit St, ME13 7DF	01795 532341	www.swanandharlequin.co.uk	-
2	27.6	33	E	Faversham	♠ ⚘ ££	Holly Cottage, Water Lane, Ospringe, ME13 8TS	01795 597597	www.hollycottagebedandbreakfast.co.uk	1.6 km (see map, via Water Ln)
2	27.6	33	F	Faversham	▲ ⚘ £	Painters Farm Camping, Painters Forstal, ME13 0EG	01795 532995	-	4.2 km (see map, via Water Ln)
2	31.3	34	A	Luddenham	♠ ⚘ £££	Rifleman Cottage B&B, ME13 0TL	01795 521638	http://riflemancottage.co.uk	-
2	35.3	34	B	Doddington	▲ ⌂ ⚘ £	Palace Farm Hostel, Down Court Rd, ME9 0AU	01795 886200	www.palacefarm.com	9.0 km (←, ↑ Station Rd), ↑ Lynsted Ln)
2	39.8	34	C	Bapchild	♠ ⚘ ££	Tonge Barn, Church Road, Tonge, ME9 9AP	01795 474743	www.tongebarn.co.uk	1.1 km (↑ to Town Centre)
2	53.7	36	A	Upchurch	♠ ⚘ £££	Suffield House, The Street, ME9 7EU (no children!)	01634 230409	www.suffieldhouse.talktalk.net	1.2 km (→, after church ↘)
2	56.1	36	B	Rainham	♠ ⚘ £	Abigails B&B, 17 The Maltings, ME8 8JL	01634 365427	www.abigailsbandb.co.uk	1.5 km (↑, at T-jct ←, 2nd →, 2nd ←)
2	63.8	37	A	Gillingham	♠ ⚘ £	Mayfield B&B, 34 Kingswood Rd, ME7 1DZ	01634 852606	-	1.1 km (←, Rosebery Rd, station route)
2	63.8	37	B	Gillingham	♠ ☏ £	The Balmoral, 57-59 Balmoral Rd, ME7 4NT	01634 365427	www.thebalmoral-guesthouse.co.uk	1.7 km (←, Rosebery Rd, station route)
2	65.3	37	C	Chatham	♠ ☏ ££	Ramada Encore Chatham, Western Av, ME4 4NT	01634 891677	www.encorechatham.co.uk	-
2	68.7	37	D	Chatham	♠ ☏ ££	St George Hotel, 7-8 New Road Av, ME4 6BB	01634 841012	www.george-hotel.co.uk	0.2 km (←, Hamond Hill, T-jct →)

Rte	Km	Page	Ref	Town	Info	Name, address and postcode	Phone	Internet	Distance to route & extra instructions
2	69.0	37	E	Rochester	⚲	Cycle King, 353-357 High St, ME1 1DA	01634 811147	-	-
2	70.1	37	F	Rochester	⌂ ⚲ ££	The Kings Head Hotel, 58 High St, ME1 1LD	01634 831103	www.kingsheadrochester.co.uk	-
2	70.3	37	G	Rochester	⌂ ⚲ ££	Grayling House Hotel, 54 St Margaret St, ME1 1TU	01634 826593	-	0.2 km (↖, St Margaret St)
2	70.3	37	H	Rochester	⌂ ⚲ ££	Greystones B&B, 25 Watts Av, ME1 1RX	01634 409565	www.greystonesbandb.org.uk	0.4 km (↖, St Margaret St, 5th ←)
3	9.5	39	A	Higham	⌂ ⚲ ££	Gardeners Arms, Forge Lane, ME3 7AS	01474 823901	www.gardenersarmshigham.co.uk	1.8 km (←, after railway ←)
3	16.4	39	B	Gravesend	⌂ ⚲ £	Shamrock Guesthouse, 118 Milton Rd, DA12 2PF	01474 365557	www.shamrockguesthouse.co.uk	1.8 km (end park ↖, go ↑, at T-jct ←)
3	16.7	39	C	Gravesend	⚲	Cycles UK, 148 Milton Rd, DA12 2RG	01474 333090	-	0.3 km (←)
3	16.8	39	D	Gravesend	⌂ ⚲ £££	Thames House B&B, 29 Royal Pier Rd, DA12 2BD	07805 477973	http://thameshousebandb.com	-
3	17.1	39	E	Gravesend	⚲	TriThe Bike Shop, 18 Windmill St, DA12 1AS	01474 533748	www.trithebike.co.uk	0.5 km (← opposite Town Pier)
3	18.8	39	F	Gravesend	⌂ ⚲ ££	Overcliffe Hotel, 15/16 The Overcliffe, DA11 0EF	01474 322131	http://overcliffehotel.co.uk	0.4 km (do not cross main rd, ←)
3	30.4	41	A	Dartford	⚲	Cycle King, 52-54 Spital St, DA1 2DT	01322 280050	-	0.5 km (←, in bend to right ↖)
3	43.9	41	B	London - Abbey Wood	▲ ⚲ £	Abbey Wood Camping Club, Federation Rd, SE2 0LS	020 83117708	www.caravanclub.co.uk	5.0 km (see map)
3	52.0	41	C	London - Woolwich	⚲	Harry Perry Cycles, 88 Powis St, SE18 6LQ	020 88542383	-	0.4 km (←, ↑ at rndabt, 1st ↖)
4	0.5	42	A	Harwich	⌂ ⚲ £	Paston Lodge B&B, 1 Una Rd, Parkeston, CO12 4PP	01255 551390	-	-
4	0.9	42	B	Harwich	⌂ ⚲ £	The Hive B&B, 81 Parkeston Rd, Dovercourt, CO12 4HE	01255 503316	-	-
4	2.8	42	C	Harwich	⚲	Howletts Ltd, 15-17 Kingsway, CO12 3AB	01255 503599	-	-
4	2.8	42	D	Harwich	⌂ ⚲ ££	The Tower Hotel, Main Rd, Dovercourt, CO12 3PJ	01255 504952	www.tower-hotel-harwich.co.uk	0.2 km (at lhts →)
4	2.8	42	E	Harwich	⌂ ⚲ £	Dudley House B&B, 34 Cliff Rd, Dovercourt, CO12 3PP	01255 504927	-	0.2 km (at lhts →, 2nd rd ←)
4	4.0	42	F	Harwich	⌂ ⚲ £	The Tudor Rose B&B, 124 Franks Road, CO12 4EQ	01255 552398	www.tudor-rose-harwich.co.uk	0.4 km (→, Beach Rd, at T-jct ←)
4	7.6	43	A	Ramsey	▲ ⚲ £	The Castle Inn, The Street, CO12 5HH	01255 880203	www.thecastleinnramsey.co.uk	1.4 km (→, Mayes Ln, T-jct ←, rndabt ↑)
4	16.6	43	B	Bradfield	▲ ⚲ £	Strangers Home Inn, The Street, CO11 2US	01255 870304	-	4.0 km (↑ via Wix, at T-jct →)
4	25.0	43	C	Great Bromley	⌂ ⚲ ££	Old Courthouse Inn, Harwich Road, CO 7 7JG	01206 250322	www.theoldcourthouseinn.co.uk	-
4	41.2	45	A	Colchester	⌂ ⚲ £	Corner House B&B, 36 West Stockwell Street, CO1 1HS	07737 533879	http://cornerhouse-bb.co.uk	0.2 km (in bend →, Northgate St, 1st ←)
4	41.6	45	B	Colchester	⌂ ⚲ ££	The Old Manse B&B, 15 Roman Road, CO1 1UR	01206 545154	www.theoldmanse.uk.com	0.5 km (←, after Hollytrees Mus. 1st ←)
4	41.6	45	B	Colchester	⌂ ⚲ £	Roman Cottage B&B, 64 Roman Road, CO1 1UP	01206 524562	www.64romanroad.co.uk	0.5 km (←, after Hollytrees Mus. 1st ←)
4	41.6	45	B	Colchester	⌂ ⚲ £	Park House B&B, 41a Castle Road, CO1 1UN	01206 765303	-	0.5 km (←, after Hollytrees Mus. 1st ←)
4	41.6	45	C	Colchester	⌂ ⚲ ££	George Hotel, 116 High Street, CO1 1TD	0871 3769900	-	-
4	41.6	45	C	Colchester	⌂ ⚲ ££	The Red Lion Hotel, 43 High Street, CO1 1DJ	01206 577986	www.red-lion-hotel.co.uk	-
4	42.0	45	D	Colchester	⚲	Colchester Cycle Stores, 50 St Johns Street, CO2 7AD	01206 563890	www.colchestercyclestores.co.uk	0.2 km (walk ←, 3rd ←)
4	42.5	45	E	Colchester	⌂ ⚲ £	Pescara House B&B, 88 Manor Road, CO3 3LY	01206 522055	www.pescarahouse.co.uk	0.1 km (←)
4	42.8	45	F	Colchester	⌂ ⚲ £	Tarquins Guest House, 26 Inglis Road, CO1 3HU	01206 579508	-	0.5 km (←, Oxford Rd, 2nd ←)
4	42.8	45	F	Colchester	⌂ ⚲ ££	Four Sevens Guest House, 28 Inglis Road, CO1 3HU	01206 546093	www.foursevens.co.uk	0.5 km (←, Oxford Rd, 2nd ←)
4	43.7	45	G	Colchester	▲ ⚲ ££	Colchester Holiday Park, Cymbeline Way, CO3 4AG	01206 545551	www.colchestercamping.co.uk	1.5 km (↑, opp church →, Spring Ln, ←)

Rte	Km	Page	Ref	Town	Info	Name, address and postcode	Phone	Internet	Distance to route & extra instructions
4	52.4	46	A	Layer Breton	🛏 🚲 ££	The Hare & Hounds, Crayes Green, CO2 0PN	01206 330459	www.thehareandhound.co.uk	-
4	69.1	47	A	Wickham Bishops	▲ 🚲 £	Opera in the Orchard, Bouncers Farm, Wickham Hall Ln	01621 894112	http://operaintheorchard.co.uk	0.6 km (in sharp bend down to right ↑)
5	0.0	48	A	Maldon	🛏 ⛺ ££	The Swan Hotel, 73 High St, CM9 5EP	01621 853170	-	0.3 km (via High St)
5	0.0	48	B	Maldon	🚲	Riverside Cycle Centre, 100 High St, CM9 5ET	01621 858240	www.riversidecyclecentre.co.uk	0.4 km (via High St)
5	0.0	48	C	Maldon	🛏 🚲 ££	The Star House B&B, 72 Wantz Rd, CM9 5DE	01621 853527	http://starhousemaldon.co.uk	0.7 km (via High St, 1st ↗)
5	0.5	48	D	Maldon	🛏 🚲 £	Tatoi B&B, 31 Acacia Dr, CM9 6AW	01621 853841	http://tatoibedandbreakfast.com	1.0 km (via Beacon Hill/St Giles Cr, ↖)
5	7.4	48	E	Danbury	🛏 🚲 ££	Chestnuts B&B, Chestnut Walk, CM3 4SP	01245 223905	-	1.7 km (1st →, 3rd ↗, T-jct ←, 1st →)
5	8.3	48	F	Danbury	🛏 🚲 ££	Wych Elm B&B, Mayes Lane, CM3 4NJ	01245 222674	www.wychelmb-b.co.uk	1.6 km (↘ Mill Ln, ↗, T-jct ←, 1st ←)
5	35.0	49/50	A	Doddinghurst	🛏 ▲ 🚲 ££	Little Lampetts B&B, Hay Green Lane, CM4 0QE	01277 822030	www.littlelampetts.com	-
5	39.4	50	B	Kelvedon Hatch	▲ 🚲 £	Kelvedon Hatch Camping Club, Warren Ln, CM15 0JG	01277 372773	www.campingandcaravanningclub.co.uk	-
5	53.0	50	C	Abridge	🛏 📶 £	Ottley's B&B, 55 Ongar Rd, RM4 1UH	01992 814967	www.ottleysbandb.co.uk	3.5 km (↗, T-jct →, 2 x 1st →, T-jct ↖)
5	58.2	51	A	London - Hainault	🚲	Ciclos Uno, 37 New North Rd, IG6 2UE	020 85001792	www.ciclosuno.com	0.9 km (at T-jct →, keep going ↑)
5	63.6	52	A	London - Ilford	🛏 🚲 £	Arran Guesthouse, 11 Argyle Rd, IG1 3BH	020 84783796	www.arranguesthouse.co.uk	2.4 km (→ Vicarage Ln, T-jct ↖, 1st ←, etc)
5	63.6	52	A	London - Ilford	🛏 🚲 £	Best Inn Hotel, 10 Argyle Rd, IG1 3BQ	020 84783779	http://bestinnhotel.co.uk	2.4 km (→ Vicarage Ln, T-jct ↖, 1st ←, etc)
5	63.6	52	A	London - Ilford	🛏 🚲 £	Cranford Hotel, 22 Argyle Rd, IG1 3BQ	020 84788403	www.cranford-hotel.com	2.4 km (→ Vicarage Ln, T-jct ↖, 1st ←, etc)
5	66.9	52	B	London - Barking	🛏 🚲 £	Barking Park Hotel, 56-60 Tanner St, IG11 8QF	020 85942720	www.barkingparkhotel.com	-
5	70.5	53	A	London - East Ham	🚲	Rob's Bikes Breakdown service, 50 Langton Av, E6 6AL	07846 738292	www.robsbikes.co.uk	0.2 km (T-jct →, 1st ←, 1st →)
6	1.8	54	A	London - Woolwich	🛏 📶 £	The White Horse B&B, 704 Woolwich Rd, SE7 8LQ	020 88542646	-	-
6B	11.0	55	A	London - Greenwich	🛏 🚲 £££	Number 37 B&B, 37 Burney St, SE10 8EX	020 82652623	www.burney.org.uk	0.2 km (←, ↑)
6B	11.0	55	B	London - Greenwich	🛏 🚲 £££	St Alfege Passage, 16 St Alfege Passage, SE10 9JS	020 88534337	www.st-alfeges.co.uk	0.4 km (←, 1st ←, ↖ and ↗, Roan St)
6	6.2	57	A	London - Rotherhithe	🛏 🚲 £	YHA Thameside, 20 Salter Rd, SE16 5PR	0845 3719756	www.yha.org.uk	-
6	7.4	57	B	London - Rotherhithe	🚲	Robinsons Cycles, 172 Jamaica Rd, SE16 4RT	020 72374679	-	0.4 km (← after house no 180)
6	9.4	57	C	London - Southbank	🚲	On Your Bike, 52-54 Tooley St, SE1 2SZ	020 73786669	www.onyourbike.com	-
7	1.7	59	A	London - Southbank	🛏 📶 £££	The Mad Hatter Hotel, 3-7 Stamford St, SE1 9NY	020 74019222	www.madhatterhotel.co.uk	-
7	3.9	60	A	London - Westminster	🚲	Action Bikes, 19 Dacre Street, SW1 0DJ	020 77992233	-	0.4 km (via 2nd exit Parliament Sq, 2nd →)
7	8.9	60	B	London - Kensington	🛏 🚲 £	Clearlake Hotel, 19 Prince of Wales Tc, W8 5PQ	020 79373274	www.clearlakehotel.co.uk	0.1 km (→)
7	8.9	60	B	London - Kensington	🛏 🚲 £££	Kensington House Hotel, 15-16 Prince of Tc, W8 5PQ	020 79372345	www.kenhouse.com	0.1 km (→)
7	9.5	60	C	London - Kensington	🛏 📶 £	Meininger Hostel, 67 Queens Gate Mews, SW7 5JS	020 33181407	www.meininger-hotels.com	0.5 km (← Cornwall G, T-jct ↖, T-jct →)
7	10.2	61	A	London - Kensington	🛏 🚲 ££	Hotel St Simeon, 38 Harrington Gdns, SW7 4LT	020 73730505	www.stsimeon.com	-
7	10.5	61	B	London - Kensington	🛏 🚲 £	YHA Earls Court, 38 Bolton Gdns, SW5 0AQ	0845 3719114	www.yha.org.uk	-
7	10.7	61	C	London - Kensington	🚲	Cyclecare Kensington, 54 Earls Court Road, W8 6EJ	020 74600495	www.cyclecarekensington.co.uk	1.5 km (→)
7	12.5	62	A	London - Fulham	🚲	Days Cycles, 213 Dawes Rd, SW6 7QZ	020 73853870	-	0.5 km (↗)
7	15.7	62	B	London - Putney	🚲	Holdsworth Cycles, 132 Lower Richmond Rd, SW15 1LN	020 87881060	www.holdsworthcycles.net	0.4 km (last rd ← Festing Rd, at jct →)

Rte	Km	Page	Ref	Town	Info	Name, address and postcode	Phone	Internet	Distance to route & extra instructions
7	28.5	63	A	Kingston upon Thames	££££	Malara Cottage B&B, 103 Lower Ham Rd, KT2 5BD	020 85499611	http://malaracottage.co.uk	0.1 km (ep ↙ via rd)
8	0.3	64	A	Kingston upon Thames	££	The Foresters, 45 High St, Hampton Wick, KT1 4DG	020 89435379	www.the-foresters.com	0.2 km (at rndabt ↗)
8	0.3	64	A	Kingston upon Thames	£££	Chase Lodge, 10 Park Rd, Hampton Wick, KT 1 4AS	020 89431862	www.chaselodgehotel.com	0.3 km (at rndabt ↗, 1st ↖)
8	4.9	65	A	Hampton Court	££	Houseboat Riverine, Hampton Court Rd, TW12 2HA	020 89792266	www.feedtheducks.com	0.3 km (→, 1st ←, 1st ← to Taggs Isl)
8B	12.9	65	B	Walton on Thames	⌁	East St Cycles, 12-14 New Zealand Av, KT12 1QD	01932 221424	-	1.1 km (↙ to main rd, → via main rd)
8B	19.1	66	B	Chertsey	⌁	Birdie Bikes, Sainsbury Centre, Guildford St, KT16 9AG	01932 560760	-	1.4 km (at cross rds ↑, at T-jct ↗, ↑ via path)
8B	19.1	66	B	Chertsey	££	Thyme at the Tavern, 20 London St, KT16, 8AA	01932 429667	www.thymeatthetavern.co.uk	1.6 km (see Birdie Bikes above, ep →)
8B	19.5	66	C	Chertsey	££	The Bridge Hotel, Bridge Rd, KT16 8JZ	01932 565644	www.bridgehotelchertsey.com	-
8B	19.5	66	D	Chertsey	££	Chertsey Camping Club, 65-67 Bridge Rd, KT16 8JX	01932 562405	www.campingandcaravanningclub.co.uk	0.2 km (westbound from bridge)
8	1.3	67	A	Laleham	££	Laleham Camping, Laleham Park, Thameside, TW18 1SS	01932 564149	www.lalehamcampingclub.co.uk	-
8	6.3	67	B	Staines	⌁	The Bike Company, 4 Thames St, TW18 4SD	01784 440666	www.thebikecompany.co.uk	-
8	6.5	67	C	Staines	££	Jolly Farmer, 2 Farmers Rd, The Hythe, TW 18 3JE	01784 452807	-	- (after bridge ←)
8	6.5	67	C	Staines	££	Anne Boleyn Hotel, 29 The Hythe. TW18 3JD	01784 455930	www.boleynhotel.com	0.1 km (after bridge ←)
8	6.5	67	C	Staines	£££	Swan Hotel, The Hythe, TW18 3JB	01784 452494	http://swanstaines.co.uk	0.2 km (after bridge ←)
8	22.1	69	A	Windsor	££	3 York Road, 3 York Rd, SL4 3NX	01753 861741	-	0.1 km (not left into York Av, but ↑)
8	22.4	69	B	Windsor	££	Alma House, 56 Alma Rd, SL4 3HA	01753 862983	www.bed-and-breakfast-windsor.co.uk	0.3 km (→ at jct with lhts, 1st →)
8	22.4	69	C	Windsor	££	The Trooper, 97 St Leonards Rd, SL4 3BZ	01753 670123	www.thetrooperinnwindsor.com	0.7 km (→ at jct with lhts, 4th →)
8	22.4	69	D	Windsor	£	Clarence Hotel, 9 Clarence Rd, SL4 5AE	01753 864436	www.clarence-hotel.co.uk	0.3 km (→ at jct with lhts)
8	22.4	69	D	Windsor	⌁	Seven Hundred , 68 Peascod St, SL4 1DE	01753 858777	www.7hundred.co.uk	0.3 km (→ at jct with lhts)
8	22.6	69	E	Windsor	££	Dee & Steves B&B, 169 Oxford Rd, SL4 5DX	01753 845489	www.deeandsteve.com	0.1 km (→ after jct with lhts 2nd rd →)
8	22.8	69	F	Windsor	££	Barbara's B&B, 16 Maidenhead Rd, SL4 5EQ	01753 840273	http://bbandbwindsor.com	0.1 km (at 2nd jct with lhts →)
8	22.8	69	G	Windsor	££	76 Duke Street, 76 Duke St, SL4 1SQ	01753 620636	www.76dukestreet.com	0.1 km (after 2nd jct with lhts 2x 1st rd →)
9	6.4	70	A	Maidenhead	££	Amerden Caravan Park, Old Marsh Lane, SL6 0DZ	01628 627461	http://amerdencaravanpark.webs.com	1.0 km (↑ via towpath, after viaduct M4 →)
9	8.6	71	A	Bray	££	Peartrees B&B, 78 Windsor Rd, SL6 2DJ	01628 624407	www.peartreesguesthouse.co.uk	1.2 km (main T-jct Bray ←, at T-jct ←)
9	9.3	71	B	Bray	££	Braywick Grange B&B, 100 Braywick Rd, SL6 1DJ	01628 625915	www.braywickgrange.co.uk	0.4 km (↑ along school, at jct →)
9	10.4	71	C	Maidenhead	££	Bridge Cottage Guest House, Bath Rd, Taplow, SL6 0AR	01628 626805	http://bridgecottagebb.co.uk	1.2 km (↑, ep ↖ via bend ↗, T-jct →)
9	10.4	71	D	Maidenhead	£££	Thames Riviera Hotel, Bridge Rd, SL6 8DW	01628 674057	www.thamesriviera.com	1.0 km (↑, ep ↖ via bend ↗, T-jct →)
9	10.7	71	E	Maidenhead	⌁	DNA Cycles, 91a High St, SL6 1JX	01628 780026	www.dnacycles.co.uk	0.7 km (end ⬦ to Town Centre ←, 2nd →)
9	10.7	71	F	Maidenhead	££	Clifton Guest House, 21 Craufurd Rise, SL6 7LR	01628 620086	www.cliftonguesthouse.co.uk	1.2 km (see above, then High St ←, end →)
9	11.0	71	G	Maidenhead	⌁	Halfords, Stafferton Wy, SL6 1AA	01628 644050	-	-
9	22.1	72	A	Warren Row	££	The Snooty Fox, Warren Row Rd, RG10 8QS	01628 825861	www.thesnootyfoxwarrenrow.com	-
9	32.6	73	A	Sonning	£££	The Bull Inn, High, St, RG4 6UP	01189 693901	www.bullinnsonning.co.uk	0.2 km (← into High St)
9	32.8	73	A	Sonning	£££	Great House Hotel, Thames St, RG4 6UT	01189 692277	www.greathouseatsonning.co.uk	-

Rte	Km	Page	Ref	Town	Info	Name, address and postcode	Phone	Internet	Distance to route & extra instructions
9	36.6	73	B	Reading	⚲	Ben Breakdown service, 97 Donnington Rd, RG1 5NE	07984 911782	www.ask-ben.co.uk	0.8 km (at bridge ← via Cumberland Rd)
9	37.9	73	C	Reading	♿ 🛜 ££	The Great Expectations Hotel, 33 Londen St, RG1 4PS	01189 503925	www.relaxinnzreading.co.uk	0.1 km (← via London St)
9	37.9	73	D	Reading	♿ 🛜 ££	La Baguette, 7 Balgrave St, RG1 1PJ	01189 560882	www.labaguettes.co.uk	0.6 km (→ via London St, towards station)
9	37.9	73	D	Reading	♿ 🛜 £££	Malmaison Hotel, 18-20 Station Rd, RG1 1JX	01189 562300	www.malmaison.com	0.6 km (→ via London St, towards station)
10	1.2	74	A	Reading	♿ 🛜 £	Arch Guest House, 92 Basingstoke St, RG2 0EL	01189 872221	www.archguesthouse.co.uk	0.9 km (↑ via Elgar Rd, at main jct ←)
10	1.2	74	A	Reading	♿ 🛜 £	Avenue Roses, 88-90 Basingstoke St, RG2 0EL	01189 313394	-	0.9 km (↑ via Elgar Rd, at main jct ←)
10	12.8	75	A	Sulhamstead	♿ 🚴 ££	Field Farm Cottage, Sulhamstead Hill, RG7 4DA	01189 302735	www.bandbwestberkshire.co.uk	1.0 km (← into Sulhamstead)
10	19.9	75	B	Upper Woolhampton	♿ 🚴 £	The Paddock, Midgham Green, RG7 5TT	01189 713098	www.midghamgreen.co.uk	2.5 km (→, T-jct ←, 2nd →)
10	21.3	75	C	Midgham	♿ 🚴 ££	Eastfield, Birds Lane, RG7 5UL	01189 713160	-	1.5 km (lock 92 ↙ & ←, T-jct ↰, 1st ←)
10	24.6	76	A	Thatcham	♿ 🛜 ££	Swan Hotel, Station Rd, RG19 4QL	01635 862084	www.swanpubthatcham.co.uk	-
10	28.8	76	B	Newbury	♿ 🛜 £	Guywood B&B, 384 London Rd, RG18 3AA	01635 41231	www.guywood.co.uk	-
10	29.0	76	C	Newbury	♿ 🛜 ££	The Limes Guest House, 368 London Rd, RG14 2QH	01635 33082	www.limesguesthouse.co.uk	0.1 km (↑ at lhts)
10	31.6	76	D	Newbury	♿ 🚴 £££	Chequers Hotel, 6-8 Oxford St, RG14 1JB	01635 38000	www.chequershotelnewbury.co.uk	0.6 km (→ via High St, rndabt ↖)
10	31.6	76	E	Newbury	♿ 🚴 £	The Pilgrims Guest House, Oxford Rd, RG14 1XB	01635 40694	www.pilgrimsnewbury.co.uk	1.4 km (see above, next rndabt ↗, ↑)
10	31.6	76	F	Newbury	⚲	Banjo Cycles, 40 Bartholomew St, RG14 5LL	01635 43186	www.banjocycles.com	0.6 km (← via High St)
10	31.6	76	F	Newbury	⚲	Supernova Cycles, 79 Bartholomew St, RG14 7AB	01635 46600	www.supernovacycles.co.uk	0.6 km (← via High St)
10	33.3	76	G	Newbury	⛺ 🚴 £	Oakley Farm, Wash Water, RG20 0LY	01635 36581	www.oakleyfarm.co.uk	8.5 km (← before canal bridge, see map)
10	40.4	77	A	Kintbury	♿ 🚴 £££	The Dundas Arms, 53 Station Road, RG 17 9UT	01488 658263	www.dundasarms.co.uk	-
10	46.0	77	B	Hungerford	♿ 🛜 ££	Wilton House B&B, 33 High St, RG 17 0NF	01488 684228	www.wiltonhouse-hungerford.co.uk	-
10	46.0	77	B	Hungerford	♿ 🛜 ££	Clevedon House B&B, 95 High St, RG 17 0NB	01488 684730	www.clevedonhousehungerford.co.uk	-
10	46.0	77	B	Hungerford	♿ 🛜 ££	Three Swans Hotel, 117 High St, RG 17 0NZ	01488 682721	www.threeswans.net	-
10	46.0	77	C	Hungerford	♿ 🚴 ££	Honeybones B&B, 33 Bourne Vale, RG17 0LL	01488 683228	www.honeybone.co.uk	1.0 km (←, rndabt →, T-jct ←, 2nd →)
11A	9.2	79	A	Marlborough	⛺ 🚴 £	Postern Hill, on A346 (use back entrance!) SN8 4ND	01672 515195	www.campingintheforest.co.uk	1.8 km (imm ← via gravel p, 2nd p →)
11A	11.5	79	B	Marlborough	⛺ 🚴 £	Church Farm, Church Ln, Mildenhall, SN8 2LU	01672 513159	-	1.5 km (←, in Mildenhall 1st →)
11A	12.5	79	C	Marlborough	⚲	Bertie Maffoons, 14 Hughenden Yard, High St, SN8 1LT	01672 519119	-	-
11A	12.5	79	D	Marlborough	♿ 🛜 £££	Castle & Ball Hotel, 117-118 High St, SN8 1LZ	01672 515201	www.oldenglishinns.co.uk/Marlborough	-
11A	12.5	79	E	Marlborough	♿ 🛜 ££	Merlin Hotel, 36-39 High St, SN8 1LW	01672 512151	www.merlin-rooms-marlborough.co.uk	-
11A	12.5	79	F	Marlborough	♿ 🛜 ££	Sun Inn B&B, 90 High St, SN8 1HF	01672 515011	www.thesunmarlborough.co.uk	-
11A	14.9	80	A	Marlborough	♿ 🚴 £££	Beech Hill B&B, Manton Drove, Manton, SN8 4HL	01672 519833	www.beechhillhouse.net	0.8 km (T-jct ←, 1st ←)
11A	24.0	81	A	Avebury	♿ 🚴 ££	Manor Farm, High St, SN8 1RF	01672 539294	www.manorfarmavebury.com	0.2 km (beyond Keiller Museum)
11A	24.0	81	A	Avebury	♿ 🚴 £££	Avebury Life, 5 Trusloe Cottages, Trusloe, SN8 1QZ	01672 539644	wwwaveburylife.com	0.9 km (beyond Keiller Museum, see map)
11B	0.2	82	A	Great Bedwyn	♿ 🚴 ££	The Cross Keys, 16 High St, SN8 3NU	01672 870678	www.thexkeys.com	-
11B	12.7	82	B	Collingbourne Ducis	♿ 🚴 ££	The Shears Inn, Cadley Rd, SN8 3ED	01264 850304	www.theshears.co.uk	-

Rte	Km	Page	Ref	Town	Info	Name, address and postcode	Phone	Internet	Distance to route & extra instructions
11B	25.5	83	A	Netheravon	⌂ ↳ ££	The Old Post Office B&B, Everleigh Rd, Haxton, SP4 9PT	01980 671640	www.theoldpostoffice-wiltshire.co.uk	0.4 km (↑)
11B	32.3	84	A	Bulford	⌂ ↳ ££	The Dovecote B&B, Watergate Ln, SP4 9DY	01980 632625	www.thedovecot.com	0.3 km (→, 1st ←)
11B	35.4	84	B	Amesbury	⌂ 🖥 ££	Fairlawn Hotel, 42 High St, SP4 7DL	01980 622103	www.fairlawnhouse.co.uk	-
11B	35.4	84	B	Amesbury	⌂ 🖥 ££	George Hotel, 19 High St, SP4 7ET	01980 622108	-	-
11B	35.4	84	C	Amesbury	⚡	Hills Cycles, 2 Smithfield St, SP4 7AL	01980 622705	www.hillscycles.co.uk	0.3 km (← via street with shops)
11B	35.4	84	D	Amesbury	⌂ ↳ ££	Antrebus Arms Hotel, 15 Church St, SP4 7EU	01980 623163	www.antrobusarmshotel.co.uk	-
11B	36.2	84	E	Amesbury	⌂ ↳ ££	Mandalay Guest House, 15 Stonehenge Rd, SP4 7BA	01980 623733	www.mandalayguesthouse.com	-
11B	18.5	85	A	Upavon	▲ ↳ £	Woodbridge Inn, North Newnton roundabout, SN9 6JZ	01980 630266	www.thewoodbridgeinn.co.uk	-
11B	21.0	85	A	Woodborough	⌂ ↳ ££	Puckshipton House, Beechingstoke, SN9 6HG	01672 851336	www.puckshipton.co.uk	1.0 km (in sharp bend to right ↑)
11B	21.4	85	C	Woodborough	⌂ ↳ £££	The Seven Stars Inn, Bottlesford, SN9 6LW	01672 851336	www.thesevenstars.co.uk	0.7 km (after sharp bend to right 1st →)
11B	24.5	85	D	Honey Street	⌂ ↳ ££	Well Cottage B&B, SN9 5PS	01672 851577	www.well-cottage.org.uk	-
11B	24.8	85	E	Honey Street	▲ ↳ £	Barge Inn, SN9 5PS	01672 851705	www.the-barge-inn.com	0.3 km (before canal bridge ←)
12	12.8	87	A	Devizes	⌂ 🖥 £££	The Bear Hotel, 2-3 Market Place, SN10 1HS	01380 722444	http://thebearhotel.net/	0.4 km (see Market Pl route)
12	12.8	87	A	Devizes	⌂ 🖥 £££	Black Swan Hotel, 25-26 Market Place, SN10 1JQ	01380 723259	www.blackswandevizes.co.uk	0.4 km (see Market Pl route)
12	12.8	87	B	Devizes	⌂ 🖥 £££	Castle Hotel, New Park St, SN10 1DS	01380 727981	www.castlehoteldevizes.co.uk	0.4 km (Market Pl route, but ped lhts ←)
12	12.8	87	B	Devizes	⌂ 🖥 ££	The White Bear, 33 Monday Market St, SN10 1DN	01380 727588	www.whitebeardevizes.co.uk	0.4 km (Market Pl route, but ped lhts ←)
12	12.8	87	C	Devizes	⚡	Bikes 'N' Boards, Unit 2, 121 Southbroom Rd, SN10 1LY	01380 729621	www.bikesnboards.co.uk	0.6 km (Market Pl route, but ped lhts ←)
12	14.2	87	D	Devizes	⌂ 🖥 ££	The Gables B&B, Bath Rd, SN10 1PH	01380 723086	www.thegablesdevizes.co.uk	0.2 km (after lock 47 use ramp ↖ to rd)
12	16.7	88	A	Rowde	▲ ↳ £	Lower Foxhangers Farm, SN10 1SS	01380 828254	www.foxhangers.com	-
12	18.6	88	B	Seend	▲ ↳ £	Devizes Camping Club, Spout Ln, SN 12 6RN	01380 828839	www.campingandcaravanningclub.co.uk	0.2 km (at bridge no 149 →)
12	24.1	88	C	Semington	⌂ ↳ ££	Bridge House B&B, Canal Bridge, BA14 6JT	01225 703281	-	-
12	32.8	88	D	Bradford on Avon	⌂ 🖥 ££	The Barge Inn, 17 Frome Rd, BA15 2EA	01225 863403	www.thebargeinn.co.uk	-
12	32.8	88	E	Bradford on Avon	⚡	TT Cycles, The Lock Inn, 48 Frome Rd, BA15 1LE	01225 867187	www.ttcycles.co.uk	-
12	32.8	88	F	Bradford on Avon	⌂ 🖥 £££	Swan Hotel, 1 Church St, BA15 1LN	01225 868686	www.theswanbradford.co.uk	0.8 km (via rd ↑, rndabt ←)
12	32.8	88	G	Bradford on Avon	⌂ 🖥 £££	Bradford Old Windmill, 4 Masons Ln, BA15 1QN	01225 866842	www.bradfordoldwindmill.co.uk	1.1 km (via rd ↑, rndabt ←, steep climb!)
12	32.8	88	H	Bradford on Avon	⌂ ↳ £££	Priory Steps B&B, Newtown, BA15 1NQ	01225 862230	www.priorysteps.co.uk	1.1 km (via rd ↑, rndabt ←, in climb ↗)
12	32.8	88	J	Bradford on Avon	⌂ 🖥 £££	Clifton House, Bath Rd, BA15 1SL	01225 309399	-	1.4 km (via rd ↑, rndabt ←, steep climb!)
12	32.8	88	K	Bradford on Avon	⌂ ↳ ££	Alisa House, Holt Rd, BA15 1TR	01225 862020	www.alisahouse.co.uk	1.6 km (via rd ↑, rndabt ↑, climb!)
12	35.1	89	A	Avoncliff	⌂ ↳ £££	Cross Guns, Avoncliff Aqueduct, BA15 2HB	01225 862335	www.crossguns.net	-
12	47.0	91	A	Bath	⌂ ↳ £££	B&B on a boat, Grand Cru House Boat, BA1 LX	01225 312935	www.bedandbreakfastonaboat.co.uk	-
12	47.4	91	B	Bath	🏠 ↳ £	YHA Bath, Bathwick Hill, BA2 6JZ	0845 3719303	www.yha.org.uk	1.0 km (↑, at rndabt ←, steep climb!)
12	47.6	91	C	Bath	⌂ ↳ £££	Edgar Hotel, 64 Great Pulteney St, BA2 4DN	01225 420619	www.edgar-townhouse.co.uk	-
12	47.7	91	D	Bath	⌂ ↳ £££	Windsor Guesthouse, 69 Great Pulteney St, BA2 4DL	01225 422100	http://bathwindsorguesthouse.co.uk	-

Rte	Km	Page	Ref	Town	Info	Name, address and postcode	Phone	Internet	Distance to route & extra instructions
12	48.8	91	E	Bath	⚲	John's Bikes, 84 Walcot St, BA1 5BD	01225 334633	www.johnsbikes.co.uk	0.4 km (via Gay/George St, ↑ into alley, ←)
12	48.8	91	F	Bath	⌂ ≈ £	YMCA Bath, Broad Street Pl, BA1 5LH	01225 325900	www.bathymca.co.uk	0.3 km (via Gay/George St, ↑ into alley)
12	49.6	91	G	Bath	⌂ ≈ ££	Brooks Guesthouse, 1 Crescent Gdns, BA1 2NA	01225 425543	www.brooksguesthouse.com	-
12	49.6	91	G	Bath	⌂ ≈ ££	Bridgnorth House B&B, 2 Crescent Gdns, BA1 2NA	01225 331186	www.2crescentgardens.co.uk	-
12	51.1	91	H	Bath	▲ ⚴ ££	Newton Mill Caravan Park, Newton St, Loe, BA2 9JF	01225 333909	www.newtonmillpark.co.uk	3.8 km (via steps onto bridge ←, →, 1st ↖)
13	11.5	92	A	Bristol - Warmley	⚲	Webbs of Warmley, 14 High St, BS15 4ND	0117 9673676	http://webbsofwarmley.com	0.3 km (← into High St)
13	11.5	92	B	Bristol - Warmley	⌂ ≈ £	Ferndale Guesthouse, 37 Deanery Rd, BS15 9JB	0117 9858247	-	0.3 km (← into High St)
14	0.9	95	A	Bristol - City Centre	⌂ ≈ ££	Brooks B&B, Exchange Av, St Nicholas St, BS1 1UB	0117 9300066	www.brooksguesthousebristol.com	- (see map)
14	1.1	95	B	Bristol - City Centre	⌂⌂ ⚴ ££	Bristol Backpackers Hostel, 17 St Stephens St, BS1 1EQ	0117 9257900	www.bristolbackpackers.co.uk	- (see map)
14	1.7	95	C	Bristol - City Centre	⌂⌂ ≈ £	YHA Bristol, 14 Narrow Quay, BS1 4QA	0845 3719726	www.yha.org.uk	- (see map)
14	1.8	95	D	Bristol - City Centre	⚲	Mud Dock Cycleworks, 40 The Grove, BS1 4RB	0117 9292151	www.mud-dock.com	0.1 km (↑ via quay rd)
14	2.2	95	E	Bristol - Southville	⌂ ≈ £	Avonside Guesthouse, 106 Coronation Rd, BS3 1AX	0117 9664544	www.avonsideguesthouse.co.uk	0.3 km (1st footbridge ←, then →)
14	2.2	95	E	Bristol - Southville	⌂ ≈ £	Glanville Guesthouse, 122 Coronation Rd, BS3 1AZ	0117 9631634	www.glanvilleguesthouse.co.uk	0.3 km (1st footbridge ←, then →)
14	28.7	97	A	Clevedon	⌂ ⚴ ££	Walton Park Hotel, Wellington Tc, BS21 7BL	01275 874253	www.waltonparkhotel.co.uk	-
14	28.9	97	B	Clevedon	⌂ ⚴ ££	Highcliffe Hotel, Wellington Tce, BS21 7PU	01275 873250	www.highcliffehotel.com	-
14	29.5	97	C	Clevedon	⚲	Bike Style, 25b Alexandra Rd, BS21 7QH	01275 876572	-	0.2 km (← opposite pier)
14	29.5	97	D	Clevedon	⌂ ⚴ ££	Cavell House B&B, 1 Elton Rd	01275 874477	www.cavellhouse.com	0.5 km (← opposite pier, at rndabt →)
14	30.5	97	E	Clevedon	⚲	Bike King, 31 Old St, BS21 6ND	01275 873551	-	1.2 km (← at petrol station, keep ↑)
14	36.3	98	A	Kingston Seymour	▲ ⚴ £	Bullock Farm, Back Ln, BS21 6XA	01934 835020	www.bullockfarm.co.uk	-
14	38.6	98	B	Yatton	⌂ ≈ £	The Bridge Inn, North End Rd, BS49 4AU	01934 839100	www.hungryhorse.co.uk	-
14	42.2	98	C	Yatton	⌂ ⚴ £££	Hollybank B&B, 1 Claverham Rd, BS49 4JT	01934 834967	www.hollybankbb.co.uk	0.9 km (via Town Centre route, then →)
14	43.6	98	D	Congresbury	▲ ⚴ £	Oak Farm Touring Park, Weston Rd, BS49 5EB	01934 833246	-	- (↑ down ramp, ← on rd pavement)
14	46.2	98	E	Congresbury	⌂ ⚴ ££	Brinsea Green Farm, Brinsea Ln, BS49 5JN	01934 852278	www.brinseagreenfarm.co.uk	2.8 km (at golf course ←, ep ←, 2x →)
14	54.5	98	F	Axbridge	⌂ ⚴ £££	Compton House B&B, Townsend, BS26 2AJ	01934 733944	www.axbridgeaccommodation.co.uk	-
14	55.0	98	G	Axbridge	⌂ ⚴ ££	The Oakhouse Hotel, 2 The Square, BS26 2AP	01934 732444	www.theoakhousesomerset.com	-
14	55.6	98	H	Axbridge	⌂ ⚴ ££	Reservoir View Motel, Cheddar Rd, BS26 2DL	01934 732180	www.reservoirviewmotel.com	-
14	55.7	98	H	Axbridge	⌂ ⚴ ££	Strawberry Line B&B, Cheddar Rd, BS26 2DL	01934 732573	strawberrylinebedandbreakfast.co.uk	-
14	57.1	99	A	Cheddar	⚲	Cheddar Cycle Store, 1E Valley Line Ind Est, BS27 3EE	01934 741300	www.cheddarcyclestore.co.uk	1.0 km (follow Strawberry Line 26 to end)
14	57.1	99	B	Cheddar	▲ ⚴ £	Cheddar Bridge Touring Park, Draycott Rd, BS27 3RJ 3EE	01934 743048	www.cheddarbridge.co.uk (no children!)	1.8 km (via Strawberry Line 26, see map)
14	58.1	99	C	Cheddar	⌂ ⚴ ££	Bramblewood B&B, Upper North St, BS27 3HX	01934 744310	http://bramblewoodbandb.co.uk/	0.1 km (→ Upper North St)
14	58.1	99	D	Cheddar	⌂⌂ ⚴ £	YHA Cheddar, Hillfield, BS27 3HN	0845 3719730	www.yha.org.uk	0.6 km (→ Upper North St, at jct ↑)
14	58.8	99	E	Cheddar	⌂ ≈ £	Cox's Mill Hotel, The Cliffs, BS27 3QE	01934 742346	-	0.1 km (←)
14	58.8	99	F	Cheddar	⌂ ≈ £££	Gordons Hotel. Cliff St, BS27 3PT	01934 742497	www.gordonshotel.co.uk	0.2 km (→)

Rte	Km	Page	Ref	Town	Info	Name, address and postcode	Phone	Internet	Distance to route & extra instructions
15	3.2	100	A	Rodney Stoke	▲ ⚒ £	Rodney Stoke Inn, Wells Rd, Draycott, BS27 3XB	01749 870209	rodneystokeinn.co.uk (no children!)	2.5 km (1st ←, T-jct →, ↖ and ↗ Eastville Ln)
15	4.5	100	B	Wedmore	⌂ ⚒ ££	Batts Farm B&B, Nyland, BS27 3UD	01934 741469	-	-
15	5.5	100	C	Wedmore	⌂ ⚒ ££	Tor Farm B&B, Nyland, BS27 3UD	01934 743710	-	-
15	11.5	100	D	Wedmore	⌂ ⚒ ££	Poplar Farm B&B, West Stoughton, BS28 4PP	01934 712087	www.poplarfarmbb.co.uk	-
15	26.2	101	A	Cossington	⌂ ⚒ ££	Brookhayes Farm, Bell Ln, TA7 8LR	01278 722559	www.brookhayesfarm.co.uk	0.2 km (just before bend to left →, Bell Ln)
15	26.9	101	B	Woolavington	▲ ⚒ ££	Fairways Caravan Park, Bath Rd, Bawdrip, TA7 8PP	01278 685569	www.fairwaysinternational.co.uk	1.0 km (↑ via rd, cross rds ←)
15	32.3	102	A	Chedzoy	⌂ ⚒ ££	Apple View B&B, Temple Farm, TA7 8QR	01278 423201	www.bramleylodge.co.uk	1.5 km (in Chedzoy at bus shelter →)
15	39.1	102	B	Bridgwater	⚒	The Bicycle Chain, Salmon Pd, TA7 5PY	01278 423640	www.bicyclechain.co.uk	0.2 km (ep ↙ via rd)
15	39.6	102	C	Bridgwater	⚒	St John Street Cycles, 91-93 St John St, TA6 5HX	01278 441500	www.sjscycles.co.uk	1.0 km (at bridge →, keep ↑ to station)
15	39.7	102	D	Bridgwater	⌂ ⚒ ££	Tudor Hotel, 21 St Mary's St, TA6 3LX	01278 422093	www.tudorhotel.co.uk	0.2 km (follow rd →, 3rd ↗)
15	39.7	102	D	Bridgwater	⌂ ⚒ £££	Old Vicarage Hotel, 45-51 St Mary's St, TA6 3EQ	01278 458891	www.theoldvicaragebridgwater.com	0.3 km (follow rd →, 3rd ↗)
15	39.7	102	E	Bridgwater	⌂ 📶 ££	Admirals Rest, 5 Taunton Rd, TA6 3LW	01278 458580	www.admiralsrest.co.uk	0.3 km (follow rd →, 2nd ←)
15	42.4	102	F	Bridgwater	⌂ 📶 ££	Boat and Anchor, Meade Cl, North Petherton, TA7 0AQ	01278 662473	www.theboatandanchor.co.uk	-
16	0.7	105	A	Taunton	⚒	Six Cycles, Pegasus Ct, Coal Orchard, TA1 1JL	01823 323130	www.sixcycles.co.uk	0.1 km (← on car park)
16	0.8	105	B	Taunton	⚒	Ralph Colman Cycles, 79 Station Rd, TA1 1PB	01823 275822	www.bike-uk.co.uk	0.3 km (→, ↗ at lhts)
16	1.1	105	C	Taunton	⌂ ⚒ £££	Castle Hotel, Castle Green, TA1 1NF	01823 272671	www.the-castle-hotel.com	0.3 km (keep ← onto Tower St)
16	1.8	105	D	Taunton	⌂ 📶 £££	Blorenge Guest House, 57 Staplegrove Rd, TA1 1DG	01823 283005	www.blorengehouse.co.uk	0.3 km (↑ after weir, onto rd, T-jct →)
16	1.8	105	E	Taunton	⌂ 📶 ££	Holly Lodge B&B, 86 Staplegrove Rd, TA1 1DL	01823 352100	-	0.3 km (↑ after weir, onto rd, T-jct ←)
16	1.3	105	F	Taunton	⌂ 📶 ££	Brookfield House, 16 Wellington Rd, TA1 4EQ	01823 272786	www.brookfieldguesthouse.uk.com	0.3 km (↑ via main rd, at T-jct lhts ←)
16	1.3	105	F	Taunton	⌂ 📶 ££	Acorn Lodge, 22 Wellington Rd, TA1 4EQ	01823 337613	http://acornlodgetaunton.co.uk	0.3 km (↑ via main rd, at T-jct lhts ←)
16	1.3	105	F	Taunton	⌂ 📶 ££	Lowdens House, 26 Wellington Rd, TA1 4EQ	01823 336586	www.tauntonguesthouse.co.uk	0.3 km (↑ via main rd, at T-jct lhts ←)
16	3.7	105	G	Bishops Hull	⌂ ⚒ ££	The Old Mill, Netherclay, TA1 5AB	01823 289732	www.bandbtaunton.co.uk	0.2 km (in sharp bend to left →, 1st ←)
16	8.6	106	A	Hillfarrance	⌂ ⚒ ££	The Anchor Inn, TA4 1AW	01823 461334	www.theanchorinn.net	-
16	22.6	106	B	Greenham	▲ ⚒ ⚒	Gamlins Farm Caravan & Camping Park, TA21 0LZ	01823 672859	www.gamlinsfarmcaravanpark.co.uk	0.7 km (↖ to Wollington, koop ↖)
16	23.1	106	C	Greenham	⌂ ⚒ ££	Greenham Hall B&B, TA21 0JJ	01823 672603	www.greenhamhall.co.uk	-
16	38.3	107	A	Bampton	⌂ ⚒ ££	Blackberries B&B, 19 Fore St, EX16 9ND	01398 331842	www.courtyard-bampton.co.uk	- (at T-jct ←)
16	38.3	107	A	Bampton	⌂ ⚒ ££	Weston House, 6 Luke St, EX16 9NF	01398 332094	www.westonhousedevon.co.uk	0.1 km (at T-jct ←)
16	38.3	107	A	Bampton	⌂ ⚒ ££	Bridge House Hotel, 24 Luke St, EX16 9NF	01398 331298	www.bridgehouse-bampton.co.uk	0.2 km (at T-jct ←)
16	49.7	107	B	Dulverton	⌂ ⚒ ££	Winsbere House B&B, 64 Battleton, TA22 9HU	01398 323278	www.winsbere.co.uk	-
17A	0.1	109	A	Dulverton	⌂ ⚒ £££	Town Mills B&B, 1 High St, TA22 9HB	01398 323124	www.townmillsdulverton.co.uk	-
17A	0.2	109	A	Dulverton	⌂ ⚒ £££	Lion Hotel, 2 Bank Sq, TA22 9BU	01398 324437	www.lionhoteldulverton.com	-
17A	1.9	109	B	Dulverton	⌂ ⚒ ££	Marsh Bridge Cottage, TA22 9QG	01398 323197	www.marshbridgedulverton.co.uk	0.1 km (↑ on rd to Hawkridge)
17A	7.7	109	C	Winsford	▲ ⚒ ££	Halse Farm, TA24 7JL	01643 851259	www.halsefarm.co.uk	2.6 km (→ via tarmac, ↑ at cross rds)

Rte	Km	Page	Ref	Town	Info	Name, address and postcode	Phone	Internet	Distance to route & extra instructions
17A	8.4	109	D	Tarr Steps	♠ ⚲ £££	Tar Farm Inn, TA22 9PY	01643 851507	www.tarrfarm.co.uk	-
17	2.7	109	E	Exmoor	♠ ⚲ ££	The Sportsman Inn, Sandyway, EX36 3LU	01643 831109	www.sportsmansinn.co.uk	0.2 km (↑ on rd to Withypool)
17	20.9	110	A	Bratton Fleming	♠ ⚲ £	Franklyn House B&B, EX31 4TG	01598 710108	www.franklynhouse.co.uk	0.2 km (↑ via rd down hill)
17	36.0	111	A	Barnstaple	♠ 🔌 ££	Sunnymead B&B, Landkey Rd, EX32 9BW	07561 326414	www.sunnymeadbandb.co.uk	0.2 km (path ↖ up hill next to school, ep ←)
17	37.8	111	B	Barnstaple	♠ ⚲ ££	Park Hotel, Taw Vale, EX32 9AE	01271 372166	www.brend-hotels.co.uk/thepark	0.1 km (end Rock Park ↘)
17	37.9	111	C	Barnstaple	♠ ⚲ £££	The Old Vicarage B&B, Barbican Tc, EX32 9HQ	01271 328504	www.oldvicaragebarnstaple.co.uk	0.2 km (end Rock Park ↘, rndabt ↙, keep ↗)
17	38.2	111	D	Barnstaple	♠ ⚲ £££	Imperial Hotel, Taw Vale, EX32 8NB	01271 345861	www.brend-hotels.co.uk/theimperial	-
17	38.2	111	D	Barnstaple	⚲	The Bike Shed, The Square, EX32 8LS	01271 328628	www.bikeshed.uk.com	-
17	38.2	111	E	Barnstaple	♠ 🔌 £££	Royal & Fortescue Hotel, 61 Boutport St, EX31 1HG	01271 342289	brend-hotels.co.uk/theroyalfortescue	- (cross square to pedestrian lights, ↗)
17	39.2	111	F	Barnstaple	⚲	Bike It, Mill Rd, EX31 1JQ	01271 323873	www.bikeitbarnstaple.co.uk	0.2 km (before high bridge ↘ gravel, at jct ↗)
17	39.4	111	G	Barnstaple (see page 112)	▲ 🔌 £	Chivenor Caravan Park, 85 Chivenor Cross, EX31 4BN	01271 812217	www.chivenorcaravanpark.co.uk	5.0 km (↑🚲 to Braunton, at rndabt →)
17	40.1	111	H	Barnstaple	♠ 🔌 ££	Cresta Guest House, 26 Sticklepath Hill, EX31 2BU	01271 374022	www.crestaguesthouse.co.uk	0.6 km (↑🚲 along main rd, ↗ up hill via 🚲)
18	9.4	112	A	Instow	♠ ⚲ £££	Wayfarer Inn, Lane End, EX39 4LB	01271 860342	www.thewayfarerinn.co.uk	0.1 km (← opposite beach entrance)
18	14.5	113	A	Bideford	♠ 🔌 £££	Royal Hotel, Barnstaple St, EX39 4AE	01237 472005	www.brend-hotels.co.uk/theroyal	- (at station, walk down ramp ↘)
18	15.2	113	B	Bideford	⚲	Cycles Scuderia, Kingsley Rd, EX39 2PF	01237 476509	www.cyclesscuderia.co.uk	0.1 km (cross main rd ←, Pill Rd)
18	15.2	113	B	Bideford	♠ ⚲ ££	Corner House B&B, The Strand, EX39 2ND	01237 473722	www.cornerhouseguesthouse.co.uk	0.2 km (cross main rd ←, Pill Rd, 1st ←)
18	16.4	113	C	Bideford	♠ ⚲ ££	Riversford Hotel, Limers Ln, EX39 2RG	01237 474239	www.riversford.co.uk	-
18	19.3	113	D	Westward Ho!	🏠 ⚲ ££	Manorville Hostel, Kingsley Rd, Fosketh Hill, EX39 1JA	01237 479766	www.manorvillehostel.com	
18	19.3	113	D	Westward Ho!	♠ ⚲ ££	Culloden House, Fosketh Hill, EX39 1UL	01237 479421	www.culloden-house.co.uk	
18	19.5	113	E	Westward Ho!	♠ ⚲ ££	Penkenna House B&B, 11 Nelson Rd, EX39 1LF	01237 470990	www.penkennahouse.com	
18	19.6	113	F	Westward Ho!	♠ ⚲ ££	Brockenhurst B&B, 11 Atlantic Wy, EX39 1HX	01237 423346	www.brockenhurstindevon.co.uk	0.1 km (→ Youngaton Rd, T-jct →)
18	20.0	113	G	Westward Ho!	♠ 🔌 ££	Waterfront Inn, Golf Links Rd, EX39 1LH	01237 474747	www.waterfrontinn.co.uk	-
18	8.3	115	A	Great Torrington	⚲	Torrington Cycle Hire, Unit 1, Station Yard, EX38 8JD	01805 622633	www.torringtoncyclehire.co.uk	-
18	8.4	115	B	Great Torrington	♠ ⚲ £	Globe Hotel, Fore St, EX38 8HQ	01805 622352	-	2.0 km (see Torrington route, major climb!)
18	8.4	115	B	Great Torrington	♠ ⚲ £	Eastmond House B&B, 4 Potacre St, EX38 8BH	01805 623411	-	2.0 km (see Torrington route, major climb!)
18	8.4	115	B	Great Torrington	♠ 🔌 ££	Windsor House B&B, New Rd, EX38 8EJ	01805 623529	www.windsorhousebandb.co.uk	2.0 km (see Torrington route, major climb!)
18	13.6	115	C	Little Torrington	▲ ⚲ ££	Smytham Manor, EX38 8PU	01805 622110	www.smytham.co.uk	0.5 km (← at rd crossing, in climb 1st ←)
18	15.6	115	D	Petersmarland	🏠 ▲ ⚲ £	Yarde Orchard, East Yarde, EX38 8QA	01805 601778	www.yarde-orchard.co.uk	-
18	27.6	115	E	Sheepwash	♠ ⚲ £££	Halfmoon Inn, The Square, EX21 5NE	01409 231376	www.halfmoonsheepwash.co.uk	-
19	7.0	116	A	Hatherleigh	♠ ⚲ ££	Pipers Cottage B&B, 8 Oakfield Rd, EX20 3JT	01837 811701	www.piperscottage.co.uk	-
19	7.2	116	A	Hatherleigh	♠ ⚲ ££	Raymont House, 49 Market St, EX20 3JP	01837 810850	www.raymonthouse.co.uk	-
19	7.3	116	B	Hatherleigh	♠ ⚲ ££	Tops B&B, The Old Police Station, Souh St, EX20 3JB	01837 811043	www.topsbedandbreakfast.co.uk	0.1 km (→ downhill)
19	20.2	117	A	Okehampton	⚲	Okehampton Cycles, North Rd, EX20 1BQ	01837 53811	www.okecycles.co.uk	-

Rte	Km	Page	Ref	Town	Info	Name, address and postcode	Phone	Internet	Distance to route & extra instructions
19	20.8	117	B	Okehampton	♠ ⚘ ££	The Fountain Inn, Fore St, EX20 1AP	01837 810454	http://fountainokehampton.co.uk	-
19	20.8	117	C	Okehampton	♠ ⚘ £££	The White Hart Hotel, Fore Street, EX20 1HD	01837 52730	www.thewhitehart-hotel.com	0.1 km (↑ via main rd)
19	21.2	117	D	Okehampton	♠ ⚘ ££	Capella B&B, 31 Station Rd, EX20 1EA	01837 53607	http://capelladevon.co.uk	-
19	21.2	117	D	Okehampton	♠ ⚘ ££	Number 59 B&B, 59 Station Rd, EX20 1EA	01837 54614	www.59bb.co.uk	-
19	21.2	117	D	Okehampton	♠ ⚘ ££	Meadowlea Guesthouse, 65 Station Rd, EX20 1EA	01837 53200	www.meadowleaguesthouse.co.uk	-
19	21.7	117	E	Okehampton	⧖ ⚘ £	YHA Okehampton, Klondyke Rd, EX20 1EW	01837 53916	www.yha.org.uk	0.1 km (↑ under viaduct, imm ↘)
19	27.4	118	A	Sourton	▲ ⚑ £	Bundu Camping Park, Sourton Down, EX20 4HT	01837 861747	www.bundu.co.uk	-
19	32.3	118	B	Bridestowe	▲ ⚘ £	Glebe Camping & Holiday Park, Glebe Park, EX20 4ER	01837 861261	-	-
19	32.8	118	C	Bridestowe	♠ ⚘ ££	Hunters Moon B&B, EX20 4EN	01837 861193	www.huntersmoon-devon.co.uk	0.2 km (→ at T-jct)
19	32.9	118	D	Bridestowe	♠ ⚘ ££	Royal Oak House, 24 Fore St, EX20 4EN	01837 861711	www.royaloakhousebandb.co.uk	-
19	35.5	118	E	Lydford	⧖ ▲ ⚘ £	The Fox and Hounds Camping Barn/Hostel, EX20 4HF	01822 820206	www.foxandhoundshotel.com	0.6 km (↑ via rd)
19	37.5	118	F	Lydford	♠ ⚘ £££	Lydford Country House, EX20 4AU	01822 820347	www.lydfordcountryhouse.co.uk	-
19	40.5	119	A	Lydford	♠ ⚘ ££	Mallard House, 2 The Mucky Duck, EX20 4BL	01822 820609	www.mallardhouselydford.co.uk	-
19	50.4	119	B	Tavistock	▲ ⚑ ££	Harford Bridge Holiday Park, Peter Tavy, PL19 9LS	01822 810349	www.harfordbridge.co.uk	1.5 km (↑ under viaduct, T-jct ⌖ ← (27))
19	52.7	120	A	Tavistock	⧖ ⚘ £	Tavistock Bunkhouse, The Union, King St, PL19 0DS	01822 613115	www.tavistockbunkhouse.co.uk	0.2 km (↑, keep ↑ at cross rds, T-jct →)
19	52.8	120	B	Tavistock	⚲	Tavistock Cycles, Paddons Row, Brook St, PL19 0HF	01822 617630	www.tavistockcycles.co.uk	0.1 km (↑ via shopping street)
19	52.8	120	B	Tavistock	♠ ⚑ ££	Tavistock Inn, 19 Brook St, PL19 0HD	01822 615736	www.thetavistockinn.co.uk	0.1 km (↑ via shopping street)
19	52.8	120	C	Tavistock	♠ ⚑ ££	Kingfisher Cottage, Vigo Br, Mount Tavy Rd, PL19 9JB	01822 613801	http://kingfishercottage.mydnd.com	0.2 km (↑ via shopping street, 2nd →)
19	52.8	120	C	Tavistock	♠ ⚑ ££	April Cottage, 12 Mount Tavy Rd, PL19 9JB	01822 613280	www.aprilcottagetavistock.co.uk	0.2 km (↑ via shopping street, 2nd →)
19	54.9	120	D	Tavistock	▲ ⚘ £	Valley View Farm, Brook Ln, PL19 9DP	07974 569620	-	0.8 km (ep ↘, follow rd ↑)
19	55.0	120	E	Tavistock	⚲	Dartmoor Cycles, West Devon Business Park, PL19 9DP	01822 618178	www.dartmoorcycles.co.uk	-
19	61.9	121	A	Yelverton	♠ ⚑ £££	The Old Diary B&B, PL20 6DW	01822 855007	www.theolddairybandb.co.uk	- (on quiet rd on north side of roundabout)
19	61.9	121	A	Yelverton	♠ ⚑ ££	The Rosemont B&B, Greenbank Tc, PL20 6DR	01822 852175	www.therosemont.co.uk	- (on quiet rd on north side of roundabout)
19	61.9	121	A	Yelverton	♠ ⚘ ££	Barnabas House, Harrowbeer Ln, PL20 6DY	01822 853268	www.barnabas-house.co.uk	- (on quiet rd on north side of roundabout)
19	83.5	123	A	Plymouth – West Hoe	♠ ⚘ £	Edgcumbe Guesthouse, 50 Pier St, PL1 3BT	01752 660675	www.edgcumbeguesthouse.co.uk	(→ on rndabt)
19	83.5	123	A	Plymouth – West Hoe	♠ ⚘ ££	Osmond Guesthouse, 42 Pier St, PL1 3BT	01752 221654	www.osmondguesthouse.co.uk	(→ on rndabt)
19	83.6	123	B	Plymouth – West Hoe	♠ ⚘ ££	Seabreezes Guesthouse, 28 Grand Pd, PL1 3DJ	01752 667205	www.plymouth-bedandbreakfast.co.uk	-
19	83.6	123	B	Plymouth – West Hoe	♠ ⚘ ££	The Rusty Anchor Guesthouse, 30 Grand Pd, PL1 3DJ	01752 663924	www.therustyanchor-plymouth.co.uk	-
19	83.8	123	C	Plymouth – West Hoe	♠ ⚘ ££	Old Pier Guesthouse, 20 Radford R, PL1 3BY	01752 309797	www.oldpier.co.uk	0.1 km (↘ at T-jct)
19	84.5	123	D	Plymouth – Hoe	♠ ⚘ ££	Tudor House B&B, 105 Citadel Rd, PL1 2RN	01752 661557	www.tudorhouseplymouth.co.uk	0.5 km (↘ at rndbt into one way -rd)
19	84.5	123	D	Plymouth – Hoe	♠ ⚘ £	The Lamplighter B&B, 103 Citadel Rd, PL1 2RN	01752 663855	www.lamplighterplymouth.co.uk	0.5 km (↘ at rndbt into one way -rd)
19	86.1	123	E	Plymouth – City Centre	⚲	Cogs Bikes, Drake Circus Mall, 1 Charles St, PL1 1QH	01752 600601	www.cogs-bikes.com	0.7 km (go to Drake Circus Mall from station)
20	18.1	125	A	Holsworthy	♠ ⚑ ££	Kings Arms Hotel, The Square, EX22 6AN	01409 259362	www.kingsarmsholsworthy.co.uk	0.1 km (walk ↑ to Square)

Rte	Km	Page	Ref	Town	Info	Name, address and postcode	Phone	Internet	Distance to route & extra instructions
20	18.1	125	B	Holsworthy	♠ ☎ £	White Hart Hotel, Fore St, EX22 6EB	01409 253475	www.whiteharthotel.co.uk	0.1 km (walk ↑ to Square, keep ←)
20	18.1	125	C	Holsworthy	♠ ☎ ££	Old Market Inn, Chapel St, EX22 6AY	01409 253941	www.oldmarketinn.co.uk	0.2 km (walk ↑ to Square, T-jct ↗)
20	18.2	125	D	Holsworthy	♠ ⚒ £	Penrose Villa Guest House, Bodmin St, EX22 6BB	01409 254185	-	0.2 km (at cross rds ← to T-jct Bodmin St)
20	22.1	126	A	Pyworthy	▲ ⚒ £	Noteworthy Campsite, Bude Rd, near Derril, EX22 7JB	01409 253731	www.noteworthy-devon.co.uk	2.5 km (→, imm ↖, T-jct →, ← main rd)
20	31.2	126	B	Marhamchurch	♠ ⚒ ££	Bullers Arms Hotel, EX23 0HB	01288 361277	-	-
20	35.1	126	C	Bude	⛺ ⚒ £	Northshore Backpackers, 57 Killerton Rd, EX23 8EW	01288 354256	www.northshorebude.com	0.7 km (from car park →, 2nd rd →)
20	35.1	126	D	Bude	♠ ⚒ £	Tee-side Guest House, 2 Burn View, EX23 8BY	01288 353351	www.tee-side.co.uk	1.0 km (via Town Centre loop, see map)
20	35.1	126	D	Bude	♠ ⚒ ££	Sunrise Guest House, 6 Burn View, EX23 8BY	01288 353214	www.sunrise-bude.co.uk	1.0 km (via Town Centre loop, see map)
20	35.1	126	D	Bude	♠ ⚒ £	Links Side B&B, 7 Burn View, EX23 8BY	01288 353410	www.linkssidebude.co.uk	1.0 km (via Town Centre loop, see map)
20	35.1	126	D	Bude	♠ ⚒ £	Sea Jade Guest House, 15 Burn View, EX23 8BZ	01288 353404	www.seajadeguesthouse.co.uk	1.0 km (via Town Centre loop, see map)
20	35.1	126	D	Bude	♠ ⚒ ££	Palms Guest House, 17 Burn View, EX23 8BZ	01288 353962	www.palms-bude.co.uk	1.0 km (via Town Centre loop, see map)
20	35.1	126	E	Bude	⚒	North Coast Cycles, 2 Summerleaze Av, EX23 8RL	01288 352974	-	1.5 km (via Town Centre, ↑, see map)
20	35.3	126	F	Bude	♠ ⚒ ££	Falcon Hotel, Breakwater Rd, EX23 8SD	01288 352005	www.falconhotel.com	0.3 km (after bridge →)
20	35.3	126	G	Bude	♠ ☎ ££	The Brendon Arms, Falcon Tc, EX23 8SD	01288 354542	www.brendonarms.co.uk	-
20	36.1	127	A	Bude	▲ ⚒ £	Upper Lynstone, Lynstone Rd, EX23 0LP	01288 352017	www.upperlynstone.co.uk	-
20	36.6	127	B	Bude	♠ ⚒ £	Upton Cross B&B, Marine, Drive, EX23 0LY	01288 355310	www.uptoncrossbedandbreakfast.co.uk	0.1 km (← via rd)
20	42.0	127	C	Widemouth Bay	⛺ ▲ ⚒ £	Penhalt Farm Holiday Park, EX23 0DG	01288 361210	www.penhaltfarm.co.uk	-
20	45.6	127	D	St Gennys	♠ ⚒ ££	Bears and Boxes Guest House, Dizzard, EX23 0NX	01840 230318	www.bearsandboxes.com	-
20	46.7	127	E	St Gennys	♠ ⚒ ££	Lower Tresmorn Farm B&B, EX23 0NU	01840 230667	www.lowertresmorn.co.uk	0.8 km (via dead end rd →)
21A	0.8	130	A	St Gennys	▲ ⚒ £	Coxford Meadow, EX23 0NS	01288 230707	-	-
21A	1.6	130	B	Crackington Haven	♠ ⚒ £	Trewartha B&B, EX23 0NN	01840 230420	-	-
21A	4.8	130	C	Trevigue	♠ ⚒ £	Trevigue B&B, EX23 0LQ	01840 230418	www.trevigue.co.uk	-
21A	21.4	131	A	Tintagel	♠ ☎ ££	Cornish Man Inn, Fore St, PL34 0DA	01840 770238	www.cornishmaninn.com	0.1 km (↑ at rndabt)
21A	21.4	131	A	Tintagel	♠ ☎ ££	Ye Olde Malthouse, Fore St, PL34 0DA	01840 770461	www.yeoldemalthouseinn.com	0.2 km (↑ at rndabt)
21A	21.4	131	B	Tintagel	♠ ☎ ££	Wootons Country Hotel, Fore St, PL34 0DD	01840 770170	www.wootons.co.uk	0.2 km (↑ at rndabt)
21A	21.4	131	C	Tintagel	♠ ⚒ ££	Bosayne Guest House, Atlantic Rd, PL34 0DE	01840 770514	www.bosayne.co.uk	0.6 km (↑ at rndabt)
21A	21.4	131	C	Tintagel	♠ ⚒ ££	Pendrin Guest House, Atlantic Rd, PL34 0DE	01840 770560	www.pendrintintagel.co.uk	0.6 km (↑ at rndabt)
21A	21.4	131	D	Tintagel	▲ ⚒ £	Headland Caravan Park, Atlantic Rd, PL34 0DE	01840 770239	www.headlandcaravanpark.co.uk	0.7 km (↑ at rndabt)
21A	22.5	131	E	Tintagel	⛺ ⚒ £	YHA Tintagel, Dunderhole Point, PL34 0DW	0845 3719145	www.yha.org.uk	1.2 km (at bend to left →, keep ↖)
21A	23.0	131	F	Treknow	♠ ⚒ £	The Willows B&B, PL34 0EN	01840 779014	-	-
21A	23.0	131	F	Treknow	♠ ⚒ £	Anneth B&B, PL34 0EN	01840 770568	-	-
21A	23.3	131	G	Treknow	♠ ⚒ £	Hillscroft B&B, PL34 0EN	01840 770551	-	-
21A	23.7	131	G	Trebarwith	♠ ⚒ £££	Mill House Inn, PL34 0HD	01840 770200	www.themillhouseinn.co.uk	-

Rte	Km	Page	Ref	Town	Info	Name, address and postcode	Phone	Internet	Distance to route & extra instructions
21A	26.5	131	H	Delabole	▲ ⚲ £	Planet Caravan Park, West Down Rd, PL33 9DR	01840 213361	-	0.9 km (at pub ←, T-jct →, 1st ←)
21A	29.3	131	I	St Teath	⌂ ⚲ ££	Paths End B&B, Trewennen Rd, PL30 3JZ	01208 850441	-	-
21B	2.3	132	A	Wainhouse Corner	⌂ ⚲ ££	The Old Wainhouse Inn, EX23 0BA	01840 230711	www.oldwainhouseinn.co.uk	-
21B	11.1	132	B	Hallworthy	⌂ ⚲ ££	Wilsey Down Hotel, PL32 9SH	01840 261205	http://thewilseydown.co.uk	0.1 km (at T-jct ←)
21B	21.8	133	C	Camelford	⌂ 📶 ££	Culloden Farmhouse B&B, 16 Victoria Rd, PL32 9XA	01840 211128	www.cullodenfarmhouse.co.uk	2.0 km (→, at T-jct ← into Camelford)
21B	21.8	133	D	Camelford	⌂ 📶 ££	Warmington House, 32 Market Pl, PL32 9PD	01840 214961	www.warmingtonhouse.co.uk	2.3 km (→, at T-jct ← into Camelford)
22	1.2	135	A	St Mabyn	▲ ⚲ ££	St Mabyn Holiday Park, Longstone Rd, PL30 3BY	01208 841677	www.stmabynholidaypark.co.uk	4.0 km (→ via rd and climb, keep ↑)
22	9.6	135	B	Bodmin	⌂ 📶 ££	Westberry Hotel, Dennison Rd, PL31 2EL	01208 72772	www.westberryhotel.net	3.2 km (route 3 to Bodmin, ep T-jct →, 3rd ←)
22	9.6	135	B	Bodmin	⚲	Bodmin Bikes, Hamley Court, Dennison Rd, PL31 2LL	01208 73192	www.bodminbikes.co.uk	3.0 km (route 3 to Bodmin, ep T-jct →)
22	18.7	135	C	Wadebridge	📶 ££	Swan Hotel, 9 Molesworth St, PL27 7DD	01208 812526	www.staustellbrewery.co.uk/swan-hotel	-
22	18.7	135	C	Wadebridge	⌂ 📶 ££	Molesworth Arms Hotel, 38 Molesworth St, PL27 7DP	01208 812055	www.moleswortharms.co.uk	0.1 km (← at rndabt)
22	25.6	135	D	Padstow	▲ ⚲ £	Dennis Cove Camping, Dennis Ln, PL28 8DR	01841 532349	-	0.3 km (before sign "🚲 P 200 yds" ← steps)
22	26.3	135	E	Padstow	⌂ ⚲ £££	Coswarth House B&B, 12 Dennis Rd, PL28 8DD	01841 534755	www.coswarthhouse.com	0.2 km (T-jct ← via climb, 1st ←)
22	26.3	135	F	Padstow	⌂ 📶 £££	St Petroc's Hotel (Rick Stein Bistro), 4 New St, PL28 8A	01841 532700	www.rickstein.com	0.2 km (T-jct ← via climb, 1st →)
22	26.7	135	G	Padstow	⌂ 📶 £££	Old Ship Hotel, Mill Sq, PL28 8AE	01841 532357	www.oldshiphotel-padstow.co.uk	(at end of alley →, not into Duke St)
22	27.0	135	H	Padstow	⌂ ⚲ £££	Tregea Hotel, 16-18 High St, PL28 8BB	01841 532455	www.tregea.co.uk	-
22	27.1	135	H	Padstow	⌂ 📶 £££	Garslade Guest House, 52 Church St, PL28 8BG	01841 533804	www.garslade.com	0.1 km (at 2nd jct ← back into Padstow)
22	28.2	136	A	Padstow	⌂ 📶 £££	Woodlands Country House B&B, Treator PL28 8RU	01841 532426	www.woodlands-padstow.co.uk	-
22	31.1	136	B	Harlyn Bay	⌂ 📶 £££	The Harlyn Inn, Harlyn Bay, PL28 8SB	01841 520207	www.harlyn-inn.co.uk	-
22	34.0	136	C	Treyarnon Bay	▲ ⚲ £	Treyarnon Bay Caravan & Camping Park, PL28 8JP	01952 581007	www.treyarnonbay.co.uk	0.5 km (2nd →)
22	34.0	136	C	Treyarnon Bay	🏠 ⚲ £	YHA Treyarnon Bay, PL28 8JR	0845 3719664	www.yha.org.uk	0.7 km (2nd →)
22	36.2	136	D	St Merryn	▲ ⚲ £	Trevean Caravan & Camping Park, PL28 8PR	01841 520772	www.treveancaravanandcamping.net	-
22	37.2	136	E	St Merryn	▲ ⚲ £	Seagull Tourist Park, PL28 8SG	01841 520117	-	-
22	37.7	136	F	St Merryn	⚲	Point Curlew, PL28 8PY	01841 620856	-	-
22	42.2	137	A	Rumford	▲ ⚲ ££	Music Water Touring Park, PL27 7SJ	01841 540257	http://musicwater.wix.com/touringpark	1.5 km (1st rd ←)
22	48.0	137	B	St Columb Major	⌂ ⚲ ££	The Cribbage Guest House, 15 Fair St, TR9 6RL	01637 881729	www.thecribbage.co.uk	-
22	49.2	137	C	St Columb Major	▲ ⚲ ££	Trekenning Touring Park, TR8 4JF	01637 880462	www.trekenning.co.uk	0.1 km (T-jct ←)
22	51.3	137	D	Trebudannon	⌂ ⚲ ££	Trebudannon Farm B&B, TR8 4LP	01637 880208	www.trebudannonfarm.com	-
22	51.5	137	D	Trebudannon	⌂ ⚲ £	Wheel Lodge Country Hotel & Restaurant, TR8 4LP	01637 880304	-	-
22	60.0	139	A	Newquay	▲ ⚲ £	Porth Beach Tourist Park, Alexandra Rd, Porth,TR7 3NH	01637 876531	www.porthbeach.co.uk/holiday-park	0.6 km (T-jct ←, Alexandra Rd)
22	60.1	139	B	Newquay	⌂ 📶 £££	Porth Veor Manor Hotel, Porth Wy, TR7 3LW	01637 873274	www.porthveormanor.com	-
22	61.0	139	C	Newquay	⌂ ⚲ £££	Hotel Riviera, Lusty Glaze Rd, TR7 3AA	01637 878000	-	-
22	61.0	139	D	Newquay	⚲	Mal Breakdown service, Indoor Mt, Chester Rd, TR7 3BP	07786 874292	www.malthebikeguy.co.uk	0.4 km (T-jct ←, 1st →)

Rte	Km	Page	Ref	Town	Info	Name, address and postcode	Phone	Internet	Distance to route & extra instructions
22	61.7	139	E	Newquay	⚲	Ideal Bikes and Boards, 32 Cliff Rd, TR7 2ND	01637 876009	-	-
22	62.3	139	F	Newquay	⚲ ≈ £	Silver Spray Lodge, 9 Trebarwith Cr, TR7 1DX	01637 440031	-	-
22	62.3	139	F	Newquay	⌂ ≈ ££	Pengilley Guest House, 12 Trebarwith Cr, TR7 1DX	01637 872039	www.pengilley-guesthouse.co.uk	-
22	63.8	139	G	Newquay	⌂ ⚲ £££	Headland Hotel, Headland Rd, TR7 1EW	01637 872211	www.headlandhotel.co.uk	-
22	65.7	139	H	Newquay	⌂ ≈ ££	Meadow View, 135 Mount Wise, TR7 1QR	01637 873132	www.meadowviewnewquay.co.uk	-
22	65.7	139	H	Newquay	⚲ ≈ £	Matts Surf Lodge, 110 Mount Wise, TR7 1QP	01637 874651	www.matts-surf-lodge.co.uk	-
22	65.7	139	H	Newquay	⌂ ≈ ££	Tir Chonaill Guest House, 106 Mount Wise, TR7 1QP	01637 876492	www.tirchonaill.co.uk	-
22	65.7	139	H	Newquay	⌂ ≈ ££	Surfside Stop Guest House, 35 Mount Wise, TR7 2BH	01637 872707	www.surfsidenewquay.co.uk	-
22	65.7	139	H	Newquay	⌂ ≈ ££	St Breca B&B, 22 Mount Wise, TR7 2BG	01637 872745	www.stbreca.co.uk	-
23	1.0	141	A		▲ ⚲ ££	Riverside Holiday Park, Gwills Ln, TR8 4PE	01637 873617	www.riversideholidaypark.co.uk	0.5 km (at cross rds →)
23	5.7	141	B	St Newlyn East	⌂ ⚲ £	Village B&B, Hillcrest, 16 Churchtown, TR8 5LJ	01872 519194	-	-
23	21.0	141	C	Truro	⚲	Clive Mitchell Cycles, 6 Calenick St, TR1 2SF	01872 276930	www.clivemitchellcycles.co.uk	- (opposite church ←)
23	21.3	141	D	Truro	⌂ ≈ ££	Baytree Guest House, 28 Ferris Town, TR1 3JH	01872 240274	www.baytree-guesthouse.co.uk	0.1 km (T-jct → St Dominic St, T-jct →)
23	21.5	141	E	Truro	⌂ ⚲ ££	Rowan Tree B&B, 3 Parkvedras Tc, TR1 3DF	01872 277928	http://rowantreetruro.co.uk	- (on Chapel Hill 1st rd →)
23	22.0	141	F	Truro	⌂ ⚲ ££	Donnington Guesthouse, 43 Treyew Rd, TR1 2BY	01872 277374	www.donnington-guesthouse.co.uk	0.1 km (← via main rd)
23	23.2	142	A	Truro	⌂ ⚲ ££	The Laurels B&B, Penweathers, TR3 6EA	07794 472171	www.thelaurelsbedandbreakfast.com	- (before bridge ↗)
23	28.2	142	B	Carnon Downs	⌂ ⚲ ££	Chycara House, Chyreen Ln, TR3 6LG	01872 865447	www.chycara.co.uk	0.7 km (T-jct ←, next jct ↖ and imm ←)
23	29.3	142	C	Bissoe	⚲	Bissoe Bike Hire & Cafe, Old Conns Works, TR4 8QZ	01872 870341	www.cornwallcyclehire.co.uk	-
23	34.0	142	D	St Day	▲ ⚲ £	St Day Holiday Park, Church Hill, TR16 5LE	01209 820459	www.stdaytouring.co.uk	0.7 km (after cross rds 1st path →, →)
23	34.0	142	E	St Day	⌂ ⚲ ££	The Cedars B&B, 22 Church St, TR16 5JY	01209 820288	www.thecedarsbandb.co.uk	0.7 km (after cross rds 1st path →)
23	38.2	143	A	Redruth	⌂ ⚲ ££	Lansdowne Guest House, 42 Clinton Rd, TR15 2QE	01209 216002	www.lansdowne-guesthouse.co.uk	0.2 km (at cross rds ← via Clinton Rd)
23	39.1	143	B	Redruth	⌂ ⚲ ££	Tre Vab Yowann B&B, 6 Trevingey Rd, TR15 3DG	01209 211453	www.trevabyowann.co.uk	-
23	44.1	143	C	Camborne	⚲	MT Cycle Services, 5a Vean Rd, TR14 7TA	01209 420165	www.mtcycleservi.co.uk	0.3 km (at cross rds →, 1st ←)
23	44.6	143	D	Camborne	⌂ ≈ ££	Cherry Villa B&B, 21 Trevu Rd, TR14 7AE	01209 610135	-	-
23	44.7	143	E	Camborne	⌂ ≈ £££	Tyacks Hotel, 27 Commercial St, TR14 8LD	01209 612424	www.tyackshotel.co.uk	(↑ over railway, rndabt ↗, T-jct ↗)
23	47.2	144	A	Barripper	⌂ ▲ ⚲ £	Bikers B&B, Palm Springs, 38 New Rd, TR14 0QS	01209 719415	www.bikers-bed-and-breakfast.com	0.1 km (at T-jct with church ↑)
23	48.5	144	B	Carnhell Green	▲ ⚲ £	Lavender Fields, Penhale Rd, TR14 0LU	01209 832188	www.lavenderfieldstouring.co.uk	-
23	54.8	144	C	Hayle	⌂ ≈ £	Tamarisk B&B, 23 Penmare Tc, TR27 4PH	01736 757920	-	0.2 km (at T-jct ↑ via main rd)
23	55.1	144	D	Hayle	⌂ ≈ ££	Madhatter B&B, 73 Fore St, TR27 4DX	01736 754241	-	0.3 km (ep ↑ via main rd)
23	55.1	144	D	Hayle	⌂ ≈ £	Cornubia Hotel, 35 Fore St, TR27 4DX	01736 753351	-	0.2 km (ep ↑ via main rd)
23	55.5	144	E	Hayle	▲ ⚲ £	Beachside Holiday Pk, Lethlean Ln, Phillack, TR27 5AW	01736 753080	www.beachside.co.uk	1.0 km (ep ↑, T-jct ↑, T-jct →, 1st ←)
23	55.5	144	F	Hayle	⌂ ⚲ £££	Penellen B&B, 64 Riviere Towans, Phillack, TR27 5AF	01736 753777	bedandbreakfasthotelcornwall.co.uk	1.2 km (ep ↑, T-jct ↑, T-jct ←)
23	57.0	144	G	Hayle	⚲	Hayle Cycles, 36 Penpol Tc, TR27 4BQ	01736 753825	www.haylecycles.co.uk	-

Rte	Km	Page	Ref	Town	Info	Name, address and postcode	Phone	Internet	Distance to route & extra instructions
23	57.2	144	G	Hayle	♠ ⅃ ££	White Heart Hotel, 10 Foundry Sq, TR27 4HQ	01736 752322	http://whitehearthotel-hayle.co.uk	-
23	65.3	145	A	Marazion	▲ ⅃ £	Wheal Rodney Holiday Park, Gwallon Ln, TR17 0HL	01736 710605	www.whealrodney.co.uk	-
23	66.9	145	B	Marazion	♠ ££	Godolphin Arms, West End, TR17 0EN	01736 710202	www.godolphinarms.co.uk	-
23	67.2	145	C	Marazion	▲ ⅃ £	Dove Meadows Camping, Green Lane West,TR17 0HH	01736 710854	www.dovemeadows.co.uk	0.3 km (leaving Marazion ↗ Green Ln)
24	0.3	146	A	Penzance	⅃	The Cycle Centre, 1 New St, TR18 2LZ	01736 351671	-	0.2 km (main rd 1st →, imm ←, 1st →)
24	0.8	146	B	Penzance - Docks	♠ ⅃ ££	The Dock Inn, 17 Quay St, TR18 4BD	01736 362833	www.dockinn.net	- (after bridge, but before bend to right ↘)
24	0.8	146	B	Penzance - Docks	♠ ⅃ £££	The Dolphin Tavern, Quay St, TR18 4BD	01736 364106	www.dolphintavern.co.uk	- (after bridge, but before bend to right ↘)
24	1.2	146	C	Penzance - Promenade	♠ 🛜 ££	Lugger Hotel, Marine Tc, TR18 4DL	01736 363236	www.theluggerhotel.co.uk	-
24	1.2	146	C	Penzance - Promenade	♠ 🛜 ££	Seawaves B&B, 4 Marine Tc, TR18 4DL	01736 368053	seawavesguesthouse-penzance.co.uk	-
24	1.2	146	C	Penzance - Promenade	♠ 🛜 ££	The Corner House B&B, 20 Marine Tc, TR18 4DL	01736 351324	www.thecornerhousepenzance.co.uk	-
24	1.2	146	C	Penzance - Promenade	♠ 🛜 £££	Queens Hotel, Promenade, TR18 4HG	01736 362371	www.queens-hotel.com	-
24	1.2	146	C	Penzance - Promenade	♠ 🛜 ££	Beachfield Hotel, Promenade, TR18 4NW	01736 362067	www.beachfield.co.uk	-
24	1.5	146	D	Penzance - West	⋔ ⅃ ££	Blue Dolphin Backpackers, Alexandra Rd, TR18 4LZ	01736 363836	www.pzbackpack.com	0.4 km (rndabt →)
24	1.5	146	E	Penzance - West	⋔ ⅃ £	YMCA Penzance, The Orchard, Alverton Rd, TR18 4TE	01736 334820	www.ymcacornwall.org.uk	0.7 km (rndabt →, rndabt ←)
24	5.7	147	A	Mousehole	♠ ⅃ £££	Old Coast Guard Hotel, The Parade, TR19 6PR	01736 731222	www.oldcoastguardhotel.co.uk	-
24	5.7	147	A	Mousehole	♠ 🛜 ££	Ship Inn, South Cliff, TR19 6QX	01736 731234	-	-
24	5.7	147	A	Mousehole	♠ 🛜 £££	Cornish Range Restaurant & Rooms, TR19 6SB	01736 731488	www.cornishrange.co.uk	-
24	8.5	147	B	Lamorna	♠ ⅃ ££	Castallack Farm B&B, TR19 6NL	01736 731969	www.castallackfarm.co.uk	-
24	11.2	147	C	Lamorna	▲ ⅃ £	Boleigh Farm Camping Site, TR19 6BN	01736 810305	-	-
24	25.5	148	A	Land's End	♠ ⅃ ££	Treeve Moor House B&B, Sennen, TR19 7AE	01736 871284	www.firstandlastcottages.co.uk/bab	0.1 km (← via private rd)
24	26.1	148	B	Land's End	▲ ⅃ £	Sea View Holiday Park, Sennen, TR19 7AD	01736 871266	www.seaview.org.uk	-
24	27.6	148	C	Sennen	♠ 🛜 £££	Sunny Bank Hotel, Sea View Hill, TR19 7AR	01736 871278	-	-
24	28.9	148	D	Sennen	▲ ⅃ £	Trevedra Farm, TR19 7BE	01736 871818	www.trevedrafarm.co.uk	-
24	33.1	148	E	St Just	⋔ ⅃ £	YHA Land's End, Letcha Vean, TR19 7NT	0045 3719043	www.yha.org.uk	-
24	36.9	148	F	St Just	♠ ⅃ ££	Boswedden House B&B, Cape Cornwall, TR19 7NJ	01736 788733	www.boswedden.org.uk	-
24	38.2	148	G	St Just	♠ 🛜 £££	Wellington Hotel, Market Sq, TR19 7HD	01736 787319	www.wellington-hotel.co.uk	-
24	38.2	148	G	St Just	♠ 🛜 ££	Commercial Hotel, 13 Market Sq, TR19 7HD	01736 788455	www.commercial-hotel.co.uk	-
24	40.4	148	H	St Just	▲ ⅃ £	Roselands Camping Park, Dowran, TR19 7RS	01736 788571	www.roselands.co.uk	0.1 km (2nd ↗)
24	49.0	146	F	Penzance - North	▲ ⅃ £	Bone Valley Holiday Park, Heamoor, TR20 8UJ	01736 360313	www.bonevalleyholidaypark.co.uk	0.6 km (cross rds ↑, 1st ←)
24	49.6	146	G	Penzance - North	⋔ ⅃ £	YHA Penzance, Castle Horneck, TR20 8TF	0845 3719653	www.yha.org.uk	1.0 km (at rndabt → via footpath A30)
24	51.1	146	H	Penzance - Station	♠ ⅃ £	Torre Vene Guest House, 11 Lescudjack Tc, TR18 3AE	01736 364103	-	0.3 km (at Corner Ways ↙, T-jct →)
24	51.1	146	J	Penzance - Station	♠ ⅃ ££	Corner Ways Guest House, 5 Leskinnick St, TR18 2HA	01736 364645	www.cornerways-penzance.co.uk	-
24	51.1	146	J	Penzance - Station	♠ ⅃ ££	Honeydew Guest House, 3 Leskinnick St, TR18 2HA	01736 364206	-	-